THE VICTORIA HISTORY OF LEICESTERSHIRE

IBSTOCK

by Pamela J. Fisher

First published 2020

A Victoria County History publication for the Institute of Historical Research

ISBN 978 1 912702 46 6

SCHOOL OF
ADVANCED STUDY
UNIVERSITY
OF LONDON

Cover image: Mining wheel at the Miners' Welfare sports grounds. The plaque reads: 'Erected by the parish council in 1993 as a tribute to those people of Ibstock who devoted their working lives to the coal mining industry'. (Photographed by Pamela J. Fisher.)

Back cover image: Architect's drawings for 106 and 108 Chapel Street (1903), typical of the working-class housing being built in the village in this period. (ROLLR, DE 3806, Market Bosworth District.)

Typeset in Minion Pro by Jessica Davies Porter

CONTENTS

LIST OF ILLUSTRATIONS

All figures are copyright of the author unless otherwise stated below.

Data for the graphs (Figures 7 and 8) was taken from agricultural returns, TNA, MAF 68/134; 68/533; 68/1103; 68/1673; 68/2243; 68/2813; 68/3356; 68/3836; 68/4205; 68/4575; 68/5037; 68/5588.

Figure

LIST OF MAPS

With thanks to Ordnance Survey, National Library of Scotland and the Record Office for Leicestershire, Leicester and Rutland for permission to republish and reuse material.

Map

FOREWORD

The Victoria County History is a great national project to write the history of every village and town in England. It was originally named after Queen Victoria, but has been recently rededicated to Elizabeth II. Each county makes its own contribution; some have completed the task, but many, of which Leicestershire is one, have made good progress but have more to do. Leicestershire has five volumes which appeared before 1964, but many more villages need to be researched and published.

Leicestershire Victoria County History Trust was founded in 2008, and I was pleased to become one of its patrons. Since then a number of parishes have had their histories written and placed online, and two have appeared in print. I am delighted that Ibstock, with which I have been closely associated, is now being published. We are all grateful to Dr Pam Fisher, who with the help of enthusiastic local volunteers, has researched and written the history of the village. She has shown great dedication and skill because the story is complicated, with boundary changes, many landowners, and numerous industries.

The story of Ibstock is a heartening one, because the people have endured many setbacks through the years, including unemployment, industrial unrest, and the decline of staple industries such as framework knitting and coal mining, yet they have recovered and rebuilt new ways of life. Pam Fisher has shown that Ibstock over the last two hundred years has kept together through friendly societies, the church, a number of strong nonconformist chapels, schools, sports clubs, scouts and guides and the Townswomen's Guild. The history society celebrates Ibstock's heritage, and a practical respect for the past has led to the restoration of buildings, notably the former Palace cinema: this has become a community hub and focal point for the modern village. This book will be read with interest and some pride by the modern inhabitants, but because it is published by a national organisation, Ibstock and its sense of community will become known outside Leicestershire.

David Wilson, CBE, DL

ACKNOWLEDGEMENTS

IT HAS BEEN A PLEASURE to research and write this history of Ibstock, which has only been possible through the help and support of many people. First and foremost, my thanks go to David Wilson CBE DL, for his interest and generous financial support for the research and publication, without which this volume could not have been produced, and also for agreeing to provide the foreword, and information to help with part of the modern economic history of the parish.

I am also very grateful to Chris Dyer, who has offered sound advice, support and encouragement every step of the way. The text has gained greatly from his willingness to share his expertise, and for his valuable and constructive criticism.

Numerous people in Ibstock and beyond have contributed in many ways to the research. The late Andrew Ward and his wife Janet pointed the way in the early stages, and Andrew's deep knowledge of Ibstock, resulting from many years of research in primary sources, was of immense help. I am very grateful to them both for their assistance and hospitality. Many members of Ibstock Historical Society have also been generous with their time and support, have provided access to their extensive archive of documents, transcripts and photographs, and have introduced me to other local people to help with specific queries. I could not hope to find a friendlier local history group anywhere. Paula and Terry Gretton and Pauline and Stephen Pettitt have supported me throughout this journey, and I am grateful to them for their friendship, kindness and help with so many aspects of this project. Also within Ibstock, I acknowledge with thanks the help of Jacqui Aucott, Pattie Bailey, Chris & Sue Bates, David and Sandra Baxter, Janet Beniston, David Cooper, Scott Cooper, Jane Davidson, Trudy Fry, Vera Harding, Brian Hall, Ian and Jennifer Holloway, Nicola Land, Alan and Jo Lovell, Jill McMinn, Steve Meadows, Roy Monks, June Newman, Tina Newton, Kevin Norman, Carol Oswin, David Ottey, Joe Reid, Steve Saunders, Joanne Sheppard, Chris Simmons, Ronnie Taberner, Roger Thomas, Ian Vickers, John and Marjorie Wood, and all those who have provided information or helpful comments on social media posts. Thanks too, to the staff at Ibstock Community Voice, who have helped to raise the profile of this project by publishing short pieces in their magazine.

I also owe a large debt of gratitude to a band of VCH volunteers outside Ibstock for their help with information, research and transcription, and to others who I have approached for information: Anne Bryan, Carol Cambers, Richard Clark, Charles Doble, Helen Edwards, Mick Gamble, Pat Guy, Simon Harratt, David Holmes, Peter Leadbetter, M. Keatley, Stacey Paling, Hazel Pearson, Chris Pickford, Nicola Taylor, Martin Watkinson, Helen Wells, Bridget Wells-Furby, James White and Neil Wilson. Any omissions from these two lists are inadvertent, and I offer my apologies if I have failed to name others who have assisted.

In the course of this research I have visited many archives, record offices, libraries and museums, and have contacted others by email. I am very grateful to the archivists, librarians and staff at the Record Office for Leicestershire, Leicester and Rutland, The National Archives, The British Library, the Church of England Records Centre, the Cinema Theatre Association Archive, the David Wilson Library at the University of Leicester, De Montfort University Special Collections, the IHR Wohl Library, Lambeth Palace Library, Lincolnshire Archives, the Museum of English Rural Life, the National Coal Mining Museum for England, the National Library of Scotland, Northamptonshire Record Office and the Parliamentary Archives for answering queries, helping me find my way around catalogues and making numerous boxes and items available to me.

I am also very grateful to the Record Office for Leicester, Leicestershire and Rutland, Leicestershire County Council (Historic Environment Record), Ibstock Historical Society and Scott Cooper (Cooper's Dimension) for permission to reproduce the image on the back cover and those images detailed in the List of Illustrations and List of Maps.

This is the third paperback in the Leicestershire VCH series, and once again I am very grateful to Cath D'Alton for her cartographic skills, and to Adam Chapman and Jessica Davies Porter of VCH Central Office for their guidance, support and professional skills in turning my draft text into this attractive volume, despite being unable to access their usual offices in the final stages of production. The many others involved at the publishers and printers are also thanked for overcoming the challenges of working under the restrictions posed by the Covid-19 pandemic.

Pam Fisher

INTRODUCTION

THE LARGE VILLAGE OF IBSTOCK is 15 miles north-west of Leicester, six miles south-east of the historic market town of Ashby-de-la-Zouch and three miles SSW of the modern town of Coalville.

Ibstock was mentioned in Domesday Book. Its medieval parish church stands to the south of the modern built area (Map 1). In the Middle Ages Ibstock was a medium-sized village in a sparsely populated rural area. Its character changed from 1825, when William Thirlby sank a coal mine in the north of the parish (at 'Brick Wks' on Map 1), and more rapidly from 1873, when a second coal mine was sunk by Joseph Joel Ellis in the east of the parish ('Wks' on Map 1). In 1901, Ibstock was the most populous civil parish in Leicestershire that was not part of an urban district. It then fell within the rural district centred upon Market Bosworth, five miles to its south, a parish then with a population of 659, against Ibstock's population of 3,922.[1]

Ibstock's fastest period of growth was between 1861 and 1911, when it developed many of the features of a town, although it failed to obtain the urban status that some residents sought. The central road through the village, 'Main Street' in 1881, had been renamed 'High Street' by 1891.[2] There were several sports fields, and a large Miners' Welfare sports ground opened in 1929. Many clubs and societies were formed, offering a wide range of activities to suit different ages and interests. Diverse religious views, more often a feature of towns, found expression in 1901 in Anglican, Baptist, Primitive Methodist, Wesleyan Methodist and Wesleyan Reform churches in the village, and four of those churches continued to hold regular Sunday worship in 2019.

The woodland shown on Map 1 was planted following the closure of the last deep coal mine in the area, Bagworth-Ellistown, in 1991. It covers an area where the ground has been extensively undermined, and forms part of the National Forest. Brickworks had been attached to the collieries almost from when the pits were sunk, and these continued. One of Britain's largest brick manufacturers, Ibstock plc, owned clay quarries and plant at the former Ibstock colliery site in 2019 which could produce 190 million bricks annually.

The civil parish of Ibstock was created in 1866. The township of Hugglescote and Donington, to the north, once part of the ancient parish of Ibstock, became a civil parish, with the division along the township boundary.[3] Houses were built for colliery and brickyard workers, in locations determined by the availability of suitable land, which paid no heed to established boundaries.

Despite their shared name, Ellistown colliery and the village which became known as Ellistown were in different civil parishes. Ellistown colliery was sunk on farmland in

1 *VCH Leics.*, III, 183, 190.

2 Census, 1881, 1891.

3 Youngs, *Admin. Units*, II, 228; OS Map 6", Leics. XXIII.SE (1885 edn); ROLLR, DE 8666; DE 144/7; DE 380/45.

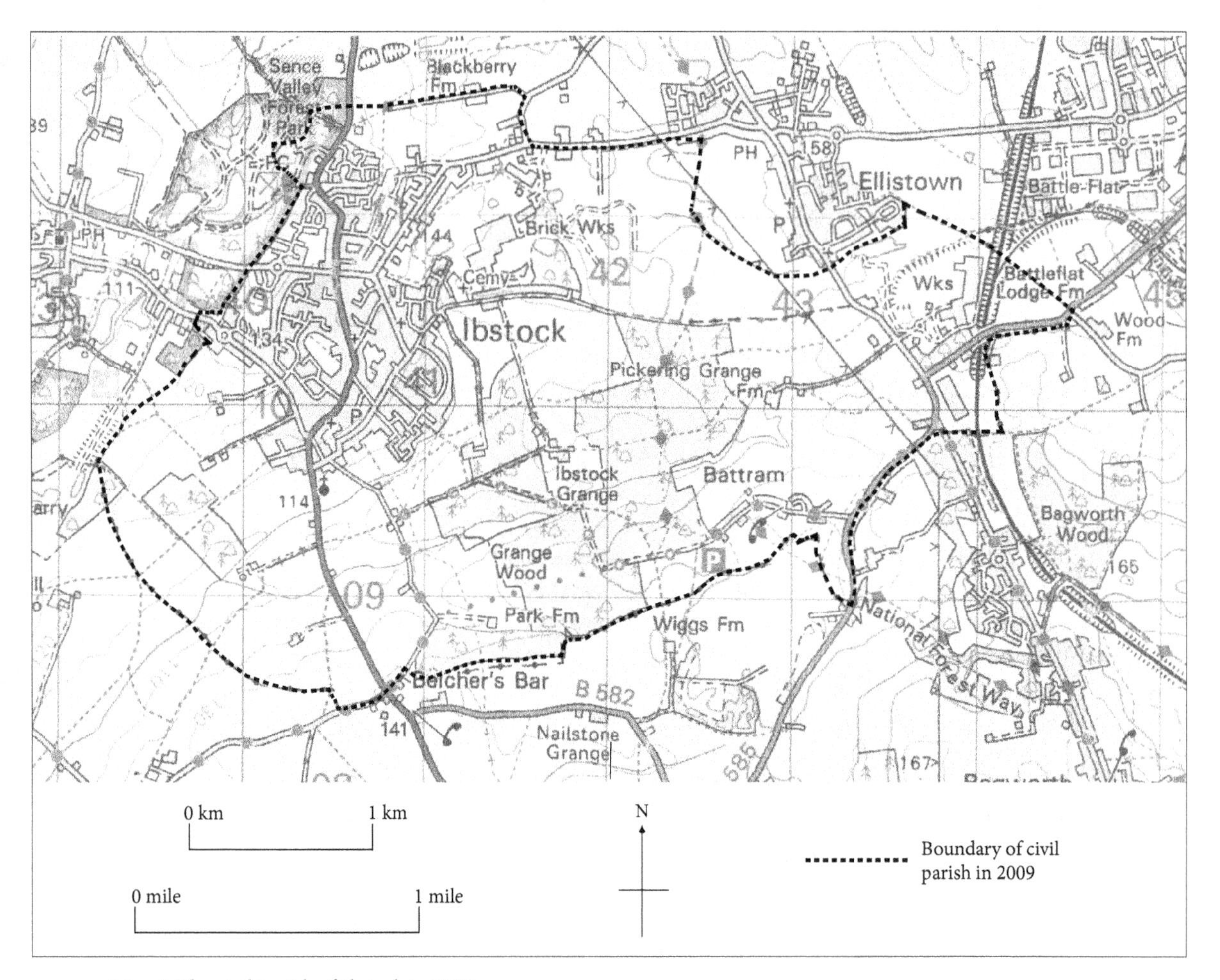

Map 1 *The civil parish of Ibstock in 2009.*

the east of Ibstock parish, and took its name from its founder, Joseph Joel Ellis, who built houses for 41 employees in the immediate vicinity. The history of the farm, colliery and neighbouring houses are included in this book. The village known in 2019 as Ellistown (formerly Whitehill) was in Hugglescote and Donington civil parish until 2001, when it became part of the new civil parish of Ellistown and Battleflat.[4] Its history sits with the histories of Hugglescote and Donington, and is not covered here.

The village of Battram, in the south-east of Ibstock parish, was developed in the 1880s around the southern boundary of Ibstock, to house workers at Nailstone colliery, ½ mile south of the houses and within Nailstone parish. Battram became a small community, with a school, chapel and sports facilities. Battram's history is therefore also included within this volume.

Like many large villages, Ibstock in the early 21st century was in some respects a dormitory settlement. Many houses were built between 1990 and 2020, but industry was encouraged to locate a few miles away, in Coalville, Bardon and Hugglescote.[5]

4 The North West Leicestershire (Parish) Order 2001.
5 Below, Local Government, local government after 1894.

Parish Boundaries

THE CIVIL PARISH IS IRREGULAR in shape. It measures 1.9 miles from north to south, and 3.4 miles from west to east, and contained 2,257 a. in 1881.[1] There were two minor boundary changes in the north-east and west of the parish in 1984 and 1986, and two more significant changes in 1984, which added *c.*100 a. in the north of the parish and *c.*50 a. in the south (Map 2).[2] The parish contained 998 ha. (2,466 a.) in 2011.[3]

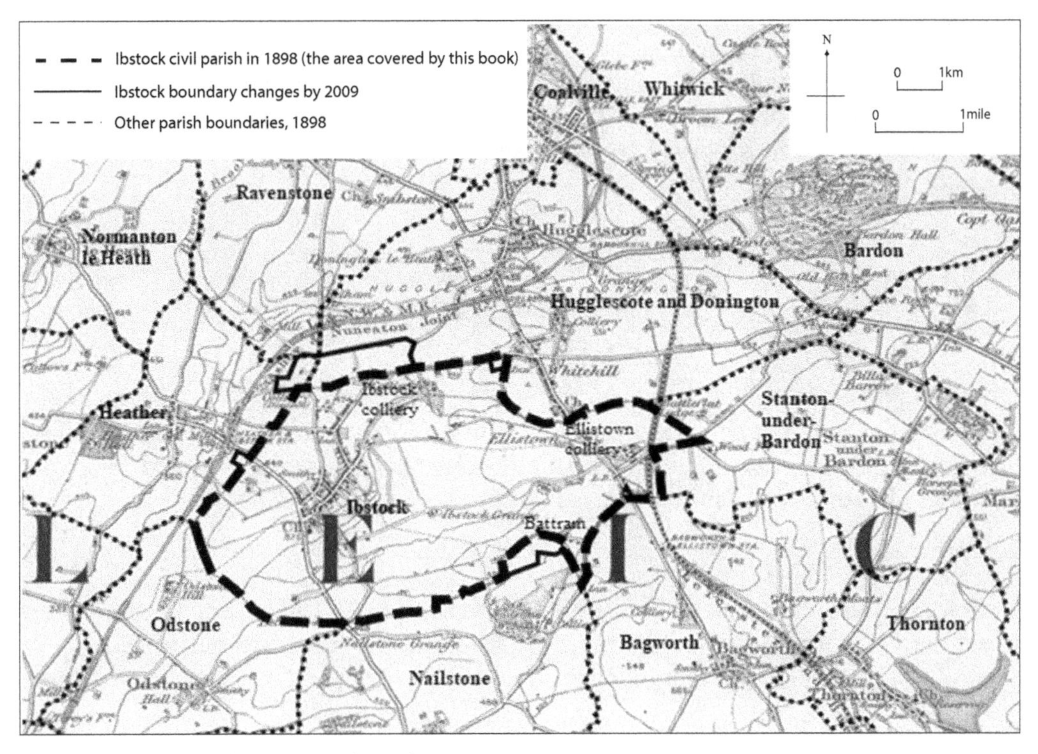

Map 2 *Ibstock and neighbouring civil parishes in 1898.*

1 http://www.visionofbritain.org.uk/ (accessed 10 Mar. 2019).
2 OS Map 1", sheet 155 (1899 edn); The North West Leicestershire (Parishes) Order 1983; The North West Leicestershire (Parishes) Order 1986; Ex inf. N. Taylor, Legal Services Team, NWL DC.
3 2011 census.

Ibstock's western boundary with Heather is almost straight. The latter place-name suggests the boundary was drawn across open heath land, with few natural features.[4] From the point in the south-west where the boundaries of Ibstock, Heather and Odstone meet, and moving anti-clockwise, the boundary traces a sweeping convex curve, perhaps indicative of the extent of land cleared for ploughing when the settlement was established. After a short, straighter, section, it picks up the course of a small brook. The boundary originally then turned north to run along Battram Road, but was moved *c.*300 m south in 1984, to include the entire village of Battram within Ibstock parish.[5] From Battram, it turns sharply to the south, then doubles back on itself to create a small 'pan-handle' shape, where Ibstock meets the parishes of Nailstone and Bagworth. This pattern is often a feature of early boundaries in areas of woodland or heath.[6] Bagworth had a large wood in 1086, measuring one league by half a league (*c.*500 a.).[7] The concave curve of the parish boundary in the south-east may mark an early boundary of Bagworth Wood.

The boundary then turns to the north, then east, then north-west to pick up the course of Ibstock's northern brook, which formed part of the boundary between the townships of Ibstock and Hugglescote. It then strikes north to Leicester Road, then originally taking an almost straight course for 1.4 miles to Heather. The name of the village to the north, Donington-le-Heath, suggests this area was also open heathland when the township boundary was established. A further boundary change in 1984 transferred land suitable for property development from Hugglescote and Donington, Ravenstone and Heather parishes into Ibstock (Map 2).

Landscape

Relief

The parish is gently undulating, rising from 110 m. above Ordnance Datum (OD) in the south-west to 165 m. above OD in the east. The village lies between 115 m. and 130 m. above OD, with the parish church unusually at the lowest point.

Geology

The Leicestershire and South Derbyshire coalfield forms an ellipse, oriented north-west to south-east, covering an area of *c.*100 square miles.[8] The Ashby anticline, near the centre of this area, is largely unproductive. The basin to the west of the anticline is known

4 B. Cox, *The Place-names of Leicestershire*, VI (Nottingham, 2014), 104.
5 Ex inf. N. Taylor, Legal Services Team, NWL DC.
6 D. Hooke, *The Landscape of Anglo-Saxon England* (1998), 80.
7 *Domesday*, 649. Area calculated as length x breadth x 0.7: O. Rackham, *Trees and Woodland in the British Landscape: The Complete History of Britain's Trees, Woods and Hedgerows* (2001), 48
8 C. Fox-Strangways, *The Geology of the Leicestershire and South Derbyshire Coalfields* (1907), 1.

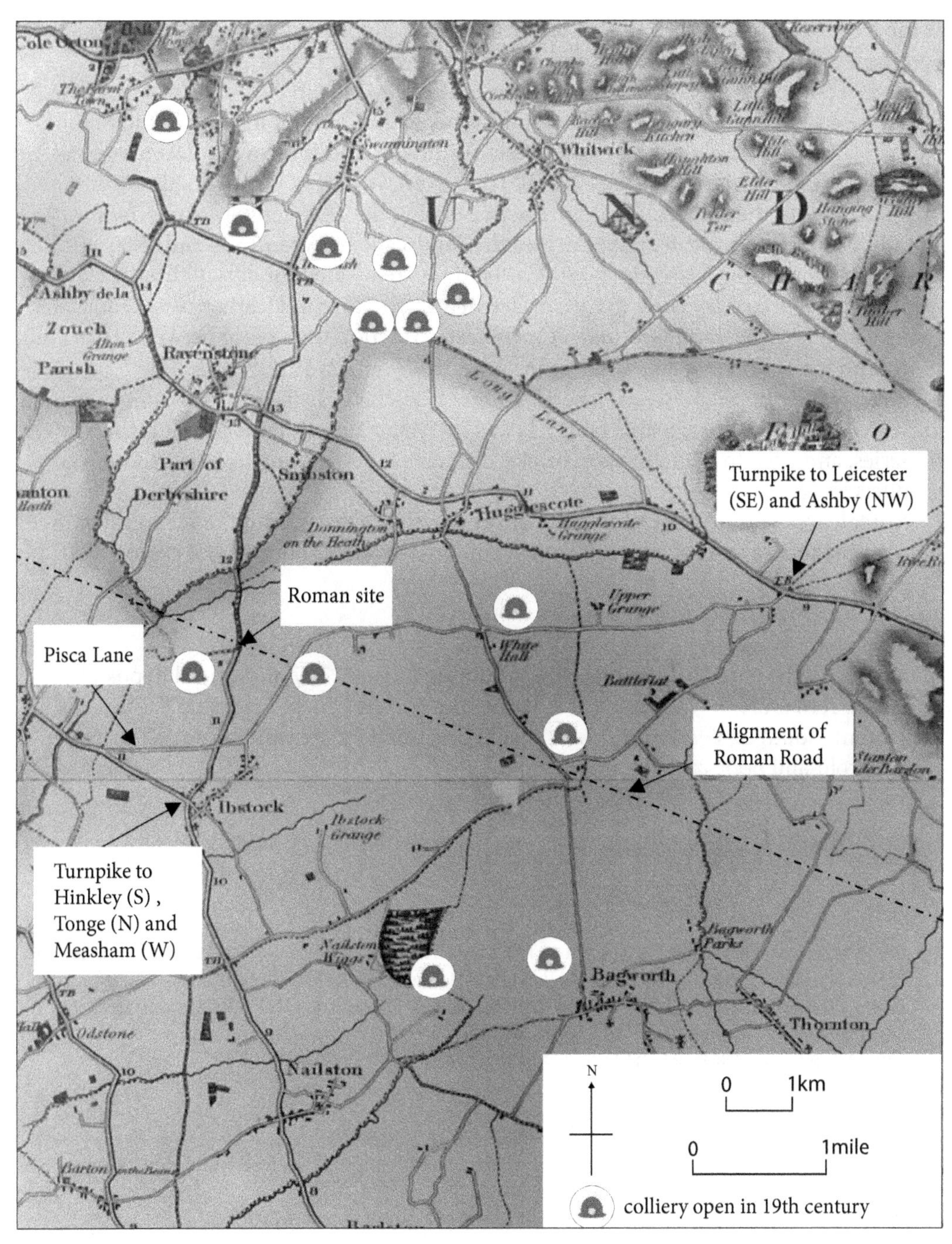

Map 3 *Ibstock and part of the Leicestershire coalfield area in 1827, also showing collieries open during the 19th century.*

as the Derbyshire coalfield, and that to the east is the Leicestershire coalfield, although both basins straddle the county boundary.[9]

In the southern part of the Leicestershire coalfield, which includes Ibstock, the coal seams are concealed beneath New Red Sandstone, with a band of igneous Whitwick Dolerite immediately above the coal between Whitwick and Ellistown.[10] Deep mining for coal began in this area in the 1820s.[11] Map 3 overlays part of Greenwood's county map (1827) with the collieries that were active during the 19th century, and provides an indication of the scale of change across this landscape between 1820 and 1900 as new mines opened, and also since 1990, as land was reinstated for agriculture, or as woodland.[12] The coal lay close to the surface in a small inlier in Heather parish, adjacent to Ibstock's western parish boundary. Open-cast extraction took place between 1976 and 1996, with the land reinstated to become Sence Valley Forest Park.[13]

Fireclay deposits sit between the coal seams.[14] Fireclay resists heat, and can be vitrified to create a smooth impermeable fabric. It was extracted at both Ibstock and Ellistown collieries, and used to make furnace bricks, drainage pipes and intricate terracotta products.[15]

A small area of sandstone in the east of the parish snakes around the medieval grange site.[16] Ironstone was found when Ellistown colliery was sunk, but was not exploited.[17]

Soils

In the west of the parish the soils are free-draining loams.[18] The superficial deposits across the remainder of the parish are clays of the Mercia Mudstone group.[19] The soils in the extreme south and east of the parish were described by the tithe commissioners in 1838 as 'cold and poor in the extreme'.[20]

9 Fox-Strangways, *Geology*, 18; K. Spink and T.D. Ford, 'The Coal Measures', in P.C. Sylvester-Bradley and T.D. Ford (eds), *The Geology of the East Midlands* (Leicester, 1968), 98; C. Owen, *The Leicestershire and South Derbyshire Coalfield*, 1200–1900 (Ashbourne, 1984), 13–15; Brit. Geol. Surv, https://www.bgs.ac.uk/downloads/start.cfm?id=2556 (accessed 1 Apr. 2018).

10 Fox-Strangways, *Geology*, 33–4; Owen, *Leicestershire and South Derbyshire*, 12, 17.

11 *VCH Leics*. III, 38.

12 ROLLR, Ma/L/29.

13 E. Hull, *The Geology of the Leicestershire Coalfield and of the Country around Ashby-de-la-Zouch* (1860), 71; 'Coalfield North Opencast Site Open Day' (leaflet, 1990); https://www.forestryengland.uk/sence-valley (accessed 11 Nov. 2019).

14 *VCH Leics*. III, 39; Brit. Geol. Surv., Mineral Planning Factsheet: Fireclay, 5.

15 Below, Economic History, extractive industries.

16 http://mapapps.bgs.ac.uk/geologyofbritain/home.html (accessed 24 Feb. 2019); below, Economic History, extractive industries.

17 ROLLR, DE 4939/352, p. 3; below, Economic History, extractive industries.

18 Cranfield Soil and Agrifood Institute, http://www.landis.org.uk/soilscapes/ (accessed 24 Feb. 2019).

19 Brit. Geol. Surv., https://www.bgs.ac.uk/downloads/start.cfm?id=2556 (accessed 1 Apr. 2018); Cranfield Soil and Agrifood Institute, http://www.landis.org.uk/soilscapes/ (accessed 24 Feb. 2019).

20 TNA, IR 18/4506.

Figure 1 *Battram Wood, one of five named woods planted in the south of the parish as part of the National Forest.*

Watercourses

Springs rise from the sandstone in many places. The northernmost of Ibstock's three brooks fed an industrial reservoir at Ibstock colliery. From there, the brook flows south-west and passes to the south of Ibstock church to reach the western parish boundary. Two springs in the east of the parish near Pickering Grange farmhouse form a second brook, which flows south-west over Overton Road (a ford in 2019) and under Hinckley Road, before joining the other brook a little further west. The southernmost brook rises in Nailstone parish to flow west, and forms part of Ibstock's southern parish boundary. On reaching Overton Road it flows north down the valley to join the second brook at the ford. The combined watercourse flows into the river Sence beyond the parish boundary, and eventually reaches the Trent near Alrewas (Staffs.).

Land Use

The soke of Ibstock belonged to Bagworth in 1066.[21] The two settlements may once have been part of a much larger estate which fragmented before the Conquest. Ibstock's place-name, which means the dairy farm of Ibba (an Old-English personal name), suggests

21 *Domesday*, 649.

that Ibstock had a specialist function within that estate.[22] Garendon abbey named their grange in the east of the parish Swynfen.[23] Their other granges were named after the places where they were located,[24] and perhaps Swynfen ('swine fen') was an old name for this area, where pigs rootled on poorly-drained land.[25]

Garendon abbey kept a large flock of sheep on their Ibstock land, and the soils across the remainder of the parish supported mixed farming. After 1775, arable farming was mostly concentrated in the west and north of the parish, and dairy farming predominated on the heavier soils to the south and east.

Mixed woodland totalling 163 ha. (404 a.) was planted from the 1990s between the southern parish boundary and Pretoria Road as part of the creation of the National Forest, which stretches across former industrial areas in Staffordshire, Derbyshire and Leicestershire (Figure 1).[26] The species include Ash, Common Alder, Corsican Pine, Douglas Fir, European Larch, Hazel, Lime, Norway Spruce, Oak, Poplar, Sweet Chestnut, Wild Cherry and Willow. A further 17 ha. (42 a.) of woodland was planted between Paget farm and the sewage works in the south-west of the parish.

There has been small-scale clay extraction since at least the 17th century. Two coal mines were sunk in the north and east of the parish in the 19th and 20th centuries, and the red marls overlaying the coal measures have been extensively quarried in the vicinities of the mines. Quarrying continued at both sites in 2019.[27] Exhausted quarries have been reinstated for agriculture or public amenities, and active quarries are screened by banks and trees. The clays hold vast quantities of water, which was directed to Leicester Corporation's Thornton Reservoir from 1893, and treated to provide piped water to the Coalville Urban Area and Ibstock from 1932.[28]

Communications

Roads

It has long been speculated that the Roman road from Colchester to Leicester, known as the *Via Devana*, continued north-west from Leicester to Chester. Margary did not recognise this road, but earthworks, cropmarks and a stretch of metalled road have been found at five separate locations on a straight alignment which stretches 21 km north-west from a few miles outside Leicester.[29]

22 Cox, *Place-Names* VI, 142.
23 *VCH Leics.* II, 5, Nichols, *History* III, 823.
24 ROLLR, DE 40/26.
25 Cox, *Place-Names* VI, 143.
26 Area calculated through https://magic.defra.gov.uk/; https://www.nationalforest.org/ (accessed 24 Feb. 2019).
27 Below, Economic History, extractive industries.
28 Ibid; below, Local Government, local government after 1894; W.W. Baum, *The Water Supplies of Leicestershire* (Leicester, 1949), 44–5.
29 I.D. Margary, *Roman Roads in Britain* (1973 edn); P. Liddle and R.F. Hartley, 'A Roman road through north-west Leicestershire', *Trans. LAHS*, 68 (1994), 186–9; Leics. and Rutl. HER, MLE 9662; MLE 4345 (at SK 310155, SK 386122, SK 407114, SK 460090, SK 488080).

An Act of 1760 authorised a turnpike trust to improve the road from Hinckley through Ibstock towards Melbourne (Derb.), to meet the turnpike road between Tamworth (Staffs.) and Nottingham at Tonge. For five months in every year teams of eight horses regularly drew loads of up to seven tons of lime south along this road from the quarries near Breedon on the Hill.[30] The road also served the collieries near Coleorton and Swannington. A westward spur from Ibstock through Heather (which became Station Road) served the southern part of the Derbyshire coalfield (Map 3). The turnpike trust was required to spend equal sums of money on the two sections, to ensure similar treatment of mineral owners.[31] A revised Act of 1828 brought Pisca Lane, which also ran from Ibstock to Heather, within the ambit of the same turnpike trust.[32] The Trust was dissolved in 1880.[33] This road crossed the turnpike road between Ashby-de-la-Zouch and Leicester.[34] This supported Ibstock's development in the late 18th century as an industrial village serving Leicester hosiers.[35]

Carriers

Two carriers operated a Saturday service between Leicester and Ibstock in 1815.[36] By 1828 there was also a weekly market-day service to Hinckley.[37] In 1835, there were services to Hinckley on Mondays, Ashby-de-la-Zouch on Tuesdays and Saturdays, Leicester on Wednesdays and Saturdays, Loughborough on Thursdays and Shepshed on Saturdays.[38] Carriers continued to operate a twice-weekly service to Leicester and weekly services to Ashby and Loughborough throughout the 19th century. The last reference to a service to Hinckley was in 1863.[39] Only the Leicester services continued from Ibstock in 1908.[40]

Bus and Coach Services

James Newman offered a horse-drawn brake service in 1912 and 1916.[41] Cherry's of Chapel Street (probably John Cherry) and Newbold's of Curzon Street (probably Thomas Newbold) also provided horse-drawn brakes to Bagworth station every Saturday for the train to Leicester.[42]

30 *Report of the Royal Commission on the State of Roads in England and Wales* (Parl. Papers 1840 [C. 280], xxvii), p. 266.
31 33 Geo. II, c. 46; 44 Geo. III, c. x; ROLLR, DE 380/2; A. Cossons, *The Turnpike Roads of Leicestershire and Rutland* (Newtown Linford, 2003), 54–56.
32 9 Geo. IV, c. v; ROLLR, DE 380/23.
33 41 & 42 Vict. c. 62.
34 ROLLR, Ma/L/1.
35 *VCH Leics.* III, 81; Below, Economic History, manufacture.
36 *Leic. Dir.* (Leicester, 1815), 77.
37 Pigot & Co., *Nat. Comm. Dir. for Leics.* (1828), 480, 492.
38 Pigot & Co., *Nat. Comm. Dir. for Leics.* (1835), 69.
39 W. White, *Hist., Gaz., and Dir. of Leics. and Rutl.* (Sheffield, 1846), 564; *PO Dir. of Leics. and Rutl.* (1855), 52; W. White, *Hist., Gaz., and Dir. of Leics. and Rutl.* (Sheffield, 1863), 678; *PO Dir. of Leics. and Rutl.* (1876), 372; *Kelly's Dir. of Leics. and Rutl.* (1895), 94.
40 *Kelly's Dir. of Leics. and Rutl.* (1908), 107
41 *Kelly's Dir. of Leics. and Rutl.* (1912), 108; (1916), 107.
42 Memories of S. Wallace in J. Carswell (ed.), *Ibstock Lives* (Coalville, *c.*1991), 25.

It was announced in 1913 that 'trial runs' of a motor-bus service for Ibstock and district had been successful.[43] No subsequent service has been identified before the First World War. Albert Hipwell of Leicester Road and William and Albert Brooks of Copson Street offered motorised bus services from *c.*1919, Brooks to local factories, and Hipwell to Coalville.[44]

The Birmingham Midland Motor Omnibus Company ('Midland Red'), began a daily service between Leicester and Ibstock in 1922, and from Leicester to Ashby on Wednesdays and Saturdays, calling at Ibstock.[45] There were three more bus and coach businesses by 1928: Hubert Bircher on High Street, G. Rudin & Son on Melbourne Road and Windridge, Sons & Riley, also on Melbourne Road.[46] By 1933 they had been joined by Harry Fowkes of Chapel Street, trading as H.F. Bus Service. Services ran to Coalville, Heather and Leicester.[47] Bircher and Midland Red offered services to Market Bosworth from 1931, following the cessation of railway passenger services from Heather and Ibstock station.[48]

Hipwell's business and depot were purchased by Browns Blue in 1946, who also bought Rudin's vehicles and services.[49] They ran buses in 1956 to Ashby, Coalville and Leicester, won some school contracts and had works contracts with Nailstone Colliery, Desford Colliery, Clutsom and Kemp's elastic factory in Coalville, the engineering company Tube Investments at Desford and footwear factories in Earl Shilton.[50] The company was acquired by Midland Red in 1963. Reliant Coaches Ltd, operating from Melbourne Road between 1963 and 2007, provided works, colliery and school services.[51]

Arriva Midlands offered a regular service between Ibstock and Coalville in 2019. Roberts Coaches, based in Hugglescote, provided a service between Hinckley and Coalville, which called at Ibstock.[52]

Post and Telecommunications

Thomas Thomas, a draper, was appointed as receiver of post for Ibstock in 1843.[53] Thomas Bailey (a tailor and draper) was postmaster from 1847 to 1888. His house in

43 *Leic. Chron.*, 8 Nov. 1913.

44 L.S. Eggington, *Ibstock: A Story of her People* (Moira, 1984), 3, 23; further details of Ibstock's bus businesses below, Economic History, retail and services.

45 P.L. Hardy, *Midland Red, Leicester and Leicestershire Route History 1920–1929* (Leicester, 1972), 1.

46 *Kelly's Dir. of Leics. and Rutl.* (1928), 115–6; Ex inf. Iris Gleeson.

47 C.S. Dunbar, 'Independent Still', in *Commercial Motor*, 4 May 1956, http://archive.commercialmotor.com/article/4th-may-1956/60/independent-still (accessed 5 Oct. 2018); Fare sheet for H.F. bus service, 1933 (priv. colln).

48 R.V.J. Butt, *The Directory of Railway Stations* (Sparkford, 1995), 129; ROLLR, DE 3640/170, pp. 81, 123.

49 The company's memorandum and articles of association contains no apostrophe in the name Browns Blue, image in M. Gamble, *Brown's Blue: The Leicestershire Bus Company that took the Community to its Heart* (Enderby, 2012), 59.

50 Gamble, *Brown's Blue*, 72–3; Dunbar, 'Independent Still'.

51 Gamble, *Brown's Blue*, 138–40; *Commercial Motor*, 5 July 1963, at http://archive.commercialmotor.com/article/5th-july-1963/74/planning (accessed 5 Oct. 2018).

52 https://bustimes.org/services/15-coalville-coalville; https://bustimes.org/services/159-hinckley-coalville (accessed 9 Oct. 2018).

53 J. Soer, *The Royal Mail in Leicestershire and Rutland* (Midland (GB) Postal History Society, 1997), 112; TNA, HO 107/601/10/25.

Deacons Lane (later renamed Gladstone Street) was described as the Post Office in 1861.[54] A money order, telegraph and savings bank service was available by 1876.[55] Edwin Badcock, a printer and bicycle-dealer, took over as postmaster between 1891 and 1908, from premises on High Street.[56] Post was originally routed through Ashby-de-la-Zouch, then Leicester, from 1895. Ibstock became a post-town in 1992, with a sorting office serving local villages. There was also sub-office on Leicester Road between 1936 and 1992.[57] Ibstock Community Enterprises Ltd, a not-for-profit company, became managers of Ibstock Post Office and sorting office in 2012.[58]

Ibstock was connected to the national telephone network in 1911.[59] BT Openreach offered fibre-optic broadband services from 2011.[60]

Railways

An Act of Parliament of 1830 authorised the Leicester & Swannington Railway Co. to construct a railway between those places, a distance of 16 miles, with branches from the collieries at Bagworth, Ibstock and Whitwick.[61] The main line opened for freight and passengers between Leicester and Bagworth in 1832, and through to Swannington in 1833.[62] The sections of the line north and south of Bagworth were linked by an incline. Wagons and carriages were detached from their locomotive and attached to a rope. The empty wagons were hauled up the 1 in 29 gradient by the weight of the full wagons descending, and another locomotive would complete their journey. A footpath was provided for passengers.[63]

The Leicester & Swannington Railway Co. was purchased by Midland Railway Co. in 1846, which obtained Acts to extend the line to Burton-upon-Trent (Staffs.), bypass the incline at Bagworth (where a replacement station was built) and connect the line to the developing national network at Knighton Junction (south of Leicester).[64]

Four trains initially ran through Bagworth in each direction on weekdays, and two on Sundays.[65] The station was renamed Bagworth and Ellistown in 1894. Bardon Hill station, on the same line and originally named Ashby Road, was closer to Ibstock by road. It closed in 1952.[66] Bagworth and Ellistown station closed in 1965.[67] Following

54 Soer, *Royal Mail*; TNA, HO 107/2083/416; RG 9/2265/67.
55 *PO Dir. of Leics. and Rutl.* (1876), 372.
56 TNA, RG 12/2507/88; *Kelly's Dir. of Leics. and Rutl.* (1908), 107.
57 Soer, *Royal Mail*, 112.
58 *Ibstock Community Voice*, Jan. 2017, 12; https://uk.linkedin.com/in/ibstock-community-enterprises-2a9a86139 (accessed 20 Dec. 2019).
59 *Leic. Daily Post*, 20 Nov. 1911.
60 https://www.ispreview.co.uk/story/2011/04/07/bt-reveals-156-new-uk-locations-for-its-next-gen-superfast-broadband-services.html (accessed 25 Feb. 2019).
61 11 Geo. IV, c. 58; *VCH Leics.* III, 110–11.
62 *VCH Leics.* III, 112–3.
63 Ibid., 111.
64 Ibid., 119; T.J. Chandler, 'Communications and a coalfield: a study in the Leicestershire and South Derbyshire coalfield, *Trans. and Papers of the Inst. of British Geographers*, 23 (1957), 166, 170.
65 Leics. Indust. Hist. Soc., *The Leicester to Swannington Update 2010: Compendium* (Leicester, 2011), 347; *Leic. Jnl*, 10 Aug. 1849.
66 Butt, *Directory*, 19, 27.
67 Ibid., 22.

the closure of the last of the Leicestershire collieries in 1991, and the decommissioning of Drakelow power station (Derb.) in 2003, the line was used almost exclusively to transport aggregates from Bardon Hill quarries to Knighton Junction for the main line south.[68] It remained open for freight in 2019, but the possibility of reopening the line to passengers was rejected by Leicestershire County Council in 2009, on cost grounds.[69] The risk of subsidence dictated speed restrictions, creating long journey times and making it unattractive to potential passengers.[70]

The Midland and London and North Western Railways opened the Ashby and Nuneaton Joint Railway in 1873, which passed through Market Bosworth. A branch extended north-east from Shackerstone station to Coalville junction, with stations in Heather and Hugglescote.[71] Heather station was renamed Heather and Ibstock in 1894. Timetabled passenger services ceased in 1931, although occasional excursions continued until 1964. The line closed in 1971.[72] The section between Shackerstone and Shenton, through Market Bosworth, reopened as a heritage steam railway (the Battlefield Line) in the 1980s.[73]

A mineral line from Nailstone colliery to the junction at Bagworth opened in 1862 and crossed the south-east of Ibstock parish at Battram Road.[74] This railway line was replaced by an overland conveyor in 1979.[75]

Population

Twenty-one tenants were recorded in Ibstock in 1086, suggesting a population of *c.*100 inhabitants.[76] In 1279, 50 families were recorded, excluding the households of the two manorial lords.[77] Only 86 people over the age of 14 years were enumerated for the poll tax in 1377, suggesting a total population of *c.*130 people.[78]

There were 29 households in the village in 1563, *c.*130 people.[79] No details were supplied to the 1603 return of the number of communicants, but there had been

68 https://www.derbytelegraph.co.uk/burton/new-power-plant-south-derbyshire-3075240 (accessed 11 Nov. 2019); https://www.railforums.co.uk/threads/leicester-burton-line.30941/ (accessed 11 Nov. 2019).

69 *Leic. Mercury*, 9 Sept. 2009.

70 *Leicester and Leicestershire Rail Strategy*, App. B (2017), 54–6 (at http://politics.leics.gov.uk/documents/s126315/Appendix%20B%20-%20Leicester%20and%20Leicestershire%20Rail%20Strategy.pdf) (accessed 10 Nov. 2019).

71 D.L. Franks, *The Ashby and Nuneaton Joint Railway together with the Charnwood Forest Railway* (Sheffield, 1975), 18–19, 21 and map.

72 A. Moore, *Leicestershire Stations: An Historical Perspective* (Narborough, 1998), 126–33; Butt, *Directory*, 129.

73 https://www.battlefieldline.co.uk/ (accessed 10 Nov. 2019).

74 *Leic. Guardian*, 15 Nov. 1862; OS map 6", Leics. XXIII.SE (1881 edn).

75 http://specialcollections.le.ac.uk/digital/collection/p15407coll7/id/128/ (accessed 19 Nov. 2019); OS Map 1:10,000, SK40NW (1983 edn); http://www.nigeltout.com/html/bagworth-rapid-loader.html (accessed 15 Dec. 2019).

76 *Domesday*, 649.

77 Nichols, *History* IV, 749–50.

78 Fenwick, *Poll Taxes*, 586–7.

79 A. Dyer and D.M. Palliser (eds), *The Diocesan Population Returns for 1563 and 1603* (Oxford, 2005), 221.

substantial population growth by 1670, when 67 houses were noted in the hearth tax.[80] This suggests a population of *c*.300, as does the return to the religious (Compton) census of 1676, which recorded 203 communicants.[81] The rector, John Laughton, estimated that there were between 60 and 70 families living in Ibstock between 1709 and 1721, suggesting a population of *c*.300.[82]

The trend of baptisms in St Denys' church suggests that the population began to rise from the 1780s,[83] perhaps through the inward migration of couples from other villages during the main period of parliamentary enclosure. The population was 763 in 1801, and 1,058 in 1821.[84] It was 1,107 in 1861, and then grew rapidly to 5,211 in 1921, as new mines were sunk in the area, including Ellistown Colliery. This growth ended when Ibstock colliery closed in 1929.[85] The population of 5,760 in 2001 was not markedly higher than the 5,365 residents in 1931.[86] It had increased to 6,201 in 2011.[87]

Settlement

Early and Roman Settlement

Flint cores and many worked flints, including arrowheads, scraper tools and blades, have been found across the parish.[88] A single Iron Age coin of the Corieltavi was found to the east of Overton Road.[89] A few sherds of Iron Age pottery have also been found, mostly alongside Roman material.[90]

A site 1¼ miles north of Ibstock church, where the assumed *Via Devana* meets Melbourne Road, has been interpreted as the location of a Roman town, occupied from the mid 1st to the early 4th centuries. A 'coherent and well-organised pattern of plot boundary ditches' extended for at least one kilometre on either side of the '*Via Devana*', and excavation uncovered three pottery kilns from the Roman period producing sandy grey ware, a tile kiln and several Roman coins (including two from the late 3rd

80 Ibid., 346, 384; *VCH Leics.* III, 172.
81 A. Whiteman, *The Compton Census of 1676: a Critical Edition* (1986), 332.
82 J. Broad (ed.), *Bishop Wake's Summary of Visitation Returns from the Diocese of Lincoln 1705–15* (Oxford, 2012), II, 879; Lincs. Arch., Gibson 12, 758.
83 ROLLR, DE 1717/4–6.
84 *VCH Leics.* III, 190.
85 Below, Economic History, extractive industries.
86 *VCH Leics.* III, 190; https://www.nomisweb.co.uk/query/asv2htm.aspx (accessed 4 Mar. 2019).
87 https://www.nomisweb.co.uk/reports/localarea?compare=E04005552 (accessed 4 Mar. 2019).
88 Leics. and Rutl. HER, Ibstock, MLE 10583 (OS: SK 422103); MLE 10584 (OS: SK 422104); MLE 10585 (OS: SK 422103); MLE 10588 (OS: SK 418104); MLE 10590 (OS: SK 423107); MLE 10591 (OS: SK 417101); MLE 10595 (OS: SK 422100); MLE 16527 (OS: SK 416104); MLE 17774 (OS: SK 402108);MLE 18789 (OS: SK 414097); MLE 18790 (OS: SK 416092).
89 Leics. and Rutl. HER, Ibstock, MLE 9190 (OS: SK 409094).
90 Leics. and Rutl. HER, Ibstock, MLE 9256 (OS: SK 421107); MLE 10580 (OS: SK 418101); MLE 10586 (OS: SK 421103); MLE 10594 (OS: SK 422100).

Figure 2 *Aerial view of St Denys' Church, from the south, with the village on higher ground to its north.*

century).[91] This area was in Ravenstone parish, but came within Ibstock following a boundary change in 1984.[92] A Roman villa, 1 km. to the south-east of this area, was discovered in a modern garden on Pretoria Road, where finds included a large quantity of Roman pottery, many roof slates, clay tiles, Roman glass, fragments of painted wall-plaster, animal bones and a coin (228 AD).[93]

Medieval and Later Settlement, to 1775

Ibstock Village

The 21 people recorded in Ibstock in 1086 probably lived in a single nucleated village. Its core may have been near the church, documented from *c.*1170 and probably on the same site as its 14th-century successor.[94] The ground here is lower than the modern built area. The church is 70 yd. from the northernmost brook, perhaps close enough to be

91 P. Liddle, 'Roman small towns in Leicestershire and Rutland', in P. Bowman and P. Liddle (eds), *Leicestershire Landscapes* (Leicester, 2004), 68; J.N. Lucas, 'A Romano-British settlement at Ravenstone', *Trans. LAHS*, 56 (1981), 104–7; Northamptonshire Archaeology, 'Archaeological Geophysical survey at Ravenstone Road, Ibstock, Report 11/287' (2011); Leics. and Rutl. HER, Ibstock, MLE 4561 (OS: SK 406114).

92 The North West Leicestershire (Parishes) Order 1983.

93 Leics. and Rutl. HER, Ibstock, MLE 10190 (OS: SK 411105).

94 Below, Religious History.

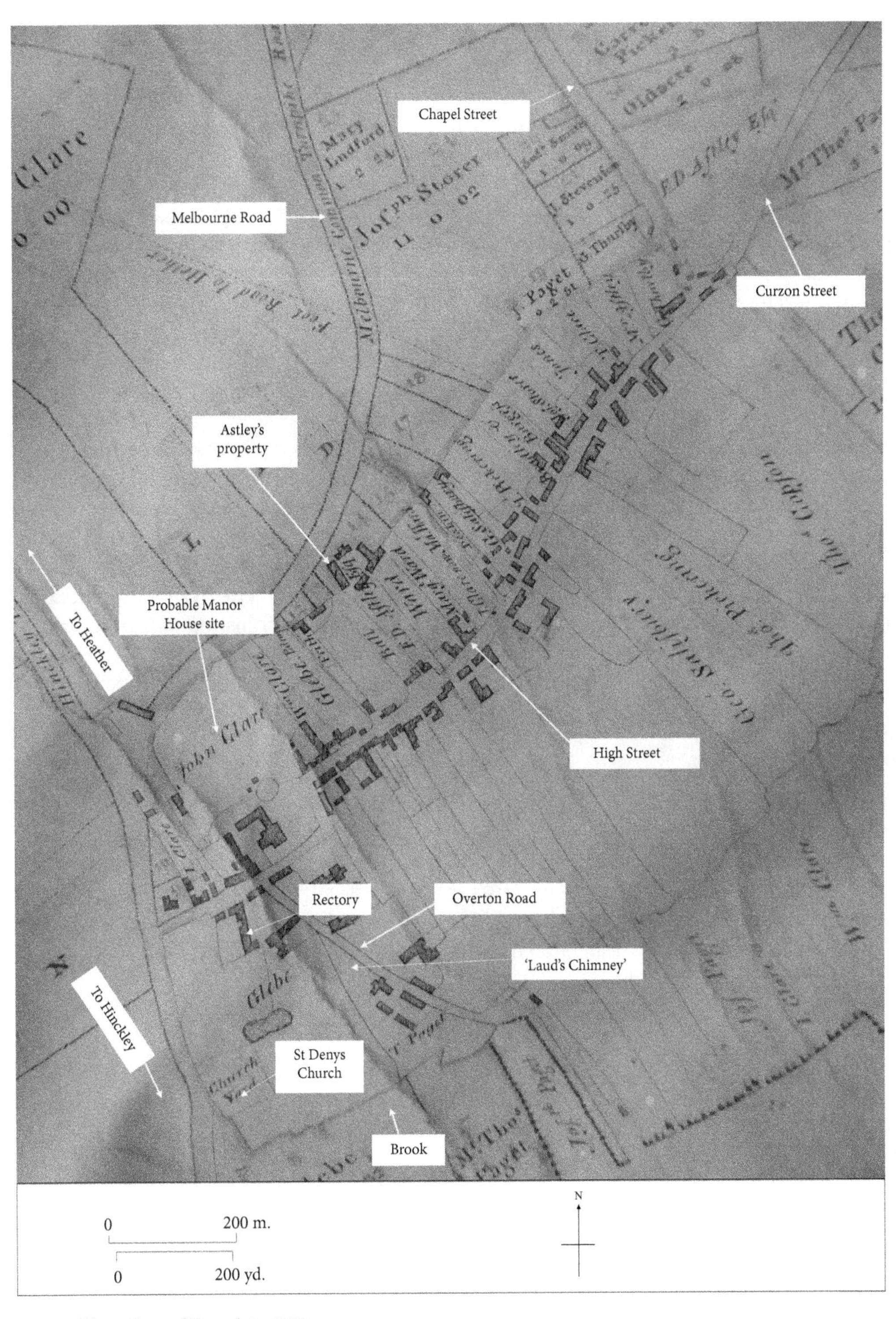

Map 4 *The village of Ibstock in 1775.*

convenient for baptisms, but away from boggy ground. The approach from High Street in 2019 is through an avenue of trees on the glebe land which extended to the north and east of the building. The subsequent growth of the village on higher ground to the north and east has the effect of making the church appear isolated (Figure 2).

The earliest surviving plan of the village, from 1775 (Map 4), suggests two distinct phases of development.[95] Between the church, Hinckley Road and the double bend towards the southern end of High Street, the village appears to have grown organically in a period when there was little pressure on land. Two houses in this part of Ibstock have some surviving architecture to suggest they were built (or more probably rebuilt) in the 16th century, including the property labelled 'John Clare' on the plan, which is probably the site of the original manor house.[96] Houses may have been built along High Street, to the north of the double bend, in the 13th or early 14th century, when the population was expanding. These plots, especially on the east of the High Street, are long and narrow, and have the appearance of being laid out over the ridges and furrows of former arable land. Many are of a similar width, some curve slightly towards the brook to their south, and several plot boundaries align with those on the opposite side of the road.[97] Further northward expansion along High Street may have taken place between 1550 and 1650, a period of significant population growth.[98]

Land to the east of the church contains the deteriorating remains of a stone chimney.[99] This is known as 'Laud's chimney', or 'Archbishop's Laud's pantry', after William Laud, the rector of Ibstock between 1617 and 1626, who was appointed archbishop of Canterbury in 1633. The ruins stood 18 ft high in the early 20th century, but only *c.*2 ft remained in 2000.[100] It lies beyond the boundary of the glebe, and is almost certainly not part of a former rectory, but probably belonged to a farmhouse.[101]

Swynfen Grange

Garendon abbey built Swynfen grange 1½ miles east of the village before the end of the 12th century.[102] The place of assessment for tax was recorded for the first time in 1524 as 'Ibstoke and Swynfeld Grange', suggesting that the monastic property had become a significant farmhouse, whose occupier was sufficiently wealthy to be assessed for tax.[103] The farm's name had changed to Pickering Grange by 1576.[104] Ibstock Grange, ¾ mile to its south-west, became a separate farm in the 17th century, but the farmhouse may not have been built until *c.*1777.[105]

95 ROLLR, DE 8666.
96 Below, Landownership, Ibstock manor.
97 ROLLR, DE 8666; OS Map 25", Leics. XXIII.15 (1903 edn).
98 Above, population.
99 NHLE, no. 1074375, Archbishop Laud's Pantry, accessed 11 Apr. 2017.
100 Cawte, 'Report', 22.
101 ROLLR, 1D 41/2/340.
102 *VCH Leics.* II, 5.
103 TNA, E 179/134/323, part 2, m. 15.
104 *Cal. Pat.* 1575–8, 162; TNA, C 66/1147, m. 18.
105 Below, Landownership, Swynfen or Pickering Grange.

Overton

A charter of the mid 12th century gave land to Garendon abbey that was partly in Ibstock and partly in the 'other Ibstock' (*alia Ybestoca*).[106] Although separately identifiable, the 'other Ibstock' was apparently not significant enough to warrant a name of its own. In another charter of an unknown date, Reginald Bartein released to Garendon abbey all his claims to land in 'Great Ibstock' and in 'Little Ibstock now commonly called Otherton'.[107] A charter of John the Porter, probably from the late 13th or early 14th century, granted 1 a. of land in 'Otherton' in Ibstock to his son Alan.[108]

It is likely that the 'Other Ibstock' became 'Otherton', which then became Overton, but this cannot be proved. 'Overton way' and 'Overton hill' are named in charters to Garendon, but the name Overton does not appear elsewhere in records before 1606.[109] Overton way was probably not the modern Overton Road, which does not lead to the former monastic land. The usual derivation of Overton is from *ofer*, a hill or a ridge,[110] and the name 'Overton hill' may support this, but the description by Ibstock's rector in 1670 of houses in Overton being on the 'Lower' side of the village supports a derivation from 'Other tūn'.[111] The interpretation is complicated by the application of the name Overton to Ibstock's southern manor by 1606, and to a broad tract of land in the southern part of the parish by at least 1654, including Pildash Close and Kimbo, which lay to the west of Overton Road, and beyond the former monastic land.[112]

There is no evidence that anyone lived in Ibstock's Overton in the Middle Ages. Ivo de Overton was assessed for tax in Ibstock in 1332, but he may have come from Coleorton, five miles away, where the two manors were known in the 14th century as Overton Saucee and Overton Quartremars.[113] The single medieval lay charter which mentions Otherton or Overton may indicate that nearly all the land named Otherton or Overton in the Middle Ages was held by Garendon abbey and remained in their hands until the abbey was dissolved. References to land in Overton become more frequent from 1536.[114]

There were 26 houses on the 'Lower or Overton Side' in 1670 which each paid 3*d.* to the rector for 'smoke and garden', and 26 houses on the 'Upper Side' which each paid 2½*d.* [115] The higher charge on the Overton side suggests these may have included the large plots near the church. The Hearth Tax of 1670 does not list any houses in 'Overton'.[116]

Two other houses lay beyond the village in 1775, between the two brooks and immediately east of what became Overton Road. These were known in 2019 as Brookside and The White House (or Swingler's Cottage).[117] The latter has a rubble-built ground

106 Nichols, *History* III, 823.
107 Ibid., 835.
108 *HMC Hastings* I, 41.
109 Nichols, *History* III, 835; TNA, C 142/294/111.
110 Cox, *Place-Names* VI, 143.
111 ROLLR, DE 464/2.
112 TNA, C 142/294/111; ROLLR, DE 365/21; Ti 155/1.
113 TNA, E 179/133/2, rot. 8d; B. Cox, *The Place-Names of Leicestershire*, VII (Nottingham, 2016), 77.
114 Cox, *Place-Names*, VI, 143; G.F. Farnham, *Medieval Village Notes*, III (Leicester, 1933), 13.
115 ROLLR, DE 464/2.
116 TNA, E 179/251/5.
117 ROLLR, DE 8666.

Figure 3 *Traces of an earlier gable end can be seen on the side of this much extended and re-fronted house at 150 High Street.*

floor, and may have originated as a squatter's cottage. There is no evidence to support the date of 1480 which appears on a plaque on the building.[118]

Settlement from 1775

Ibstock Village and Farms

John Throsby visited Ibstock in 1790 and noted '160 dwellings, which form one long street', including many 'well built' houses.[119] The southern end of High Street (a conservation area from 1992), appears to have been a fashionable place in the late 18th century.[120] Some older houses were extended or enlarged through the absorption of neighbouring houses within their structure, and refronted. One example is the large

118 NHLE, no. 1177329, The White House, accessed 1 Apr. 2017; Cawte, 'Report', 23.

119 J. Throsby, *Supplementary Volume to the Leicestershire Views, containing a series of Excursions in Leicestershire* (1790), 476.

120 NWL DC, 'Ibstock Conservation Area Appraisal and Study' (2001), 1.

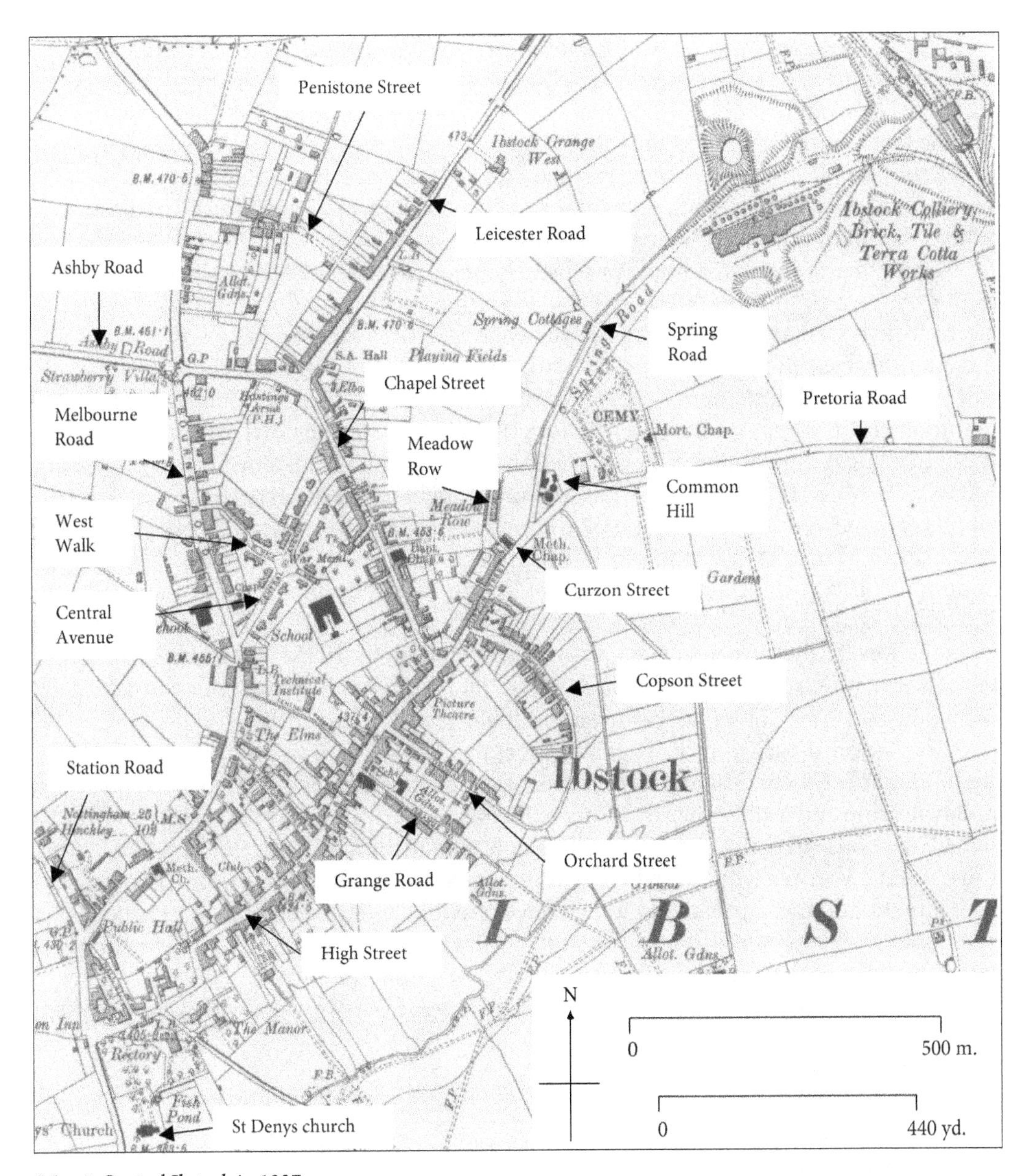

Map 5 *Central Ibstock in 1927.*

house at 150 High Street (Figure 3). This appears to have originated as a two-room cottage with rubble walls which was later extended, with a brick façade added in 1792.[121] A two-storey 'Georgian' house at 119 High Street (Glebe House) hides its origins as three older cottages.[122] The rear of its neighbour at 121 High Street, ostensibly a three-storey Georgian 'town house', also suggests more humble origins.[123]

121 Ibid., 14; NHLE, no. 1074372, 150 High Street, accessed 11 Apr. 2017; Cawte, 'Report', 14–15.
122 Cawte, 'Report', 26; NHLE, no. 1361246, 119 High Street, accessed 11 Apr. 2017.
123 Cawte, 'Report', 25; NHLE, no. 1074373, 121 High Street, accessed 11 Apr. 2017.

Three farmhouses (in different locations) were named Ibstock Lodge: one in the east, on old enclosures and possibly built by 1775, was renamed Ellistown Farm after it was purchased by Colonel Ellis in 1873,[124] one was 'lately erected' in 1825 at the site which became Ibstock colliery,[125] and the third was built by Thomas Paget (d. 1862) adjacent to Overton Road, *c.*1841.[126] Pasture Farm, on glebe land near Ibstock Colliery, had been built by 1881, but was lost to the clay quarry between 1973 and 1991.[127] Park Farm was built to the south of Ibstock Grange, *c.*1850.[128]

The number of inhabited houses in Ibstock increased from 228 in 1831 to 474 in 1881.[129] Almost all the new houses were added along existing roads. Signs of planning for future growth started to appear from 1880, when Orchard Street and Copson Street were laid out to the east of High Street.[130] By 1901, 21 houses had been added in School Fields (later Grange Road) and there was further ribbon development along Chapel Street, Common Hill and Pegg's Lane (later Pretoria Road). Land to the north of Ashby Road began to be developed in the early 20th century, and became Penistone Street.[131] Most houses were built of the local red brick, and many included decorative terracotta features such as ornamented bands, tiles and date tablets, manufactured and sold by the local brickworks.[132] Ibstock Gas Company was formed in 1877 and opened a gas works on Common Hill.[133] It was claimed in 1881 that 'Nearly all public and private houses, places of worship, &c., are now lighted with gas'.[134]

In the west of the parish, Cottage Farm had been built by 1885,[135] probably replacing a farmhouse which stood to its north east in 1838, which was no longer there in 1881,[136] and a new farmhouse at Valley Farm was built between 1881 and 1901.[137]

Pairs of semi-detached properties and short terraces of up to five homes were predominant between 1880 and 1930, reflecting the longstanding fragmentation of landownership and a strong market for small plots of land. There were 119 people who owned one house in Ibstock in 1910, 118 people who owned between two and five houses, and 43 people who owned six or more houses. Some of those owning two houses were miners, and their investment would have provided a secure income in summer months and when physical fitness declined.[138] Miss Sarah Hind, whose family fortune had been made in the slate industry at Swithland, ten miles to the east, owned numbers 136 to 148 High Street in 1910 (Figure 4).[139] This terrace of six houses with a shop at the

124 ROLLR, Ti/155/1; DE 1536/55/1–22.
125 ROLLR, DE 41/1/59.
126 Cawte, 'Report', 24.
127 ROLLR, DE 2072/176; OS Map 6", Leics. XXIII.SE (1885 edn); 1:2500, SK4110 (1973 edn), (1991 edn).
128 Cawte, 'Report', 24.
129 Census.
130 OS Map 6", Leics. XXIII.SE (1885 edn).
131 Census, 1901; OS Map 25", Leics. XXIII.11 (1903 edn).
132 ROLLR, DE 4939/326.
133 TNA, BT 31/14563/11153; *Kelly's Dir. of Leics. and Rutl.* (1881), 536; OS Map 6", Leics. XXIII.SE (1904 edn).
134 *Leic. Chron.*, 15 Jan. 1881.
135 OS Map 6", Leics. XXIX.NE (1885 edn).
136 ROLLR, Ti/155/1; OS Map 6", Leics. XXIII.SE (1885 edn).
137 OS Map 6", Leics XXIII.SE (1885 edn), (1904 edn).
138 ROLLR, DE 2072/176; 1911 census.
139 ROLLR, Wills, 1773 C–Z; Wills, 1822 A–H; TNA, IR 130/6/253; ROLLR, DE 2072/176.

Figure 4 *142–148 High Street, built at the turn of the 20th century.*

end, provided good-quality accommodation for colliery workers and their families, and five of the houses were occupied by miners in 1910.[140] Ibstock Colliery Company owned just 14 houses in 1910, all near the colliery. Their director Robert Thomson owned the 16 houses in Meadow Row.[141]

The first council houses in Ibstock, 52 in number, were built from 1921 in Central Avenue, East Walk and West Walk, surrounding the war memorial, which was unveiled in 1921 (Map 5).[142] The closure of Ibstock colliery in 1929 brought the period of population growth to an end, but new houses eased chronic overcrowding, and replaced those unfit for habitation. Market Bosworth RDC purchased 4 a. on the west of Leicester Road in 1931, where it built 20 pairs of semi-detached houses.[143] Plans for 60 council houses off Hinckley Road were rejected by the government in 1932, but a smaller estate of 24 houses proceeded.[144] There was a 'scarcity of houses at low rent' in 1936.[145] Owing to limited funds, the council surveyor was asked to consider renovating existing buildings, 'having special regard to old cottages having antiquarian value or otherwise possessing aesthetic merit'.[146] All the houses in the village were supplied with piped

140 ROLLR, DE 2072/176; 1911 census.

141 TNA, IR 130/6/249; ROLLR, DE 2072/176.

142 ROLLR, DE 3640/166, pp. 83, 122, 173; OS Map 6", Leics. XXIII.SE (1931 edn); NHLE, no. 1440138, Ibstock War Memorial; *Nottingham Jnl*, 21 Feb. 1921.

143 ROLLR, DE 3640/170, parochial mins, p. 10, planning and housing mins, pp. 13, 16, 26.

144 ROLLR, DE 3640/170, planning mins, 14 Sept. 1932, 7 Dec. 1932, 24 May 1933.

145 ROLLR, DE 3640/171, parochial min., 20 Oct. 1936.

146 ROLLR, DE 3640/171, planning and housing min., 24 Mar. 1937.

water from 1932.[147] Battram was supplied with fresh water in 1935.[148] The occupants of Ibstock's council houses requested electric light in 1934, suggesting many other houses had been connected.[149] Redholme Bungalow Farm, to the north of Ibstock Grange, was built on the site of the isolation hospital that closed in 1932.[150]

In 1943, it was estimated that a further 250 houses needed to be built to relieve poor living conditions.[151] Little could be done during the Second World War, and just 14 were built by the council in 1946 on what became known as Sunnyside estate (off Station Road), with 40 pre-fabricated bungalows added in 1948.[152] The temporary properties were replaced by permanent houses from 1963.[153] The district council was reluctant to build in the 1950s, due to fears of subsidence. Instead, it built 200 properties at Newbold Verdon in 1955, five miles away, and transferred people on the Ibstock council housing list to the Newbold Verdon list.[154]

Ibstock Brick and Tile Company formed a housing association in 1947 to build houses for its employees on Leicester Road.[155] Twenty houses were built by 1960, known as the Redlands Estate.[156] The 1960s saw private and council developments off Penistone Street and between Copson and Orchard Streets.[157] The last council houses erected in the village were built on West Walk in 1987, replacing those built by the council from 1921.[158]

By 1973, a housing estate had been built adjacent to a site off Melbourne Road where it was planned to build an infant school. Another estate was added to the west of the infant school by 1980, bounded by a new spine road (Parkdale) giving access from Ashby Road. Between 1980 and 2019, further houses were added between Parkdale and the parish boundary, and in the triangular area to the north of Ashby Road, between the sports ground and the parish boundary to the west and north. These estates included children's play areas, and homes of various types and sizes, for private ownership, and for rent or purchase at below market rates by those with modest incomes.[159]

Ellistown Colliery Area and Battram

Joseph Ellis built ten houses on farmland, along Victoria Road, between 1875 and 1879, two for the managers of his colliery and brickworks, and eight for senior employees. He also built three terraces for miners on farmland along Ellistown Terrace Road in 1879.[160] A Primitive Methodist church, a shop and allotments created a small community (Map

147 ROLLR, DE 1524/129, pp. 705, 918; DE 3640/167, pp. 363, 375; below, Local Government, local government after 1894.
148 ROLLR, DE 3640/170, pp. 51, 62, 63, 66.
149 Ibid., pp. 53, 55.
150 Ibid., p. 205.
151 ROLLR, DE 3640/172, parochial min., 19 Jan. 1943.
152 ROLLR, DE 3640/173, parochial mins, 9 May 1946, 16 July 1946, 19 Oct. 1948.
153 ROLLR, L 711, 'Ibstock Village Survey Rpt' (1963).
154 *Leic. Mercury*, 15 Dec. 1955.
155 ROLLR, DE 3640/173, parochial mins, 19 Mar. 1947, 9 Apr. 1947.
156 Ibid.; OS Map 25" SK4111 (1960 edn); M. Cassell, *Dig it, Burn it, Sell it: The Story of Ibstock Johnsen, 1825–1990* (1990), 46.
157 ROLLR, L 711, 'Ibstock Village Survey Rpt' (1963).
158 Ex inf. M. Keatley, Legal Services Team, NWL DC.
159 OS Map 1:2500, SK 4010 (1960, 1973, 1980 edns).
160 ROLLR, DE 490/16, p. 5; TNA, RG 13/2966/63.

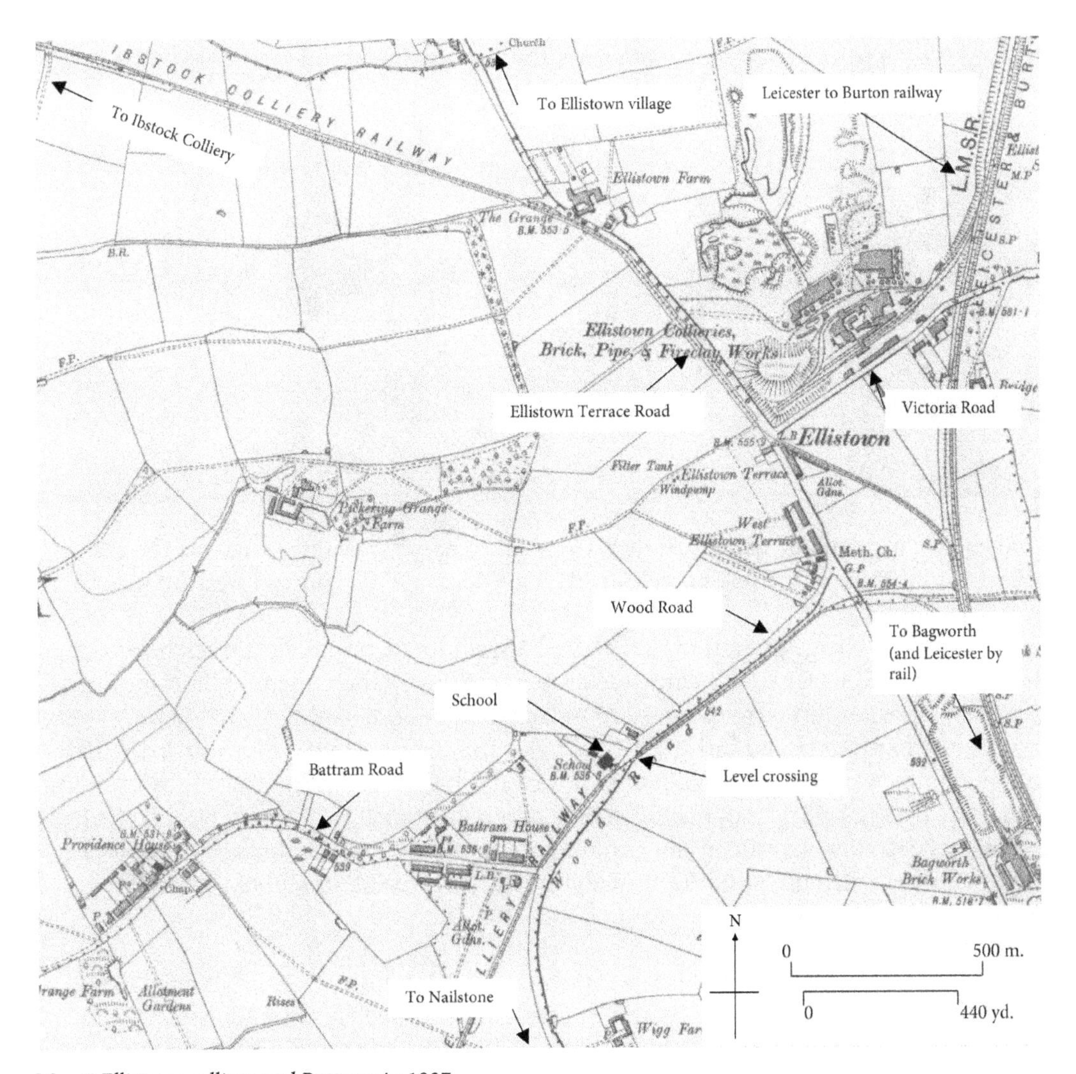

Map 6 *Ellistown colliery and Battram in 1927.*

6).[161] Subsidence had 'badly' affected the properties by 1907,[162] and buttresses were added (Figure 5). The houses, shop and chapel were demolished in the late 20th century.[163]

The place-name Battram is not recorded until 1713 (Battram Heath).[164] The suggestion that Ibstock's medieval Bertram family were originally 'of Battram' cannot be ruled out,[165] but the lack of any early form of the place-name, and lack of the preposition 'de' before the family name in early 14th-century records, makes this connection

161 OS Map 6", Leics. XXIII.SE (1931 edn); below, Religious History, Protestant Nonconformity.

162 ROLLR, DE 4939/366.

163 OS Map 6", SK 41 SW (1967 edn); memories of Ken Bowley in J. Carswell and T. Roberts (eds), *Getting the Coal: Impressions of the Twentieth-century Mining Community* (Coalville, 1992), 55–6.

164 Cox, *Place-names* VI, 144.

165 B. Cox, *Dict. of Leics. and Rutl. Place-names* (Nottingham, 2005), 8.

Figure 5 *West Ellistown Terrace (built 1879) and Primitive Methodist Chapel (built 1883–4),* c.*1910.*

unlikely.[166] The surname usually derives from a first name,[167] and that may be the case here, with Bertram of Ibstock noted in 1301, and Reginald' *fil'* (son of) Bert'am recorded in Ibstock in 1327.[168]

The modern village of Battram lies along Battram Road, originally a track between Bagworth and Hinckley Road. Only one property stood on the unnamed Battram Road in 1838,[169] apparently a farmhouse surrounded by its enclosed fields. Its name was recorded as Battram House in 1882, when it was still the only house on this road.[170] Land in this vicinity was owned by William James FitzWilliam Hall, the owner of Nailstone colliery.[171] By 1910, 58 houses had been built along this road, 37 of which were owned by Nailstone Colliery Company, including three terraces of eight houses.[172] A Wesleyan Reform chapel was built on Battram Road, *c.*1903, and a primary school was built on Wood Road in 1907 (Map 6).[173] The district council planned to build 30 houses in Battram in 1932.[174]

Subsidence was affecting the houses by the mid 20th century.[175] The National Coal Board announced plans in 1975 to undermine the east of the village, and expected subsidence to affect another 13 properties, the school and the sports ground.[176] The chapel, which had already closed, was demolished in the 1990s, also due to subsidence.[177]

166 TNA, E 179/133/2, rot. 8d (1332); Fenwick, *Poll Taxes*, 586–7.

167 J. Titford, *Penguin Dict. of British Surnames* (2009), 69.

168 Farnham, *Medieval Village Notes*, III, 4, citing TNA, CP 40/139, m. 87; W.G.D. Fletcher, 'The earliest Leicestershire lay subsidy', *Assoc. Archit. Soc. Rep. & Papers*, 19 (1887–8), 280.

169 ROLLR, Ti/55/1.

170 OS Map 25", Leics XXIII.16 (1883 edn).

171 Electoral Register 1883, Hugglescote Polling District.

172 TNA, IR 130/6/254; ROLLR, DE 2072/176.

173 OS Map 6", Leics. XXIII.SE (1931 edn); ROLLR, DE 3806/1903/77; DE 3806/1907/307; below, Religious History, Protestant Nonconformity; below, Social History, education.

174 ROLLR, DE 3640/170, planning and housing committee, pp. 52–3.

175 Memories of Edith Roberts, who spent her childhood in Battram, in Carswell and Roberts (eds), *Getting the Coal*, 56.

176 *Ibstock Par. Mag.*, Aug. 1979.

177 Ex. inf. Vera Harding, owner of the building when it was demolished.

The Pattern of Landownership

THERE WAS ONE MANOR IN Ibstock in 1086, which was divided between coheirs in the 13th century, and reunited in the hands of the Stafford family, probably in the late 16th century. William Stafford sold the manor in 1654 to Samuel Bracebridge and Thomas Clare, when a new partition was agreed. The title to the Clare portion of the manor was last recorded in 1714, and to the Bracebridge portion in 1728, but several claimants appeared following the sinking of Ibstock colliery in 1825, when mineral rights became attractive. The claim of Earl Howe (d. 1870) to be lord of the manor was generally accepted from 1855.

Two cartularies survive for Garendon abbey,[1] which was granted five carucates of land (*c*.600 a.) in Ibstock in the mid 12th century, probably from the manorial waste, and built a grange which they named Swynfen. This estate took the name Pickering Grange in the 16th century, from its lay tenants when the abbey was dissolved, and a prominent house was built on the grange site. This land had become five farms by the early 18th century, the most important of which were Pickering Grange and what became Ibstock Grange.

The rector's glebe was a significant landholding until the 20th century.[2] It is difficult to estimate other estate or farm sizes, due to the two-phase enclosure of the parish and an active land market. The Paget landholding was the most significant, with 465 a. in 1775 and 770 a. in 1910. This estate was broken up in 1919.

Ibstock Manor

Overlordships

Ibstock's overlord in 1086 was Robert de Beaumont, count of Meulan.[3] When Robert de Burton gave land to Garendon abbey in 1145, Geoffrey de Clinton (junior) remitted one-third of the service of one knight, and William, 3rd earl of Warwick, remitted the service of half a knight to both Clinton and Burton.[4] Ibstock was therefore presumably one of

1 One in BL (Lansdowne, MS 415) and one in private hands. Transcriptions of both are given in Nichols, *History* III, 805–6, 823, 834–5.
2 Below, Religious History, church origins and parochial organisation.
3 *Domesday*, 649.
4 Nichols, *History* III, 805.

the manors that Robert had transferred to his brother Henry, earl of Warwick, in 1088,[5] which Henry's son Roger, 2nd earl of Warwick, was compelled to grant to Geoffrey de Clinton (senior), *c.*1124. These manors were seized by Warwick after the deaths of Henry I and Geoffrey, but restored *c.*1138 to the younger Geoffrey de Clinton, subject to the earl of Warwick as overlord.[6] Ibstock manor was listed in some later records as being held for service of 1½ knights' fees, but just one knight's fee was recorded in others.[7]

The Hastings family had acquired the overlordship by marriage or purchase before 1279, when Henry Hastings was named as Ibstock's overlord.[8] He had died in 1269, but his son and heir John was a minor in 1279.[9] John, Lord Hastings, died in 1313, and was succeeded by his son John II (d. 1325).[10] On John II's death in 1325, the overlordship became part of the dower of his widow, Juliana, the daughter of Sir Thomas Leybourne, who outlived their son Laurence, earl of Pembroke (d. 1348).[11] After Juliana's death in 1367, the overlordship passed in turn to Laurence's son John, 2nd earl of Pembroke (d. 1375),[12] to John's widow Anne in dower (d. 1384),[13] then presumably to their son, also John, who died without issue in 1389.[14] Reynold, Lord Grey of Ruthin (d. 1440), the great-grandson of John, Lord Hastings (d. 1313) through John's daughter Elizabeth, was overlord in 1427.[15] The overlordship does not appear in later records.

Ibstock Manor before 1220

Ingulf, described as one of the 'men of the count of Meulan', held the manor in 1086.[16] He also held Bourton-on-Dunsmore and, with a certain Arnulf, part of Seckington and part of Wilnecote (Warws.) of Robert, count of Meulan. Ingulf's family appear to have taken the name de Burton.[17] Robert de Burton was Ibstock's lord in 1145. His brother was Ingulf, and they may have been direct descendants of Ingulf, Ibstock's lord in 1086. Robert's son was Richard, and Richard's sons were William and Henry.[18] Henry's three daughters inherited the manor as co-heirs: Ada, the wife of Robert of Garshall, Matilda, the wife of Philip of Ashby, and Joan, who married Robert of Verdun. Matilda's son

5 *ODNB*, s.v. 'Beaumont, Robert de, count of Meulan and first earl of Leicester (*d.* 1118)' (accessed 16 May 2017); ibid., 'Beaumont, Henry de, first earl of Warwick (*d.* 1119)' (accessed 16 May 2017).
6 D. Crouch, 'Geoffrey de Clinton and Roger, earl of Warwick: new men and magnates in the reign of Henry I', *Bulletin of the Institute of Historical Research*, 55 (1982), 119–22.
7 *Cal. Inq. p.m.* V, pp. 236, 397; VI, p. 389; Nichols, *History* I, cxv (transcript of Hundred Rolls, no longer extant).
8 Nichols, *History* I, cxv.
9 *Complete Peerage* VI, 345–6.
10 *Cal. Inq. p.m.* V, p. 236.
11 *Cal. Inq. p.m.* VI, pp. 385, 389–90; *Cal. Close* 1323–7, 433–4.
12 *Cal. Pat.* 1367–70, 21; *Cal. Inq. p.m.* XIV, p. 157.
13 *Cal. Close* 1374–7, 190–1.
14 *Cal. Inq. p.m.* XIV, p. 157; *Complete Peerage*, X, 396.
15 *Complete Peerage*, VI, 152; *Cal. Inq. p.m.* XXIII, pp. 65–6.
16 *Domesday*, 649.
17 *Domesday*, 657; *VCH Warws.* IV, 198, 249; VI, 39; http://domesday.pase.ac.uk/ 'Ingulf 1' and 'Ingulf 7' (accessed 14 Jan. 2020).
18 Nichols, *History* III, 806.

Thomas is believed to have died without issue.[19] This may have occurred by 1220, when Robert of Garshall and Roland of Verdun jointly presented Thomas of Verdun as rector.[20] Thomas Garshall and Robert Verdun held approximately equal shares of the manor in 1279.

The Garshall Manor, 1220–1654

Thomas Garshall, probably the grandson of Robert and Ada, held a demesne containing four virgates of land in 1279.[21] Thomas (or possibly a descendant of the same name) was lord in 1325.[22] His son Robert, who held the manor in 1331, succeeded him.[23] Robert's heir was his daughter Elizabeth, who married Sir Robert Burdet of Huncote.[24]

Burdet died in 1349, leaving one messuage, one carucate of land (the demesne) and 10 marks (£6 13*s.* 4*d.*) of rent in Ibstock to his son, also named Robert.[25] Robert (junior) died without issue. His heir was his brother John, who held the manor in 1376.[26] John's daughter and heir Elizabeth married Sir Humphrey Stafford of Grafton (Worcs.).[27] The manor remained in the Stafford family until the attainder of Sir Humphrey Stafford, executed for treason in 1486. It was granted by Henry VII in 1488 to his loyal and successful military leader, Sir Edward Poynings.[28]

Poynings died in 1521, leaving no legitimate children.[29] Stafford's attainder had been reversed by Henry VIII in 1514, and Ibstock manor was restored to Stafford's son, also Humphrey, who had been Poynings' ward.[30] It remained in the hands of the Stafford family until 1654, passing through the hands of William Stafford (d. 1606) and his son William (d. 1637).[31] The latter William had three sons, Edward, Charles and William. Edward inherited but died in 1638 leaving a young son, also Charles.[32] The manor was held by William Stafford in 1654, possibly the third son of the William who died in 1637.[33]

19 *VCH Warws.* VI, 39–40; Nichols, *History* IV, 749–50; W. Dugdale, *Antiquities of Warwickshire* (1730 edn), 289–91; G.F. Farnham, *Leicestershire Medieval Pedigrees* (Leicester, 1925), 39; R. Dace, 'The Bourton family and their lords in the 12th-century Midlands', *Prosopon Newsletter*, 13 (2003), 3.

20 W.P.W. Phillimore (ed.), *Rotuli Hugonis de Welles, Episcopi Lincolniensis, A.D. MCCIX-MCCXXXV*, II (Lincoln Rec. Soc. 6, 1913), 280.

21 Nichols, *History* I, cxv; IV, 749; Farnham, *Leicestershire Medieval Pedigrees*, 39.

22 *Cal. Inq. p.m.* V, p. 236; *Cal. Inq. p.m.* VI, pp. 389–90.

23 *VCH Warws.* VI, 40; TNA, CP 25/1/125/56 no. 37, online at http://www.medievalgenealogy.org.uk/fines/abstracts/CP_25_1_125_56.shtml#37 (accessed 22 Apr. 2020).

24 *VCH Warws.* VI, 40; W. Dugdale, *Antiquities of Warws.* (1730 edn), 289.

25 *Cal. Inq. p.m.* IX, p. 308.

26 *Cal. Close* 1374–7, 190–1; *VCH Warws.* VI, 40.

27 *VCH Warws.* VI, 40.

28 *Cal. Pat.* 1485–94, 250; S. Gunn, 'Sir Edward Poynings: an Anglo-Burgundian hero', *Publications du Centre Européen d'Etudes Bourguignonnes*, 41 (2001), 165.

29 *L&P Hen. VIII*, III (2), p. 1580.

30 *L&P Hen. VIII*, I (2), p. 1134; *Rot. Parl.*, VI, 526; *Cal. Pat.* 1494–1509, 84; *Hist. Parl. Commons*, 1509–1558, III, 146.

31 TNA, C 142/294/111; C 142/545/69; Nichols, *History* IV, 750.

32 Nichols, *History* IV, 750.

33 ROLLR, DE 365/39a.

The Verdun Manor, 1220–1654

Joan, daughter and co-heir of Henry de Burton, married Roland of Verdun. Roland was pardoned by Henry III for his rebellion against King John.[34] Rose Verdun held half a knight's fee in Ibstock in 1235.[35] Robert Verdun was lord in 1279, with a demesne of 3½ virgates.[36] He probably died before 1327, when Emma Verdun was assessed for tax in Ibstock.[37] John Verdun was lord in 1376.[38] He sold the manor and its lands to Sir Robert of Swillington in 1380.[39]

The manor was not mentioned on the death of Sir Robert in 1391, or on the death of his son and heir Roger in 1417. It appears to have been settled on Sir Roger for life, then successively for the benefit of Roger's widow Joan for life, their sons (in turn) and their heirs, then their daughter Margaret Gra (née Swillington) and her heirs, then Robert's half-brother Thomas Hopton and Hopton's male heirs, then other named beneficiaries.[40]

Sir Roger's widow Joan died in 1427, holding four messuages and four virgates in Ibstock in dower.[41] Their two sons had died without issue, so the manor passed to Margaret Gra (d. 1429). At her death, she held a life interest in four messuages and four virgates of land 'by name of a moiety of the manor of Ibstoke', and in the absence of children, this passed to John Hopton, the son and heir of Thomas Hopton.[42] John Hopton paid £1,000 in 1431 to Margaret's distant cousin Elizabeth Sampson (née Swillington), the great grand-daughter of Sir Robert of Swillington's older brother Adam, to remove any potential interest in the manors and lands.[43] Margaret's widower John Gra conceded any claim to the properties in 1435.[44] Ibstock was a substantial distance from Hopton's main estates in Yorkshire and Suffolk, and this gave him the clear title he needed to sell the manor and its lands. Nicholas Dixon, William Derby, John Tailboys, John Fulnetby and William Stanlow purchased the manor from Hopton in 1435 for 300 marks.[45] They were almost certainly acting as feoffees for Ralph, Lord Cromwell, who had inherited other entailed Leicestershire lands from Margaret Gra.[46]

34 *Rott. Lit. Claus*, I, 311.
35 *Book of Fees*, I, 520.
36 Nichols, *History* I, cxv.
37 Nichols, *History* IV, 750; W.G.D. Fletcher, 'The earliest Leicestershire lay subsidy', *Assoc. Archit. Soc. Rep. & Papers*, 19 (1887–8), 280; *Cal. Inq. p.m.*, V, p. 236.
38 *Cal. Inq. p.m.*, VI, pp. 389–90; *Cal. Close* 1374–7, 190–1.
39 *Cal. Close* 1377–81, 346–7, 352, 379, 498; *Cal. Close* 1381–5, 92; *Cal. Close* 1385–9, 264.
40 *Cal. Inq. p.m.* XVII, pp. 54–5, 58; XX, p. 246; *Cal. Pat.* 1413–16, 55; C. Richmond, *John Hopton: a Fifteenth-century Suffolk Gentleman* (Cambridge, 1981), xviii–xix, 2–3.
41 *Cal. Inq. p.m.* XXIII, pp. 61, 65–6.
42 *Cal. Inq. p.m.* XXIII, pp. 209, 215–7; *Cal. Fine 1422–30*, 317.
43 *Cal. Inq. p.m.* XXIII, pp. 209, 215–7; TNA, CP 25/1/292/67 no. 113; *Cal Close 1429–35*, 120, 130; Richmond, *John Hopton*, xviii–xix, 21–22.
44 *Cal. Close* 1429–35, 43.
45 TNA, CP 25/1/292/68, no. 179, online at http://www.medievalgenealogy.org.uk/fines/abstracts/CP_25_1_292_68.shtml#179 (accessed 27 Aug. 2020).
46 *Cal. Inq. p.m.* XXIII, p. 215; S.J. Payling, 'Inheritance and local politics in the later Middle Ages: the case of Ralph, lord Cromwell, and the Heriz inheritance', *Nottingham Medieval Studies*, 30 (1986), 76; S.J. Payling, 'The "grete laboure and the long and troublous tyme": the execution of the will of Ralph, lord Cromwell, and the foundation of Tattershall college', in L. Clark (ed.), *The Fifteenth Century, XIII, Exploring the Evidence: Commemoration, Administration and the Economy* (Woodbridge, 2014), 10; R.L. Friedrichs, 'The two last wills of Ralph lord Cromwell', *Nottingham Medieval Studies*, XXXIV (1990), 93.

Ralph, Lord Cromwell died in 1456. His will directed that all his land and properties that were not entailed were to be sold, and the proceeds given to charitable causes chosen by his executors.[47] The manor disappeared from view and was presumably sold: the longest-lived of Lord Cromwell's co-heirs, his niece Maud Stanhope, had no holdings in Ibstock on her death in 1497.[48] It is reputed to have been held by Sir Richard Sacheverell, who sold it to someone named Imin.[49] Sacheverell mentioned his lands and tenements in Ibstock when he made his will in 1534, but made no mention of the manor.[50]

In 1606, William Stafford (d. 1637) owned 'the manors of Ibstock and Overton'.[51] This is the earliest documentary reference to one of the manors being named Overton, but how and when he acquired this second manor is not known.

Ibstock Manor from 1654

William Stafford sold the two manors in 1654 to Robert Abbott and John Morris of London for £2,300.[52] They resold them almost immediately to Samuel Bracebridge of Atherstone Hall (Warws.), John Savage of Wilnecote (Warws.), Thomas Clare of Ibstock, and Thomas's brother William Clare of Atherstone.[53] Bracebridge and Thomas Clare immediately agreed a formal partition of the manors between them, on a new basis, with each having land in both Ibstock and 'Overton'. Bracebridge received eight yardlands of open-field land, 12 closes and 11 houses or cottages; Clare received the manor house, eight yardlands in the open fields, eight closes, 12 other houses and a smith's shop with a forge. Other manorial assets, including the right to hold courts, were shared equally.[54]

Clare Portion

The Clare family had been in Ibstock since at least 1543, when Thomas Clare was assessed for tax.[55] He owned a sizeable mixed farm at his death in 1558, with 19 cattle, 60 sheep and significant arable land.[56] When it became known that William Stafford was going to sell the manors, a later Thomas Clare (d. 1668) may have been keen to seize the opportunity to acquire land, to set up each of his two sons with a substantial farm. Bracebridge appears to have had no links to Ibstock, and did not move to the village, but he may have been known to William Clare, as both lived in Atherstone, and Thomas may have been introduced to him as someone who could facilitate the purchase by sharing the cost.

In his will, Thomas Clare (d. 1668) left the manor house, three yardlands and five closes of meadow and pasture to his eldest son Thomas (d. 1714), and two yardlands and two closes to his second son John (d. 1728).[57] His share of the manor, which is not

47 Friedrichs, 'Two last wills', 108.
48 *Cal. Inq. p.m. Hen. VII*, II, pp. 18–22, 34–5.
49 Nichols, *History* IV, 750.
50 TNA, PROB 11/25/187.
51 TNA, C 142/294/111.
52 ROLLR, DE 365/39a, indenture 15 Jan. 1653/4.
53 ROLLR, DE 365/39a, indenture 20 Jan. 1669.
54 ROLLR, DE 365/21.
55 TNA, E 179/134/323 pt 5, rot. 2.
56 ROLLR, W & I file 1558 A–F/146–7.
57 ROLLR, Wills, Leicester archdeaconry and Vicar General's court, 1668/91.

mentioned in his will, passed by survivorship to his brother and co-purchaser William Clare, who resigned his interest in 1670 in favour of Thomas (d. 1714).[58] From 1714, the land and share of the manor probably passed in turn to Thomas's two sons, Thomas, who died in 1732 without issue,[59] then John (bapt. 1677, date of death unknown),[60] then to John's son William (d. 1761),[61] followed by William's son John (d. 1783).[62] John (d. 1783) owned 76 a. of old enclosures in the south and east of the parish in 1775 and 101 a. of new enclosures in the north, in four separate parcels of land .[63] He left no children, and his will directed the sale of his estate, with the proceeds divided between his two sisters, Mary and Elizabeth.[64] Mary appears to have received some of the land in her own name, and some or all of the remainder may have been purchased by Mary's husband, Thomas Paget (d. 1818).[65]

John, the second son of Thomas Clare (d. 1668), died in 1728,[66] when the land may have passed to his son John (bapt. 1680, date of death unknown).[67] John (II) was probably the father of William (bapt. 1731, d. 1801),[68] who was allotted 88 a. in the enclosure award of 1775 and owned a total of 174 a. in Ibstock in 1798.[69] William left a son, John (III),[70] whose son Henry was listed as a chief landowner in Ibstock in 1863.[71] Henry moved to his wife Ann's native parish of Knipton, in the Vale of Belvoir, and died in 1880.[72] He had sold most of the land by 1873, when he owned just 16 a. in the county.[73] No one named Clare owned any farmland in the parish in 1910.[74]

Bracebridge Portion

The partition of the manor in 1654 provided Samuel Bracebridge with a half-share of the manor, eight yardlands and 12 closes.[75] The share of the manor with two yardlands and one close was sold by (a later) Samuel Bracebridge to Richard Power in 1707.[76] These passed by settlement to Richard's son Harrington, and in due course to Harrington's only child Ann, who married William Heatley.[77] Ann outlived William, and died in 1773. They had no children. Under the terms of the settlement, the land and share of the manor passed to the seven children of William Heatley's sister, Elizabeth Harding, as

58 ROLLR, DE 365/29; DE 1717/2; Wills, 1715 C–PA.
59 TNA, PROB 11/663/63; ROLLR, DE 1717/2; Nichols, *History* IV, 754.
60 ROLLR, DE 1717/2.
61 Ibid.; ROLLR, DE 1717/3; Wills and Admons, 1761 A–M.
62 ROLLR, DE 1717/3; DE 8666.
63 ROLLR, DE 8666; 109'30/94.
64 ROLLR, DE 1717/7.
65 ROLLR, QS 62/156.
66 ROLLR, DE 1717/2; Wills and Admons, 1729, A–G.
67 ROLLR, DE 1717/2.
68 Ibid.; ROLLR, DE 1717/6; Nichols, *History* IV, 754–5.
69 ROLLR, DE 8666; TNA, IR 24/18/9256; IR 23/44/138, ff. 188–9.
70 ROLLR, Wills and Admons, 1803 A–J.
71 ROLLR, DE 1717/6; W. White, *Hist. Gaz. and Dir. of Leics. and Rutl.* (Sheffield, 1863), 677.
72 ROLLR, DE 2811/9; DE 1717/6; TNA, HO 107/2102/328/12; ROLLR, DE 1505/5.
73 *Return of Owners of Land* (1873), Leicestershire, 8.
74 ROLLR, DE 2072/176.
75 ROLLR, DE 365/21.
76 ROLLR, DE 41/1/59 Lease and release 1706/7.
77 ROLLR, DE 41/1/59 Abstract of title of George Salisbury; DE 436/1; DE 365/105b.

tenants in common.[78] The land was purchased by George Thirlby in 1777, the tenant of Pickering Grange Farm.[79] The descent of the manorial share cannot be traced.

Astley Landholding

Samuel Bracebridge's remaining six yardlands passed through three further generations of the Bracebridge family.[80] In 1737, his great-grandson Samuel Bracebridge sold seven yardlands and seven closes in Ibstock to Sir John Astley, then of Patshull (Staffs.).[81] In his will of 1771, Sir John devised his lands and houses in Ibstock to his cousin Francis Dugdale Astley and heirs.[82]

Astley was lord of the adjacent manors of Nailstone and Odstone.[83] He may have claimed to be the lord of Ibstock manor, as Ibstock's enclosure Act awarded him the freeholds of cottages standing on the manorial waste.[84] This became an allotment of 9 p. bounded by a road, the parish boundary and Astley's personal allotment, and was absorbed into the latter. Astley's total allotment was 141 a., 12 per cent of the land enclosed at that time, and possibly then his only landholding in the parish.[85] He settled his Ibstock land on his eldest son, John Dugdale Astley, in 1799. Ibstock manor was not named, but the recovery of that year, to bar the entail, lists the view of frankpledge in Ibstock.[86] In 1826, John Dugdale Astley sold 184 a. of land and two houses in Ibstock.[87] The purchasers included '[John] Brentnall, Dean and Dormer, [Thomas] Bradley and Ward'.[88] Shortly afterwards, John Brentnall claimed his purchase included manorial rights.[89]

Claimants in 1831

It was said in 1831 that 'Earl Howe claims to be Lord of the manor; but the manorial rights are claimed by the Freeholders, and also by Mr Brentnall, of Bagworth, who purchased the manor house and its land from Sir John Astley'.[90] Ibstock colliery had recently opened, and the possibility of claiming mineral rights probably provided the motivation for the multiple claims.

John Brentnall died in 1837, and made no mention of the manor in his will.[91] His claim was implied to be current in 1846, but there is no evidence that anyone had stepped forward to take his place.[92] Lord Howe (d. 1870) continued to claim ownership

78 ROLLR, DE 41/1/59, abstract of title of Wm Thirlby and his mortgagees, 1831; DE 365/105a.
79 ROLLR, DE 41/1/59.
80 ROLLR, DE 41/1/59, abstract of deeds.
81 ROLLR, DE 41/1/59, abstract of title of Francis Dugdale Astley.
82 TNA, PROB 11/974/380.
83 Nichols, *History* IV, 808, 916.
84 14 Geo, III, c. 3.
85 ROLLR, DE 8666.
86 ROLLR, DE 41/1/216/2.
87 *Derby Merc.*, 25 Oct. 1826; ROLLR, DE 41/1/216/2; Copy of sales particulars with plan held by Ibstock Historical Society.
88 ROLLR, QS 62/156.
89 J. Curtis, *A Topographical History of the County of Leicester* (Ashby de la Zouch, 1831), 80.
90 Curtis, *Topographical History*, 80.
91 ROLLR, Wills, administrations and inventories, 1837.
92 W. White, *Hist., Gaz. and Dir. of Leics. and Rutl.* (Sheffield, 1846), 564.

of the manor in 1853.[93] His claim appears to have been generally accepted by 1855.[94] He paid no land tax in Ibstock in 1831, and the Curzon estate records show no landholdings in Ibstock until 1855, when he purchased 38 a. from the trustees of the late Thomas Bradley, previously owned by Francis Dugdale Astley.[95] This may have been instrumental in the general acceptance of his claim to be the manorial lord. Lord Howe's two sons (George, d. 1876 and Richard, d. 1900) and grandson (Richard, d. 1929), the successors to his peerage, were also accepted as the lords of Ibstock.[96]

Manor House

Only one manor house was listed when the manor was partitioned in 1654, and the detail within that document suggests that if there had been two, both would have been mentioned. It was included in the half-share of the manor purchased by Thomas Clare (d. 1668), who devised it at his death to his son Thomas (d. 1714).[97] Thomas II's estate was held in 1775 by John Clare (d. 1783), who lived in a house on a large corner plot at the south of High Street (later, the White House, 156 High Street). The size and location of this site makes it a prime candidate for the historic manor house (Map 4).[98] The eastern part of this site was severed, and two houses built on it in the early 20th century (152 and 154 High Street). The older 'White House' at the rear of the plot includes an east range containing windows which appear to be from the 16th century.[99]

A plan of Francis Dugdale Astley's estate in Ibstock at the time of its sale in 1826 includes just one property. This stood on Melbourne Road (indicated on Map 4). It was described in 1826 as the 'farmhouse of Sampson Massey',[100] and is presumably the property purchased by John Brentnall which he claimed to be the manor house. Later known as 73 Melbourne Road, this property was labelled 'Manor House' on early Ordnance Survey maps.[101] Its position, far from the church and isolated from the heart of the village, suggests it was never more than a farmhouse, as does its appearance, a brick property, with a central stair tower. It was divided into two dwellings in the 1920s.[102]

A property on the east side of Overton Road, opposite the former rectory, was known as 'The Manor' in 1903, but its name had been 'Ibstock House' in 1883.[103] The earliest part of this house may date from the 16th century.[104] It may have been named 'The Manor' by T. Guy F. Paget, the owner in 1910.[105]

93 *Complete Peerage* VI, 601–2; *Leic. Chron.*, 17 Sept. 1853.
94 *PO Dir. of Leics. and Rutl.* (1855), 52; W. White, *Hist. Dir. and Gaz. of Leics. and Rutl.* (Sheffield, 1863), 677.
95 ROLLR, QS 62/156; DE 3541, ff. 58v–59, 260–260v.
96 *Kelly's Dir. of Leics. and Rutl.* (1922), 107; ibid. (1928), 115.
97 ROLLR, DE 365/21; ROLLR, Leicester archdeaconry and Vicar General's court, 1668/91.
98 ROLLR, DE 8666.
99 Cawte, 'Report', 13.
100 Plan held by Ibstock Historical Society.
101 OS Map 25", Leics. XXIII.15 (1903).
102 Cawte, 'Report', 30–31.
103 OS Map 25", Leics. XXIII.15 (1883; 1903).
104 NHLE, no. 1074371, The Manor House, High Street, accessed 11 Apr. 2017; Cawte, 'Report', 6–12.
105 TNA, IR 130/6/253; ROLLR, DE 2072/176.

Swynfen or Pickering Grange

Robert de Burton gave 3½ carucates of land in Ibstock to Garendon abbey in 1145 in thanksgiving for a ransom of 30 marks (£20) paid by the abbot to release him from captivity, and for receiving his brother Ingulf as a monk. Robert's son Richard gave the abbey a further half a carucate in Ibstock and half a carucate in the 'other Ibstock (*alia Ybestoca*), to thank the abbot for paying six marks for his release.[106] The two charters were made at Leicester in the chamber (*thalamo*) of Arnold de Bosco, steward to the earl of Leicester.[107] He may have brokered the release, with the abbot agreeing to pay the ransom against an understanding that the charters would be given.[108] In a treaty concluded by the earls of Leicester and Chester between 1147 and 1153, both earls agreed that Ravenstone castle, two miles north of Ibstock, was to be destroyed, which hints at the lawlessness in this area during Stephen's reign.[109] Further gifts increased the abbey's landholding in Ibstock to five carucates (*c*.600 a.)[110]

The abbey built a grange on their land before the end of the 12th century, which they named Swynfen.[111] It was let to William White for an unknown term in the early 16th century, then in 1530 for 50 years to Thomas, John and Margaret Pickering.[112]

Garendon abbey was dissolved in 1536.[113] Its land and grange in Ibstock were granted in 1541 to Thomas Manners, earl of Rutland (d. 1543).[114] They were settled on the earl's son Henry (d. 1563) in 1542.[115] By 1553, the land was again in the hands of the crown (for unknown reasons) and was granted by Edward VI to brothers Thomas and Humphrey Cox in 1553, and settled on Thomas, his wife and their heirs.[116]

Thomas Cox was granted a licence in 1576 to alienate 100 a. known as 'New Close', part of 'Swynstede grange al[ia]s Pickering grange', to Gregory Cox and John Cox.[117] This is the earliest record of the name 'Pickering Grange'. Gregory and John Cox were licenced to transfer this close to Thomas's son George in 1581.[118] On Thomas's death in 1586, George inherited the remainder of the Pickering Grange land.[119] George agreed to lease 170 a. to Robert White in 1589, for 61 years.[120] In 1592, George settled New Close on his

106 Nichols, *History* III, 823.
107 Ibid., 834.
108 D. Postles, '*Defensores Astabimus*: Garendon abbey and its early benefactors', in B. Thompson (ed.), *Monasteries and Society in Medieval Britain* (Stamford, 1999), 109; Dace, 'The Bourton family', 2.
109 *VCH Leics.* III, 80.
110 Nichols, *History* III, 806, 827.
111 *VCH Leics.* II, 5.
112 ROLLR, DE 40/26; TNA, SC 6/HenVIII/1825, m. 20; Nichols, *History* IV, 759; *Valor Eccl.*, IV, 173.
113 *VCH Leics.* II, 6.
114 *L&P Henry VIII*, XVI, 325–6.
115 TNA, E 326/8835; E 326/8836; A Collins, *The Peerage of England*, I (1791), 246; *Cal. Pat. Edward VI*, V, 90, 92.
116 *Cal. Pat. Edward VI*, V, 90, 92; *Cal. Pat.* 1554–5, 4–5.
117 *Cal. Pat.* 1575–8, 162; TNA, C 66/1147, m. 18.
118 *Cal. Pat.* 1580–81, 53; TNA, C 66/1202, m. 35.
119 G.F. Farnham, *Medieval Village Notes*, III (Leicester, 1933), 14, citing Inq. p.m. Thomas Cocks, 1587 (TNA, C 142/214/239).
120 TNA, C 2/JasI/L3/4; ROLLR, 44'28/516.

son Thomas (d. 1619) and Thomas's wife Joan.[121] George died in 1598, and Thomas (d. 1619) inherited the land, with the lease in place to White.[122]

Thomas Cox arranged to sell Pickering Grange with all its land to Bartholomew Laxton of Hinckley in 1606 for £1,450, payable in three instalments.[123] Laxton claimed that White and White's widow Elizabeth had allowed the building to fall down.[124] His claim may be fictitious, possibly to excuse his failure to pay later instalments, as although Thomas mentioned in his will that he had sold land in Ibstock,[125] Pickering Grange and its lands were held by the Cox family in 1638. That year, Robert Cox, presumably a relative of Thomas, sold a messuage and 590 a. in Ibstock to Nicholas Harman for £320 (perhaps an initial payment).[126] In 1649, Harman sold this for £400 to William Noel (later Sir William, 2nd baronet, d. 1675).[127] Noel's purchase comprised two houses, 160 a. of arable land, 30 a. of meadow, 300 a. of pasture and 100 a. of heath, which was probably all the former monastic land.[128]

This land had been divided into several 'parts' by 1671, with different occupiers, one of which was 'Barnwell's part' (later Ibstock Grange farm).[129] There were five farms in 1729, when George Thirlby, renting from the Noel family, paid 39 per cent of the tithes, William Pool, renting from widow Weston, paid 23 per cent (Jane Weston, widow of Benjamin, who had died in 1724), John Wilson paid 21 per cent, William Scott paid 10 per cent and Henry Burton paid 7 per cent.[130] An undated (18th-century) plan of 'Mr Wilson's Inclos'd Estate at Ibstock Grange' shows a farm of 78 a. partly bounded by the lands of Messrs Noel, Weston and Tylecoat.[131]

Pickering Grange farmhouse and a substantial part of the land remained in the hands of the Noel family after the death of Sir William in 1675, and was owned by his grandson, William Noel, at his death in 1762. William (d. 1762) had no sons, and left his estate by his will to be divided equally between his three daughters, Susanna Maria Hill (wife of Thomas Hill), Frances Sherard, countess of Harborough (wife of Bennet Sherard, 3rd earl of Harborough) and Elizabeth Noel.[132] One third passed to Elizabeth, but his other two daughters had died during the life of their father, so their two thirds were divided equally between Noel's three co-heirs, who each received two-ninths. They were Lady Frances Morgan, the only child of the earl and countess of Harborough, who had married general George Catchmaid Morgan, Samuel Hill, the elder son of Thomas and Susanna Hill and . William's daughter Elizabeth Noel, whose two-ninths were added to her existing one-third, giving her a total of five-ninths of her father's estate. Samuel Hill died intestate and

121 Farnham, *Medieval Village Notes*, III, 14, citing Inq. p.m. George Cocks, 1598 (TNA, C 142/253/133 catalogued as George Coke).
122 Ibid.
123 ROLLR, 9D 45/3.
124 TNA, C 2/JasI/L3/14.
125 TNA, PROB 11/133/285.
126 Farnham, *Medieval Village Notes*, 16, citing Fine, Easter 14 Chas. I.
127 Ibid., 17, citing Fine, 1649, octave of Purification.
128 Farnham, *Medieval Village Notes*, III, 17, citing fine, octave of the Purification, 1649.
129 ROLLR, DE 464/2; DE 436/1; wills and inventories 1724 Q–Z.
130 ROLLR, DE 464/2.
131 ROLLR, PP 454.
132 TNA, PROB 11/882/371.

Figure 6 *Pickering Grange Farmhouse (south elevation).*

without issue, and his two ninths passed to his brother Noel, later 1st Baron Berwick of Attingham (d. 1789).[133]

Under her marriage settlement and will, after Elizabeth's death without issue (1789) and the remarriage of her husband Stephen Sayre in 1790, her share passed to her niece, Lady Frances Morgan.[134] In 1860, George Robert Morgan purchased the remaining two-ninths share of the surface land from Richard Noel-Hill, lord Berwick (d. 1861), while Lord Berwick purchased the mineral rights held by Morgan.[135] All this land was owned by T. Guy F. Paget in 1910.[136]

The Pickering Grange tenancy passed through several generations of the Thirlby family, and was held by George Thirlby in 1729,[137] another George Thirlby in 1838,[138] and Richard Thirlby in 1863.[139]

Pickering Grange Farmhouse

Earthworks confirm that Pickering Grange farmhouse stands on the site of the monastic grange, but no medieval buildings survive.[140] At an unknown date, water from two springs which rose within this land was diverted into channels which formed the west, south and east sides of an area of 9 a. known as the Mottes, perhaps to create a moat

133 ROLLR, DE 4939/596 (abstract of title); *Complete Peerage*, II, 167.
134 TNA, PROB 11/1338/69; J.R. Alden, *Stephen Sayre: American Revolutionary Adventurer* (1983), 49, 162.
135 ROLLR, DE 4939/482; DE 4939/601.
136 ROLLR, DE 2072/176.
137 ROLLR, DE 464/2.
138 ROLLR, Ti/155/1.
139 W. White, *Hist., Gaz. and Dir. of Leics. and Rutl.* (Sheffield, 1863), 677.
140 R.F. Hartley, *The Medieval Earthworks of North-West Leicestershire* (Leicester, 1984), 25.

around a post-medieval house.[141] The farmhouse with Mottes Close was described as a mansion in 1589.[142] The prominence of this property by 1610, and its importance as a landmark, is demonstrated by its inclusion within John Speed's map of Leicestershire.[143]

The oldest part of the farmhouse is a stone chimney, perhaps from a 16th-century house. Adjoining it on the west is a south-facing 17th-century timber-framed property with brick infill, with a large modern extension to the rear. Immediately east of the chimney, and also adjoining, is a 19th-century brick-built farmhouse (Figure 6).[144]

Ibstock Grange Farm

Ibstock Grange was named on John Prior's county map (1777), indicating a significant farmhouse had been built. This is the earliest appearance of this name.[145] Benjamin Weston (d. 1724) bequeathed his lands 'in Pickering Grange ... which I purchased of Mr Barnwell' to his son Benjamin (d. 1777).[146] This was the 'Barnwell's part' of the Pickering Grange land mentioned in 1671.[147] There is no indication that Benjamin (d. 1724) lived on the farm. In his will, the younger Benjamin Weston (d. 1777) described himself being 'of Pickering Grange', and devised his farmhouse and lands 'known as Pickering Grange' in trust for his son, also Benjamin (d. 1810).[148] The 1777 burial entry for Benjamin II, and a memorial in Ibstock church, describe him as being 'of Ibstock Grange', suggesting that this name had been adopted very recently.[149] Nichols recorded in 1811 that Benjamin Weston's farm 'is now considered to be totally distinct from Pickering Grange', although he gave its name as Swynfen Grange.[150]

Benjamin III (d. 1810) acquired more land in the south of the parish when Thomas Paget (d. 1818) scaled down his farming activities in 1793.[151] On the death of Benjamin (III) in 1810,[152] his land passed to Samuel Weston,[153] who in 1838 owned Ibstock Grange farmhouse and 97 a. of land attached to it, as part of 332 a. he owned and farmed himself in the south of the parish.[154]

Samuel Weston sold the house and 342 a. of land in 1844.[155] It was almost certainly purchased by Thomas Paget (d. 1862), the brother of Samuel's wife Elizabeth.[156] By 1910

141 Hartley, *Medieval Earthworks*, 25; ROLLR, DE 4939/482.
142 ROLLR, DE 44'28/516.
143 ROLLR, Ma/L/22.
144 NHLE, no. 1074369, Pickering Grange Farmhouse, Ellistown Terrace Road (accessed 11 Apr. 2017); https://media.onthemarket.com/properties/777130/doc_1_0.pdf (accessed 1 Mar. 2018).
145 ROLLR, Ma/L/1; B. Cox, *The Place-names of Leicestershire*, VI (Nottingham, 2014), 142–3.
146 ROLLR, Wills, 1724 Q–Z.
147 ROLLR, DE 464/2.
148 TNA PROB 11/1042/178.
149 ROLLR, DE 1717/3; Nichols, *History* IV, 759.
150 Nichols, *History* IV, 759.
151 ROLLR, QS 62/156; below, 'Paget estate'.
152 ROLLR, DE 1717/6.
153 ROLLR, QS 62/156.
154 ROLLR, Ti/155/1.
155 *Leic. Jnl*, 21 Jan. 1844.
156 ROLLR, PR/T/1850/176; 24D65/D10 (PRs).

this land was owned by T. Guy F. Paget.[157] It was put on the market in 1919,[158] and later owned for a period with Park Farm (to its south), a total of 385 a., by Henry Thorpe Hincks of Keyham Hall, a racehorse breeder and auctioneer, who also owned 700 a. in Keyham and 2,000 a. in Berkshire.[159]

Ibstock Grange farmhouse and outbuildings were badly affected by subsidence, and demolished *c.*1965. They were replaced by another farmhouse on the same site.[160]

Other Estates

Paget Estate

The Paget family claimed that Grange Farm 'was granted by Henry VI to Thomas and John Paget in 1456'.[161] No royal grant is recorded, but the date coincides with the death of Ralph, Lord Cromwell, whose will directed the sale of his lands in Ibstock and elsewhere,[162] and Thomas and John Paget may have purchased part of Lord Cromwell's land. A Thomas Paget was living in Ibstock in 1469,[163] and many land purchases were made in the parish by family members between 1590 and 1910.[164]

Joseph Paget (d. 1789) was allotted 142 a. through the enclosure award, and may have owned other land in Ibstock.[165] His brother Thomas (d. 1818) was allotted 58 a. in the enclosure award of 1775,[166] and a plan of his estate made that year shows he owned 465 a., mostly in a horseshoe-shaped 'ring farm' around the west, south and east of the village.[167] Thomas married Mary Clare, who inherited half of her father John's 177 a. landholding in Ibstock on John's death in 1783. The other half was left to Mary's sister Elizabeth, and Elizabeth's land may have been purchased by Thomas Paget.[168]

When Thomas Paget retired from farming in 1793, he sold part of his land to Benjamin Weston (d. 1810) of Ibstock Grange.[169] Paget's son, also Thomas (d. 1862), lived in Humberstone Hall, Leicester, and owned 84 a. in the south of Ibstock in 1838, possibly with other land beyond the bounds of the 1838 survey. He is reputed to have built the farmhouse on Overton Road known as Ibstock Lodge, *c.*1841.[170] He almost certainly purchased Ibstock Grange farmhouse and 342 a. of land from Samuel Weston in 1844, the husband of Paget's sister Elizabeth, when Weston retired from farming.[171]

157 ROLLR, DE 2072/176.
158 *Leic. Jnl*, 25 July 1919.
159 ROLLR, DE 4674/202, 675; *Leic. Mercury*, 31 Jan. 1939.
160 Ex inf. Stephen Saunders, Ibstock Historical Society Facebook posts (9 Feb. 2020).
161 G. Paget and L. Irvine, *Leicestershire* (1950), 198.
162 Above, Ibstock manor.
163 ROLLR, DE 365/1a.
164 ROLLR, DE 365/2–107.
165 ROLLR, DE 8666.
166 ROLLR, DE 8666.
167 ROLLR, 109'30/95.
168 Below, Economic History, agriculture.
169 ROLLR, QS 62/156.
170 Cawte, 'Parish warden's report', 24.
171 *Leic. Jnl*, 21 Jan. 1844; ROLLR, PR/T/1850/176; 24D 65/D10.

Thomas Paget (d. 1862) had two sons, Thomas Tertius (d. 1892) and John. John's grandson, Thomas Guy Frederick Paget (d. 1952) owned 770 a. in Ibstock in 1910, including Pickering Grange (231 a.), Ibstock Grange (340 a.) and Ibstock Lodge (185 a.), which each had separate tenants.[172] Pickering Grange, Ibstock Grange and another unnamed farm, totalling 651 a., were offered at auction in 1919.[173]

172 ROLLR, DE 2072/176.
173 *Leic. Jnl*, 25 July 1919.

ECONOMIC HISTORY

Overview

AGRICULTURE WAS THE MAINSTAY OF Ibstock's economy until the late 18th century. Few records relating to medieval farming survive, but rents were consistently very low between the late 14th and late 15th century, possibly because it was difficult to find tenants for the heavy clay soils. Garendon abbey kept a large flock of sheep on their enclosed estate in the south-east, with the remainder of the land supporting traditional mixed farming. The open fields were rearranged after the division of the manor between co-heirs in the 13th century, one manor having three open fields across the north of the parish, and the other having three fields in the south. The fields of the southern manor were enclosed by piecemeal agreement over the late 16th and the 17th centuries, and the three northern fields were enclosed by parliamentary award in 1775.

There is no direct evidence of those who lost access to land in 1775 turning to framework-knitting, but this industry provided work for some by the 1770s, and their number grew over the next 50 years. Of the 163 families living in Ibstock in 1811, 75 were 'chiefly employed in agriculture' and 71 were 'chiefly employed in trade, manufactures or handicraft'.[1] By 1831 the population had grown to 242 families, but the families employed in agriculture had fallen to 60, while the number of families working in trade, manufacture or handicrafts had increased to 150.[2] The proportion involved in manufacture fell over the later 19th century, as more men found work in the expanding collieries.

Only 12 residents were employed as labourers in coal mines in 1831.[3] In 1911, Ibstock had 1,093 residents employed in the mines, equating to two thirds of the 1,646 male residents aged over 12 and under 66.[4] Others worked in the brick and pipe yards attached to the collieries. The major employer based within the parish in the early years of the 21st century was Ibstock Brick, which had its origins in coal mining and operated from the former Ibstock and Ellistown colliery sites.

Small textile factories appeared in the 20th century, and shoe 'closing rooms' were set up as satellites of footwear factories in Leicester and elsewhere, which employed mostly women to stitch together the upper parts of shoes.

Ibstock's potential to become a retail centre serving other local villages is evident from a probate inventory of 1705, but this early promise was never fully realised. Although

1 Census, 1811.
2 Census, 1831.
3 *VCH Leics*. III, 204.
4 Data from Integrated Census Microdata Project, https://icem.data-archive.ac.uk/ (accessed 4 Mar. 2019).

there were many shops in the late 19th and early 20th century, Ibstock's role in serving other villages had been eclipsed by 1900 through the growth of Coalville.

Agriculture

The Agricultural Landscape

From the 12th century, Garendon abbey had a large estate of *c.*540 a. in the south-east of the parish, with a grange known as Swynfen, which became Pickering Grange Farm after the abbey was dissolved. The monastic land extended south as far as the parish boundary and east to the road which runs from Bagworth to Hugglescote, but probably not across that road. The northern boundary mostly followed tracks which ran east from Ibstock into Charnwood Forest. The western boundary of Garendon's land is more difficult to define. The reconstruction in Map 7 is based on the acreage given to the abbey and post-medieval documentary sources.

The fields were rearranged after the manor was divided between co-heirs in the 13th century, and were farmed as two manors. Although reunited by 1606, this division facilitated the piecemeal enclosure of the southern part of the parish by private agreements in the 17th century, with the land across the north enclosed by Act of Parliament in 1775.

The *c.*1,000 a. of farmland in the north is simpler to reconstruct. This was arranged in three open fields, Nether Field, Bufton (Abovetown) Field and Upper (formerly Over) Field, and an area known in 1775 as 'Upper Pasture'. The open-field boundaries recorded in 1775 were mostly prominent physical features, including the northernmost brook, the road to Heather, and the tracks which marked the northern bounds of the monastic estate.[5] The Upper Pasture may once have been part of the arable fields, possibly untilled since the population decline of the late 14th century. This may be the 100 a. of heath recorded in Ibstock in 1722.[6] Meadow extended to the south of Ibstock's two main brooks, with the south-western meadow divided between Nether Field (northern manor) and Church Field (southern manor).[7] Some of the meadow in Over (later Upper) Field was described as 'dole meadow', suggesting it was divided into portions, allocated each year by lot.[8]

The southern field system was smaller, *c.*730 a. in total, and also comprised three open fields. Little documentary evidence has survived for the period before their piecemeal enclosure by agreement in the late 16th and early 17th century, and their boundaries are partly conjecture. Their names, Church Field, Lane Field and Breach Field, provide some clues to their location.[9] Church Field almost certainly extended south of the church and west of Overton Road. Lane Field was accessible by two bridges,[10] and the name attached

5 ROLLR, DE 8666.

6 ROLLR, DE 41/1/59, abstract of deeds and fine of 1722.

7 ROLLR, DE 8666; Ti/155/1.

8 ROLLR, 1D 41/2/340–1; J. Field, *English Field-Names: A Dictionary* (Newton Abbot, 1972), 65.

9 ROLLR, DE 365/4a; ROLLR, 1D 41/2/339a–b.

10 ROLLR, Wills and Inventories, 1558 P–Z/23.

to land immediately east of Overton Road until at least 1838.[11] The 'Lane' (Overton Road) would have formed the western boundary of this field. There were still two bridges (the road and a footbridge) over the brook in 2019. The eastern field boundary would have been the monastic land.[12] Breach Field probably extended east from the monastic land to the parish boundary. The name 'breach' often refers to land on the edges of a parish, 'newly broken' when the field was named.[13]

The reunification of the manors in the hands of the Stafford family before 1606 was probably a catalyst for change.[14] The relatively small size of the open fields belonging to the southern manor, and the cold clay soil which gave rise to the field-name 'Hunger Hill' between Overton Road and Hinckley Road, would have influenced the decision that this land should be enclosed.[15] Some small-scale enclosure was underway by 1590.[16] The southern land was probably wholly enclosed by 1700.

Arable agriculture in the 21st century was concentrated in the west and north of the parish, where the soil is lighter and free draining.[17] Between 1700 and the late 20th century, dairy farming predominated elsewhere. In the early 21st century some of the southern and eastern farmland is also arable, some supports other rural businesses, including equestrian pursuits, and much is woodland.

Agriculture before 1540

Open-field Farming

Six carucates of land were recorded in Ibstock in 1086, which would have provided *c.*720 a. of arable land.[18] This would probably have been close to the church and village, on the better soils in the south-west of the parish. The neighbouring place-names of Heather and Donington-le-Heath to the north and west, and Bagworth Heath to the east, suggest that the remainder of the modern parish may have been open heath. The 11 bordars recorded in 1086, half of Ibstock's households, may have been converting heath to arable land.[19]

Four ploughs were recorded in 1066, with one of these on the lord's demesne, which was presumably one quarter of the tilled area.[20] This would leave *c.*540 a. for the peasants. Assuming each bordar held between 5 a. and 15 a. for his own use,[21] there would be an average of between 37 and 48 a. for each sokeman. Their individual holdings may have

11 ROLLR, Ti/155/1.
12 Ibid.
13 Field, *English Field-Names*, 27.
14 Above, Landownership, Ibstock manor.
15 ROLLR, Ti/155/1.
16 ROLLR, DE 365/2.
17 Cranfield Soil and Agrifood Institute, http://www.landis.org.uk/soilscapes/ (accessed 24 Feb. 2019).
18 *Domesday*, 649.
19 Ibid., S.P.J. Harvey, 'Evidence for settlement study: Domesday Book', in P.H. Sawyer (ed.), *Medieval Settlement: Continuity and Change* (1976), 197–9.
20 *Domesday*, 649.
21 Harvey, 'Evidence for settlement', 197–9.

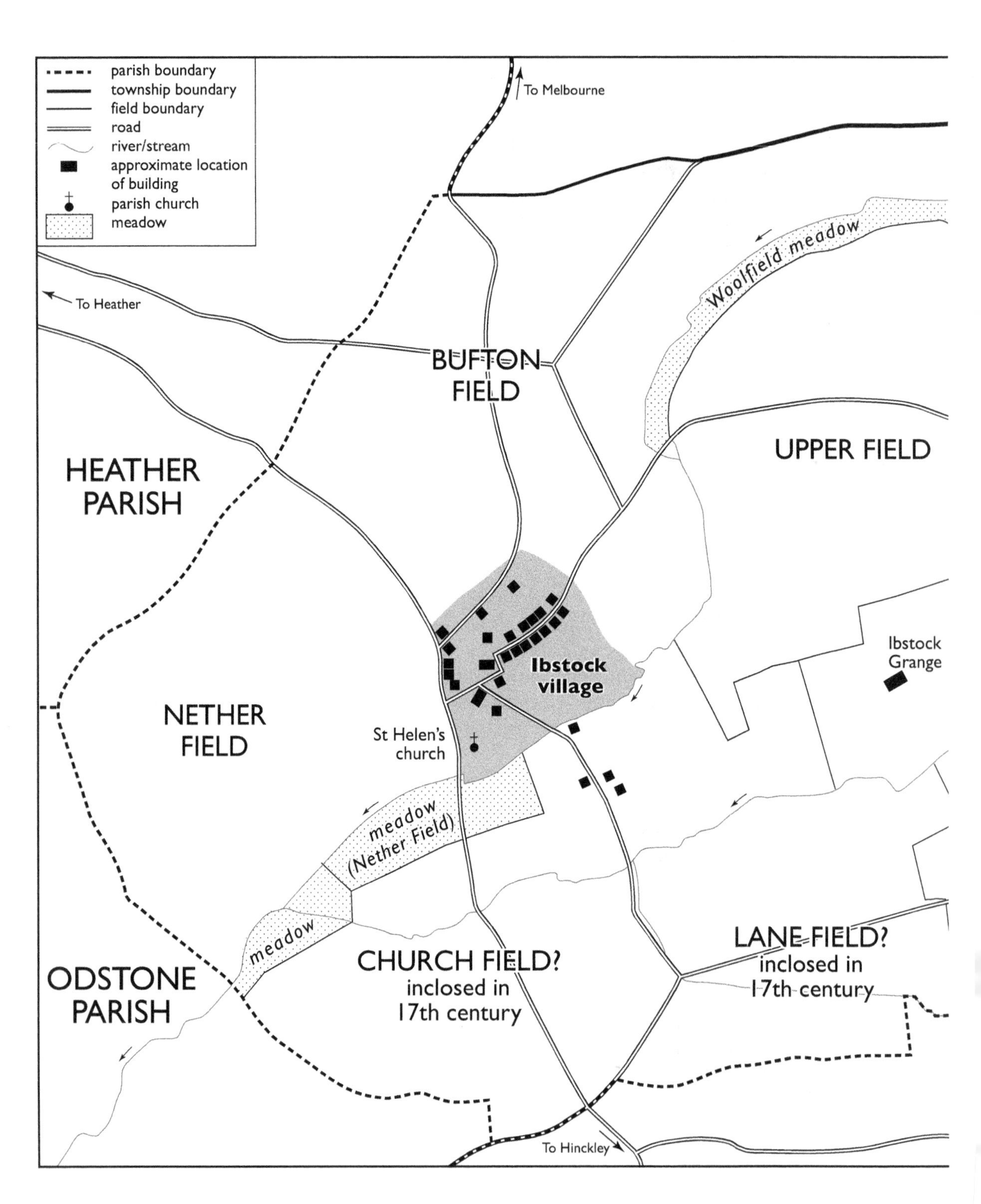

Map 7 *Ibstock's agricultural landscape, c.1630.*

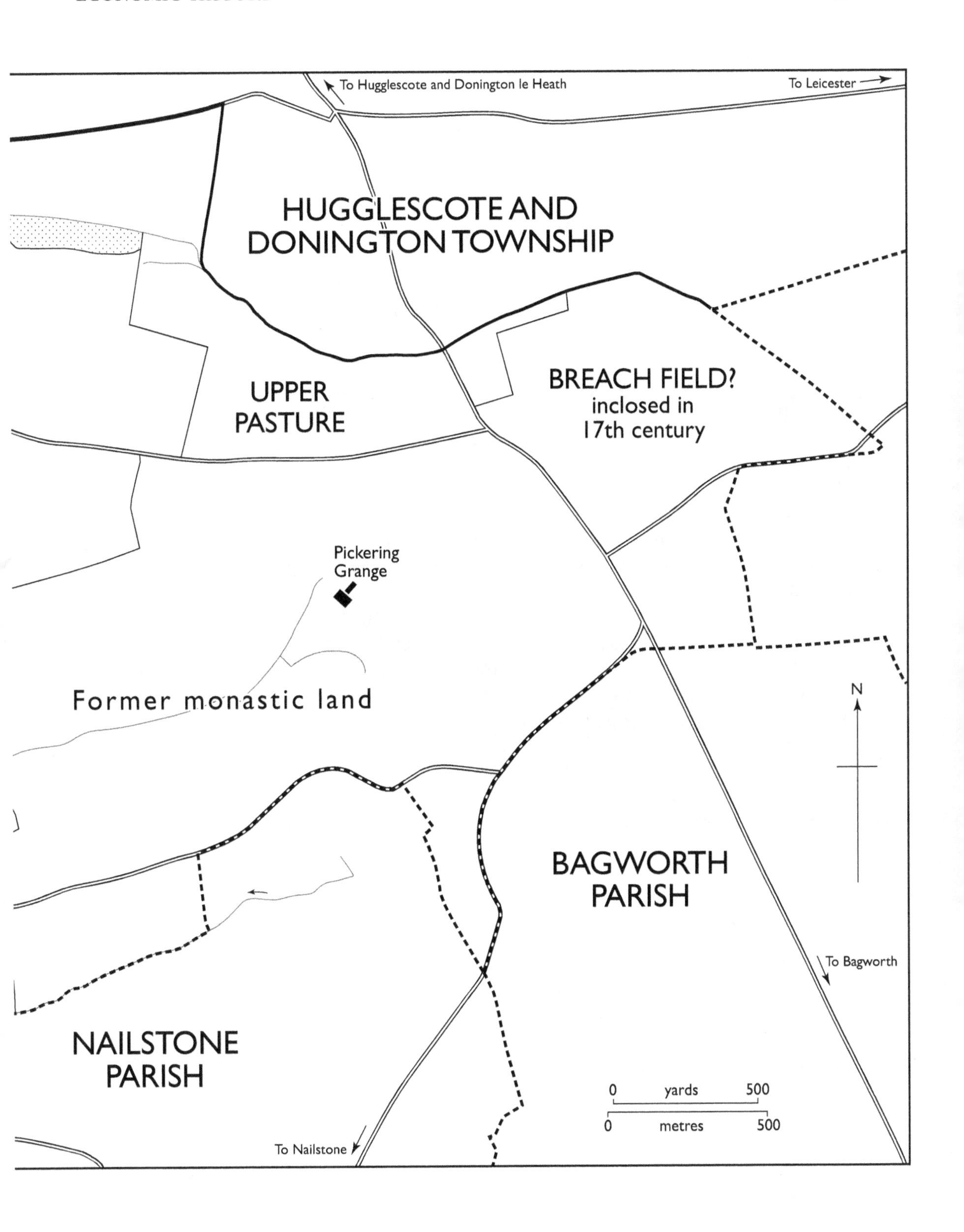

To Hugglescote and Donington le Heath
To Leicester
HUGGLESCOTE AND DONINGTON TOWNSHIP
UPPER PASTURE
BREACH FIELD? inclosed in 17th century
Pickering Grange
Former monastic land
N
BAGWORTH PARISH
To Bagworth
NAILSTONE PARISH
0 yards 500
0 metres 500
To Nailstone

differed widely, as sokemen were defined by their status, not by the amount of land they held.[22]

There were still four ploughs in 1086, but more land had probably been brought into production, as the value of the manor had risen eight-fold, from 5*s.* to 40*s.* This was a greater increase than seen in most Leicestershire villages, and four times that seen on the nine-carucate manor of Bagworth, Ibstock's eastern neighbour, which had doubled in value from £2 to £4.[23] Six carucates of land remained in Ibstock in 1145, after the gift of 4½ carucates to Garendon abbey,[24] suggesting all or most of the monastic land had been waste when it was given.

The manor was divided in the early 13th century, and held by two co-heirs in 1279. More land had been brought under the plough, and most peasants appear to have had holdings of either one or half a virgate. There were 7½ virgates of demesne land (4 virgates held by Thomas Garshall and 3½ by Robert Verdun). The peasants (*servi*) held 29¾ virgates (18 peasants with 15¾ virgates on Thomas's manor and 15 peasants with 14 virgates on Robert's manor). There were also 11 free tenants, who held a total of 24 virgates.[25] The parish contained 2,257 a. in 1831,[26] so the total farmland of 80 virgates in 1279 (including Garendon abbey's holding) suggests each virgate contained less than 28 a. of arable land.

By the mid 14th century there was no longer a resident lord.[27] An account of 1384 records rental income of 37*s.* from the two demesnes, and £7 7*s.* 11*d.* collected for the tenants' lands.[28] This would be just 2¼*d.* per acre for the *c.*200 a. demesne, a remarkably low figure.[29] Assuming a rent collector for both demesnes would also collect from the tenants of both manors, and if the average rent paid by the tenants was at a similar level to the demesne rent, then no more than 800 a. was let. With *c.*1,450 a. of tenant land available across the two manors, this suggests a contraction in wealth, and a difficulty in finding tenants in the wake of the Black Death. One positive feature was the collection of arrears of 30*s.* 1*d.*, which may indicate some recovery in tenant fortunes from the previous year.[30]

A valuation of Ralph, Lord Cromwell's estates of *c.*1456, lists rent of £4 7*s.* 9*d.* from lands and tenements in Ibstock, 'lately of John Hopton'.[31] He held one half of the manor, and the amount is approximately half the sum collected in 1384, indicating there had been little, if any, recovery in fortunes.

22 C. Lewis, P Mitchell-Fox and C. Dyer, *Village, Hamlet and Field: Changing Medieval Settlements in Central England* (Manchester, 1997), 179–80.
23 *Domesday*, 649.
24 Nichols, *History* III, 805, 834.
25 Nichols, *History* IV, 749–50.
26 http://www.visionofbritain.org.uk/ (accessed 10 Mar. 2019).
27 Above, Landownership, Ibstock manor.
28 TNA, SC 6/908/17.
29 E. Miller, 'People and land', in J. Thirsk (ed.), *The Agrarian History of England and Wales*, III (Cambridge, 1991), 8–9; R. Britnell, *Britain and Ireland 1050–1530: Economy and Society* (Oxford, 2004), 439–42.
30 TNA, SC 6/908/17.
31 TNA, SC 11/822, m.1; C. Richmond, *John Hopton: a Fifteenth-century Suffolk Gentleman* (Cambridge, 1981), 25.

Accounts for the rents collected by Henry Watts for Sir Humphrey Stafford over two years from 1477 to 1479 show annual fixed rents (rents of assize) of 14*s.* 6*d.*, and £5 8*s.* 3*d.* each year from tenants at will.[32] Stafford held only one of the manors, so assuming this rental was for *c.*800 a., the average rent paid remained at *c.*2¼*d.* per acre, with the consistency in the figures over 100 years reflecting stable population levels.

There are no surviving sources to show how the land was farmed, but the tenants may have agreed to reduce the size of the open fields and lay down some areas to grass, or to allow them to revert to heath.

Pastoral Farming

Garendon abbey held five carucates of land in Ibstock (*c.*600 a.).[33] The two surviving cartularies give no indication that significant amounts of land were purchased or exchanged to achieve the compact estate apparent from later records.[34] This suggests that all or most of their land had never been part of the open fields. Two of the gifts explicitly mentioned heathland.[35]

The abbey built a grange on this land in the 12th century, which they called Swynfen.[36] As the abbey owned 14 granges,[37] they were able to specialise on some of their land. A courtyard (*curia*), 'houses', possibly for shepherds, and sheepcotes (*domorum et berchariarum*) were constructed, and may account for some of the earthworks which survive near the modern Pickering Grange farmhouse.[38] Sheepcotes were long rectangular buildings which provided shelter for sheep in poor weather and storage for fodder beneath the roof.[39] The abbey became a major wool producer, obtaining permission to export wool in 1225.[40] It was selling the fleeces of *c.*5,000 sheep annually in the early 14th century, probably not all from their own flocks.[41]

Reginald of Ibstock claimed in 1369 that the abbot had chased his sheep to Bardon and impounded them there without food, claiming they were on the abbey's land. In a second case in 1370, possibly relating to the same incident, the abbot claimed that Reginald of Ibstock and Reginald Palmer of Ibstock had depastured the abbot's herbage.[42] Unknown criminals broke into the sheepcotes on at least one occasion.[43]

The earliest surviving rental for Garendon's land at Ibstock is probably from the early 16th century, and records that William White paid £4 6*s.* 9*d.* annually.[44] Assuming he

32 Staffs. RO, D 641/1/2/262–3.
33 Nichols, *History* III, 827.
34 Ibid., 805–6, 819, 821, 823, 834–5.
35 Ibid., 835.
36 *VCH Leics.* II, 5.
37 ROLLR, DE 40/26.
38 Nichols, *History* III, 806, 823, 829, 835; R.F. Hartley, *The Medieval Earthworks of North West Leicestershire* (Leicester, 1984), 25.
39 C. Dyer, 'Sheepcotes: evidence for medieval sheepfarming', *Medieval Archaeology*, 39 (1995), 136–164.
40 *Cal. Pat.* 1216–25, 522; *VCH Leics.* II, 5.
41 *VCH Leics.* II, 190; Sister James Eugene Madden, 'Business monks, banker monks, bankrupt monks: English Cistercians in the thirteenth century' *Catholic Historical Review*, 49 (1963), 343–4.
42 G.F. Farnham, *Medieval Village Notes* III (Leicester, 1933), 8, citing CP 40/436, mm. 75, 386d; CP 40/437, m. 154d; *VCH Leics.* II, 190–1.
43 Nichols, *History* III, 829.
44 ROLLR, DE 40/26 (other names on the document suggest it was written between 1490 and 1527).

rented *c.*600 a., this equates to 1¾*d.* per acre, less than the rent achieved by the manor, perhaps because some of the land was still unbroken heath. He would presumably have been a mixed farmer and self-sufficient, with a surplus for sale. A lease of the grange and its land in 1530 to Thomas Pickering, his son John and John's wife Margaret set a higher annual rent of £7.[45] Thomas Pickering died in 1547, leaving 18 lands (strips in the fields) of wheat and rye, four oxen, 19 dairy cows and calves and 60 sheep.[46]

Agriculture 1540–1775

Open-field Farming

The Upper Pasture enabled more livestock to be kept than the open fields alone would support. There are relatively few surviving probate inventories from the 16th century. John Perryant's land cannot be identified, but he had a large farm at his death in 1559, with corn in the field worth £22, 12 quarters of wheat and 'monkcorn' (mixed wheat and rye) worth £7, four quarters of peas and oats and 20 loads of hay. His livestock comprised ten oxen, 11 horses, 29 head of cattle, 200 sheep and 14 pigs, valued at £110 in total.[47] Thomas Sadler, who died in 1567, had a smaller farm, but his livestock were also worth many times the value of his crops. He left corn worth £4 and livestock worth £25, including 17 head of cattle, five horses and 40 sheep.[48]

A tithe book records that the main crops in 1670 (in terms of yield) were peas and barley, closely followed by 'blencorn' (mixed wheat and rye), then wheat and a little rye grown on their own; there were also small quantities of oats and hemp. No beans were recorded. The following year 160 lambs were born on 15 farms, with no more than 17 lambs born on any one farm. No cattle were noted. The figures exclude the farms on the former monastic land, where a composition had been agreed for the tithes, and where there may have been large flocks and herds.[49]

By the late 17th century, most of the southern fields had been enclosed. Thomas Copson farmed two yardlands in the open fields and four closes in 'Overton'.[50] On his death in 1687 he had wheat, barley, peas, beans, oats and hay, together valued at £64, and livestock valued at £81 7*s.*, comprising nine horses and foals, 18 cows, 61 sheep and lambs and two pigs.[51] Thomas Jackson (d. 1682) had wheat, rye, 'blencorn' and barley worth £31, peas worth £7, hay worth £11, but only six horses, six cows and three sheep, worth a total of £30.[52] The greater proportion of value held in crops by this period is striking. Nationally, the price of wheat per quarter increased substantially between the 1580s and 1680s.[53] In Ibstock, the open fields had contracted through enclosure, and

45 TNA, SC 6/HenVIII/1825, m. 20; S. Jack, 'Monastic lands in Leicestershire and their administration at the eve of the dissolution', *Trans. LAHS* 41 (1966), 23.

46 ROLLR, Wills 1547/39a.

47 ROLLR, Wills and Inventories, 1558 P–Z/24.

48 ROLLR, Wills and Inventories, 1567/104.

49 ROLLR, DE 464/2.

50 Ibid.

51 ROLLR, PR/I/90/140.

52 ROLLR, PR/I/184/196.

53 J.M. Stratton and J.H. Brown, *Agricultural Records, AD 220–1977* (1978), 249–51.

the population was increasing,[54] so the price of corn may also reflect local supply and demand.

The holder of a yardland could graze 25 sheep and two cows on the common pasture, and another cow on the heath under bylaws agreed in 1638. Cottagers could graze ten sheep and one cow on the heath, and two cows on the common pasture after Lammas (1 August).[55]

New articles agreed in 1697 may mark the enclosure of the final land in the former southern manor, and show a small reduction in grazing rights. Heathland grazing was no longer mentioned, and this land may have been enclosed. Perhaps to compensate, all holders of a yardland had to convert two of their arable lands in Nether Field to 'cow pasture'. They also had to spent one day each winter stocking the coneygree (rabbit warren), to provide another source of food.[56] This was probably in 'Connery Close', at the edge of Nether Field, on the south side of what became Station Road.[57] For each yardland held, two beasts could be kept on the cow pasture until Lammas, and six between Lammas and the sowing of crops, with one horse standing for two beasts. The stint for sheep was complex, and depended on which field was fallow, as the three open fields were different sizes. It varied from 15 to 25 sheep for each yardland, and between six and ten sheep for a cottage.[58]

Enclosed Farming

The former monastic land had been divided into five farms by 1729.[59] Valentine White, who occupied part of the Pickering Grange land in 1671, was a mixed farmer.[60] On his death in 1683 he owned six horses, 13 cows, 60 sheep and four swine worth a total of £68 4*s*. 9*d*., cheese, corn and wool worth another £6, and corn, peas and hay valued together at £60 3*s*. 4*d*.[61] Others farming this land concentrated on dairy. Thomas Farmer, alias Ward, 'of Swinfeild Grange' was a dairy farmer at his death in 1635, when he owned seven kyne, eight calves, one bull, bullocks and a mare, together worth £42 6*s*. 8*d*., one pig, no sheep and no crops.[62] John Wilson 'of Pickering Grange' was also a dairy farmer when he died in 1707, owning six cows, a yearling and a bull calf (valued at a total of £15 19*s*.), mares, two foals, 'pasture sheep' (an unrecorded number, but worth only £1 15*s*.), some swine and hay, corn worth £6 and cheese worth £2 10*s*. in his 'cheese chamber'.[63]

Some enclosure of the open fields was underway by 1590, when Leonard Paget sold a close of 4 a. which was one of at least three lying between Nether Field and the brook flowing from Pickering Grange.[64] Thomas Paget purchased two 'little closes' in 1633.[65]

54 Above, Ibstock Parish, population.
55 ROLLR, 1D 41/2/339a–b.
56 ROLLR, DE 390/57/1.
57 ROLLR, DE 8666.
58 ROLLR, DE 390/57/1; below, Local Government, manor courts.
59 ROLLR, DE 464/2.
60 Ibid.
61 ROLLR, PR/I/85/143.
62 ROLLR, PR/I/38/83.
63 ROLLR, PR/I/114/11.
64 ROLLR, DE 365/2.
65 ROLLR, DE 365/11.

Three years later, he purchased Lanefield Close (5 a., presumably once part of Lane Field), Grymesholme Close (3 a.) and Suthwell Close, all said to be in Overton, from Thomas Barwell for £90. The conveyance included the condition that 'if the closes or any of them happen to be thrown open or used in common in such manner as used to be used before they were inclosed', then Paget's purchase money would be returned together with any expenses he had incurred 'in manuring dressing and husbanding the closes', as determined by independent arbiters.[66] Paget purchased further land in 1637, including a small close 'newlie inclosed' in Over Grymesholme, in Overton.[67]

Ibstock's manorial lord, William Stafford, also appears to have been purchasing or exchanging land, probably with the intention of creating an enclosed farm. The lands on both sides of 12 strips of glebe land in Church Field and Breach Field in 1638 were held by 'Mr Stafford', and the rector had exchanged one ley and a hade (headland) in the Townsend Leys for two leys in the Church Close.[68] By 1690, the rector had no lands in Church Field or Breach Field, but had acquired a 'New Close' (7 a.) adjacent to the rectory garden.[69]

Agriculture from 1775

The enclosure award of 1775 redistributed 1,098 a. in the north of the parish between 29 people.[70] Almost all of this land (988 a.) was allotted to just ten people, with the largest awards made to the rector (282 a.), Joseph Paget (147 a.), Francis Dugdale Astley (141 a.) and John Clare (101 a.).[71] Some of these men owned other land, for example, John Clare also owned closes in the south of Ibstock containing 76 a. in 1775.[72] The time taken for some farmers to create a ring farm through land sales and purchases delayed the building of farmhouses in the fields.[73] At the other end of the scale, 13 allotments were of less than 4 a.[74] Some probably sold holdings which were uneconomic to hedge, while others may have retained or added to their land. Thomas Waine, for example, was allotted 2 a. 2 r. in 1775,[75] and remained a landowner in 1798, when he was assessed for annual land tax of *7s. 5½d.*[76]

Thomas Paget (d. 1818) was allotted 58 a. in the enclosure award of 1775, but also owned 407 a. of old enclosures in the south of the parish.[77] Paget was an associate and follower of Robert Bakewell of Dishley (1725–95). Bakewell strove to increase food supply through the selective breeding of livestock and the improvement of grassland by

66 ROLLR, DE 365/12a.
67 ROLLR, DE 365/14.
68 ROLLR, 1D 41/2/339 a–b.
69 ROLLR, 1D 41/2/340.
70 Private Act, 14 Geo. III, c. 3; ROLLR, DE 8666.
71 ROLLR, DE 8666.
72 ROLLR, 109'30/94.
73 Above, Ibstock Parish, settlement.
74 ROLLR, DE 8666.
75 Ibid.
76 TNA, IR 23/44/138, f. 189. It is not possible to quantify his acreage from the tax assessment.
77 ROLLR, 109'30/95; above, Landownership, other estates.

irrigation.[78] Paget experimented with fertilisers, mixing bones with lime to reduce them to powder, and using soot as a top dressing.[79] He grew up to 14 a. of cabbages each year as winter fodder, and was praised by agricultural writer William Marshall as 'the greatest cabbage grower I have anywhere observed'.[80] He was also lauded by Marshall as 'a master of the art of draining by sod or turf drains', teaching his labourers to cut channels and place turfs on the 'shoulders' of the ditch to produce a cheap and long-lasting drain.[81] Through effective irrigation, Paget was able to cut hay from grass 'which has received no manure for 40 years'.[82] On retiring to a smaller farm in 1793, a sale of Paget's improved cattle, sheep and rams realised premium prices, including 400 guineas for a bull named Shakespear, up to 84 guineas each for heifers and 62 guineas for sheep.[83]

A 'great proportion' of Ibstock's farmland in 1801 was pasture and meadow, and there were 'Large dairies for cheese'.[84] The arable land was planted with 264½ a. of barley, 177½ a. of oats, 146 a. of wheat and 115 a. 'beans, turnips or rape' for fodder, and there were 4 a. of potatoes.[85]

The tithe survey of 1838 covered the 1,153 a. of land enclosed before 1775, including the former monastic estate. It identified 406 a. of arable land (35 per cent), 687 a. of pasture (60 per cent) and 60 a. of meadow (5 per cent).[86] Samuel Weston's 332 a. was largely (80 per cent) meadow and pasture, but John Clare's land (87 a. in three small blocks) was all arable. The proportions would have varied, as convertible husbandry had been adopted across 'much of the land'. Grass was laid down for between four and six years before ploughing up for an annual rotation of different cereal crops, with the cycle then repeated. The Tithe Commissioners commented that the parish contained 'some peculiarly fine turnip land', suggesting this had become a common fodder crop in Ibstock.[87]

Reviewing the annual agricultural returns between 1867 and 1977 at ten-year intervals, the acreage of crops rose from 792 a. in 1867 to a peak of 881 a. in 1877, before falling to just 205 a. in 1937. Largely through the 'ploughing up' campaign of the Second World War, this had increased to 620 a. in 1947. Conversion to arable continued and there was 885 a. of arable land in 1967.[88] The main cereal crops are shown in Figure 7. These were influenced by market conditions and the needs of the livestock shown in Figure 8. The large quantities of barley grown from 1967 helped to feed an increasing number of pigs.

In common with trends across the country, the number of sheep fell from the later 19th century, from 1,647 in 1867 to 504 in 1907, and just 82 in 1967. Between 1867 and

78 W. Marshall, *The Rural Economy of the Midland Counties*, I (1790), 385; *ODNB*, s.v. 'Bakewell, Robert (1725–95), stock-breeder and farmer' (accessed 10 Mar. 2019).
79 W. Pitt, *A General View of the Agriculture of the County of Leicester* (1809), 194.
80 Marshall, *Rural Economy*, I, 259–62.
81 Ibid., 191–5.
82 Ibid., 287.
83 Pitt, *General View*, 221–2, 251–2.
84 *Home Office Acreage Returns*, 1801, II (List & Index Society, vol. 190, 1982), 56.
85 Ibid., 46.
86 ROLLR, Ti/155/1.
87 TNA, IR 18/4506; Marshall, *Rural Economy* I, 187–8.
88 TNA, MAF 68/134; 68/533; 68/1103; 68/1673; 68/2243; 68/2813; 68/3356; 68/3836; 68/4205; 68/4575; 68/5037; 68/5588.

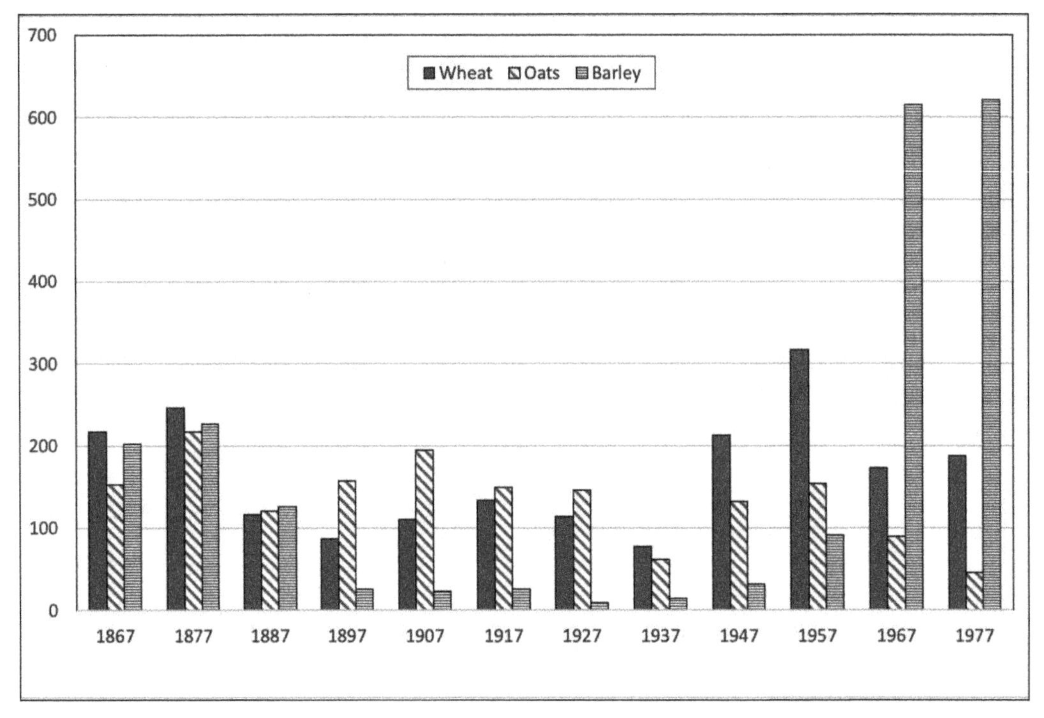

Figure 7 *Acreage of cereal crops grown on Ibstock's farms.*

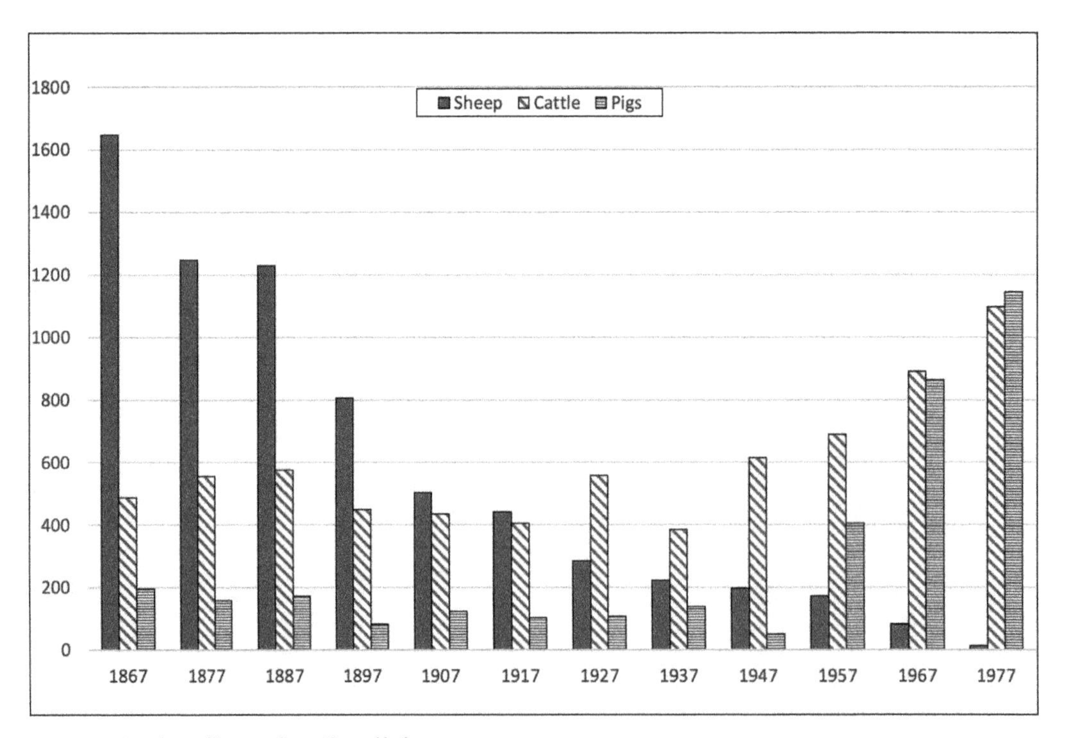

Figure 8 *Number of livestock on Ibstock's farms.*

1937 the number of cattle fluctuated between 575 (1887) and 385 (1937), and then rose steadily to 1,097 in 1977.[89] Denser stocking had become possible through improved farming methods, and the price support provided by the Milk Marketing Board from 1933 may have encouraged dairy farming.[90] Relatively little land was needed: in 1942, two Ibstock milk producer-retailers had dairy farms of 27 a. and 39 a.[91] The number of pigs increased from 51 in 1947 to 1,305 in 1985,[92] but changes in the economics of pig production meant that by 2010 they were no longer kept on any scale.[93]

Most farms were very small. In 1907, 45 of Ibstock's 54 farms contained less than 50 a., and several were run by people with another business which used farm produce, for example, butcher Walter Crane farmed 11 a. in 1916, and John Palmer, landlord of the Ram Inn, had 4 a. on which he bred between 40 and 80 pigs each year.[94] Leicestershire County Council purchased Valley Farm (114 a.) in 1920 for division into tenant smallholdings, and Clare Farm and Paget farm were built by the council on this land, the latter in 1954.[95] In 1957, there were still 21 farms of less than 50 a.[96]

The period between 1970 and 2019 has seen several changes. With the help of grants, 180 ha. (446 a.) of woodland was planted in the south, east and west of the parish, as part of the creation of the National Forest.[97] Large housing estates have been built on farmland in the west of the parish, including on part of the council smallholdings.[98] The economics of dairy farming changed with the introduction of milk quotas in 1984,[99] the abolition of the Milk Marketing Board and the rising purchasing power of supermarkets. The long-established dairy farm at Pickering Grange, which had a 110-cubicle milking parlour in the early 21st century, became an equestrian centre, and Ibstock Grange Farm also became an equestrian business.[100] By 2010, the total number of farms in the parish had reduced to 15, several of which operated another business alongside.[101]

Mills

Robert Verdun's manor had a windmill in 1279.[102] Two mill locations have been identified, possibly one for each manor. Mill Hill Close in Overton was recorded in 1670.[103] This was almost certainly Million Close, recorded in 1838, which stretched along

89 TNA, MAF 68/134; 68/533; 68/1103; 68/1673; 68/2243; 68/2813; 68/3356; 68/3836; 68/4205; 68/4575; 68/5037; 68/5588.
90 S. Baker, *Milk to Market: Forty Years of Milk Marketing* (1973), 20.
91 TNA, MAF 32/386/213.
92 TNA, MAF 68/134; 68/533; 68/1103; 68/1673; 68/2243; 68/2813; 68/3356; 68/3836; 68/4205; 68/4575; 68/5037; 68/5588.
93 Information collected from local farmers by Andrew Ward, 2010.
94 *Coalville Times*, 12 May 1916.
95 *Leic. Daily Post*, 19 July. 1920; date tablet of farm, extant 2019.
96 TNA, MAF 68/2813; MAF 68/4575.
97 https://www.nationalforest.org/about/grant-opportunities/changing-landscapes-scheme (accessed 1 May 2019).
98 https://www.richboroughestates.co.uk/project/ibstock/ (accessed 23 Dec. 2019).
99 *The Times*, 7 Apr. 1984.
100 https://media.onthemarket.com/properties/777130/doc_1_0.pdf (accessed 1 Mar. 2018); https://www.facebook.com/Pickering-Grange-Equestrian-103077147758043/ (accessed 12 Dec. 2019).
101 Information collected by Andrew Ward, 2010.
102 Nicholls, *History* IV, 749.
103 ROLLR, DE 464/2.

the west side of Overton Road from the brook closest to the church to the exposed crest of the hill to its south.[104] There is no record of when that windmill was taken down. Another windmill stood in 1775 to the north of the junction between Melbourne Road and what became Station Road.[105] This was a timber-clad post-mill on a brick base, which survived into the 20th century.[106]

Extractive Industries

Ibstock colliery was sunk in 1825. For most of its existence it suffered from a lack of capital investment, and there were several changes of ownership, often following insolvency. It closed in 1929. Ellistown colliery, 1½ miles to its south-east, began to be sunk in 1873. It was owned by wealthy financier Joseph Joel Ellis until his death in 1885. Ellistown was merged with Bagworth colliery in 1986, and the combined pit closed in 1991.

Small-scale clay extraction for bricks took place in several locations from the 17th century. The two collieries extracted the fireclay which lay between the coal seams, and used it to manufacture fire bricks, terracotta ware and, increasingly, sanitary pipes. The red marls above the coal, suitable for facing bricks, were extracted at Ibstock colliery from *c.*1854, and at Ellistown colliery from *c.*1879. The introduction of open-cast methods since the Second World War has enabled greater quantities of this clay to be quarried at a lower cost.[107] Active quarries at both former collieries were owned by Ibstock plc in 2019, a major United Kingdom brick manufacturer.

Sandstone was dug from pits in the parish in the 14th century. Ironstone lay 500 ft beneath the surface and was extracted at Ellistown Colliery in 1880, but this does not appear to have become a regular part of the business.

Coal

Ibstock Colliery

William Thirlby, a lace manufacturer, inherited a farmhouse and land in the north of the parish when his father George died in 1812, and decided to turn to mining in 1825.[108] The venture was beset with difficulties. Geological issues, poor management, the indifferent quality of the coal and (initially) a lack of cheap transport to market all played their part, but the overriding issue for much of the colliery's history was a lack of capital.

104 ROLLR, Ti/155/1.
105 ROLLR, DE 8666.
106 Photograph in Ibstock Historical Society archive.
107 Leics. CC, 'Leicestershire Minerals, Local Plan, Rpt of Survey' (1984), 67.
108 *London Gaz.*, 29 Apr. 1817, 1039; 2 Sept. 1817, 1884; ROLLR, DE 1717/6; DE 41/1/59 abstract of title of William Thirlby.

Thirlby borrowed £6,550 between 1825 and 1830 from Revd Thomas Storer of Wigston (probably a relation by marriage),[109] Joseph Jephcote of Exhall (Warws.),[110] Thomas Swinnerton of Caldecot (Warws.),[111] and John Storer, largely against mortgages.[112] This purchased engines, pumps, other equipment and sufficient labour to sink the first shaft.[113] Needing further capital, Thirlby and his son George entered into partnership in 1830 with Leicester ironfounders James and Benjamin Cort, who paid £750 for a half-share of the buildings and plant.[114] The Corts soon took over Jephcote's loan (at £1,985) and his mortgage,[115] and injected another £1,400 into the business, probably to repay Swinnerton.[116] Benjamin Cort agreed to purchase the house, farmland and colliery, 'in complete repair and full work' in 1830,[117] for £8,250.[118] A few months later, Thomas Storer called in his loan, and petitioned successfully for William Thirlby's bankruptcy.[119] In an out-of-court settlement, it was agreed that the Corts' security would rank ahead of that of John Storer, and Benjamin Cort's agreement to purchase the business would be set aside.[120] John and Joseph Storer began to run the business, at a modest level.[121] There were '12 labourers, 20 years old' living in Ibstock in 1831 who were colliery employees.[122] By 1833, Ibstock Colliery had 70 employees, about one third of whom were boys, the youngest aged about eight.[123] Some women were employed above ground, including Harriet Tunley, employed in 1834 to weigh coal for sale locally.[124]

There was no convenient water transport. The Leicester and Swannington Railway Act included provision for a branch line from Ibstock Colliery.[125] When the line between Leicester and Bagworth opened in 1832, the railway company is said to have provided a rebate of 6*d.* per ton to Ibstock colliery to cover land carriage to Bagworth.[126] By October 1832, Joseph Storer had spent 'a considerable sum' on laying a 'railway or tramway' from the colliery to the railway line.[127] No figures are available for annual output in the 1830s, but in one week out of season in August 1833, 141 tons of Ibstock coal were carried by

109 ROLLR, DE 41/1/61, indenture of 31 Aug. 1831. Four people named Thirlby married people named Storer at Ibstock and Nailstone between 1780 and 1810: ROLLR, DE 1717/7–8; DE 2707/8–9.
110 ROLLR, DE 41/1/59, abstract of Title of William Thirlby.
111 ROLLR, DE 41/1/59, abstract of three several mortgages of land at Ibstock and Donington, 1831.
112 ROLLR, DE 41/1/223/3.
113 Ibid.
114 ROLLR, DE 41/1/223/1.
115 ROLLR, DE 41/1/223/2; DE 41/1/59, abstract of title of William Thirlby.
116 ROLLR, DE 41/1/223/2.
117 ROLLR, DE 41/1/59, abstract of title of William Thirlby; *Leic. Jnl*, 31 Dec. 1830.
118 ROLLR, DE 41/1/223/2.
119 *London Gaz.*, 12 Aug. 1831, 1644–5; 10 Jan. 1832, 68; 7 Feb. 1832, 281; *The Law Advertiser for 1831*, 292.
120 ROLLR, DE 41/1/223/2; C. Owen, *The Leicestershire and South Derbyshire Coalfield, 1200–1900* (Ashbourne, 1984), 195–6; M. Kinder, 'Ibstock Colliery', *Archives*, 72 (2011), 35–6.
121 ROLLR, DE 41/1/223/3.
122 *VCH Leics.* III, 204.
123 *Report of the Royal Commission on the Employment of Children in Factories, Second Report* (Parl. Papers 1833 (519) xxi), p. 103.
124 ROLLR, DE 4939/759, Ellis v. Ibstock Colliery Co., vol. III.
125 11 Geo. IV, c. 58.
126 11 Geo. IV, c.58; C.R. Clinker, 'Leicester and Swannington Railway', *Trans. LAHS*, 30 (1954), 69; above, Ibstock Parish, communications.
127 ROLLR, DE 41/1/223/3.

train to Leicester.[128] It has been asserted that Ibstock colliery bought a steam locomotive in 1833,[129] but witnesses in two separate court cases of 1863 and 1877 remembered the mineral line being a horse-drawn tramway for nearly 20 years. This was altered for locomotives and larger wagons in 1851, when an embankment was also built between the railway and the road.[130]

The proprietors in 1837 were the 'Ibstock Coal Company'.[131] A prospectus was issued that year by the Leicestershire Coal Company seeking to raise share capital to purchase the land, shafts, engines, railway track, colliery business and an on-site brickworks for £30,000, based on a valuation by mining engineer William Willis Bailey. Two seams were being worked, with 17 a. extracted from the top seam and 3 a. from the bottom seam. Annual sales of 30,000 tons were anticipated.[132] Many of the same people were involved in both the Ibstock Coal Company and the Leicestershire Coal Company, and the prospectus seems intended to raise fresh capital from new investors. Both company names appear in subsequent records.[133]

A court case in 1839, when a spark from colliery lamps ignited the thatch on a barn belonging to the company's tenant, provides some details of how the colliery was worked. Two lamps had been erected when a new shaft was sunk less than three years previously. These were conical iron cages, open at the top, with bars round the sides, filled and lit with coals, and raised to a height of 6 ft. Shortly after 5 a.m. on the day in question, there was 'a fresh gang of men going down to relieve the others who had been working early in the night'.[134] No more than six men were permitted to ascend or descend at any one time.[135] It took 45 minutes for all the workers to reach the coal face, and as the light was needed during that period, fresh coals were added to the lamps. This created the spark which caused the blaze. The court found in favour of the farmer.[136]

The coal was extracted by the 'long wall' system. The owners contracted with 'butties' or 'stallmen', who were each allocated a length of the coal face and were responsible for safety. The butties employed workers including 'holers' (paid by the yard) to undercut the coal face and 'loaders' (who loaded the coal into tubs). Butties and loaders were paid by the ton for the coal sent out.[137] A bonus was paid in 1855 to the most productive team each fortnight, with ale when development work was completed.[138] There were 28 pit ponies providing underground haulage in 1864.[139]

128 *Leic. Chron.*, 24 Aug. 1833.

129 First suggested by C.E. Stretton, 'The history of the Ibstock colliery (private) railway' (paper read at Ibstock, 1904), 4.

130 *Leic. Chron.*, 25 July 1863; ROLLR, DE 4939/759, Ellis v. Ibstock Colliery Co., 3 vols.

131 *Leic. Herald*, 25 Nov. 1837; 2 Dec. 1837.

132 *Leic. Chron.*, 22 Apr. 1837; below, clay.

133 *Leic. Chron.*, 22 Apr. 1837; *Leic. Jnl*, 11 Jan. 1839; *Leic. Chron.* 12 Jan. 1839; 30 Mar. 1839; ROLLR, DE 41/1/31.

134 *Leic. Jnl*, 11 Jan. 1839; *Leic. Chron.* 12 Jan. 1839; a description and painting of a Leicestershire working colliery with such lamps in 1827 can be found in Univ. of Leic., David Wilson Libr. Special Collections, MS 149, William Fry's excursions, pp. 77–80.

135 *Royal Commission on children's employment in mines and manufactories* (Parl. Papers, 1842 (C. 380), xv), p. 138.

136 *Leic. Jnl*, 11 Jan. 1839; *Leic. Chron.* 12 Jan. 1839; 30 Mar. 1839.

137 *Leic. Daily Post*, 5 July 1888.

138 ROLLR, DE 41/1/131; C. Griffin, *The Leicestershire and South Derbyshire Miners*, I (Coalville, 1981), 83.

139 *Leic. Jnl*, 28 Oct. 1864.

A report on the colliery in 1840 by John Laurance identified many deficiencies. The shafts were not deep enough, were close to the edge of the geological stratum and too close to the property boundary, so the mine could not be worked outwards in all directions. The ventilation and underground roads were 'bad', the coal was poor quality and the 'the greater part of the coal which could be worked with the present shafts is nearly exhausted'.[140] Two new shafts had begun to be sunk.[141]

The 1841 census listed 42 miners in Ibstock.[142] The colliery, 'partially opened about twenty years', but only 'in full work about ten years' was offered at auction in 1846. The sale included farmland of 98 a., the farmhouse, colliery buildings, pumping and winding engines, the railway track, and shafts reaching two seams of coal, where 32 a. had been extracted from the top seam and 23 a. from the lower seam.[143] Ashby solicitor Edward Mortimer Green purchased the colliery, *c.*1848.[144] Production problems may have continued, as only 21,438 tons were sold in 1855, well below the anticipated 30,000 tons suggested to prospective investors in 1837.[145] Green appears to have lost interest by 1862, when he agreed a lease to Edwin Bray, John Roseby and John Child, who had capital of just £6,000. Within two years they had been declared bankrupt, with debts of £34,000, and the business closed.[146]

The colliery and its accompanying brickyard were purchased in 1865 by Joseph Whetstone, of Whitwick Colliery Company.[147] After Joseph's death in 1868, the two collieries and their brickyards at Whitwick and Ibstock were managed by Joseph's brother William. Leicester banker Thomas Tertius Paget (whose late father Thomas Paget (d. 1862) had been born in Ibstock) became a partner in 1871 and injected £20,000 of capital, matching Whetstone's stake.[148] The partnership between Paget and Whetstone was dissolved in 1873, probably because Whetstone wished to retire. At that point Ibstock colliery was raising 60,000 tons annually. It owned 75 a. of surface land, freehold mineral rights over 540 a. and leasehold mineral rights over 237 a., with 52 years unexpired.[149] Agreement was reached for Whetstone to pay Paget £25,000 immediately, with two subsequent payments each of £25,000.[150] Two new companies were formed, one to carry on the business of the Whitwick colliery and the other (Ibstock Colliery Company Ltd) to take over the Ibstock mine and brickworks. William Whetstone was not a director of either. His son Joseph became a director of the new Whitwick company, but was not a director of the Ibstock company.[151]

The new Ibstock company paid £95,000 for the business in 1873, £50,000 of which was deferred. The main shareholders were George Wilkinson, Thomas Webb and Henry

140 ROLLR, DE 41/1/324.
141 *Leics. Merc.*, 24 Aug. 1839.
142 Census, 1841.
143 ROLLR, DE 40/17/4.
144 *Leic. Jnl.* 24 July 1863.
145 ROLLR, DE 41/1/131; *Leic. Chron.*, 22 Apr. 1837.
146 *London Gaz.*, 4 Oct. 1864, 4735; *Loughborough Monitor*, 8 Dec. 1864.
147 *Loughborough Monitor*, 2 Feb. 1865.
148 ROLLR, DE 462/11; 1D 43/29/4.
149 *Leic. Jnl*, 22 Aug. 1873.
150 ROLLR, 1D 43/29/5; 1D 43/29/13
151 *Leic. Jnl*, 22 Aug. 1873.

May, all of London. Joshua Stallard was appointed managing director.[152] Within one year, Ibstock colliery recorded daily output of 450 tons.[153] The company was forced to close its roadside wharf in 1877, which sold coal to local people, following a case brought against them by Joseph Ellis, the owner of Ellistown Colliery, who was able to show that the wharf was on his land.[154] The financial impact may not have been significant, but the business appears to have struggled to repay the deferred consideration, and in 1884 Whetstone foreclosed on his loan, forcing the company into liquidation.[155]

A partnership was formed in 1884 to take over the business, comprising Scottish physician Samuel Thomson, who been managing director of Ibstock colliery since 1875, his son Robert, William Sheppard, a general practitioner and surgeon from Kent, and William's son William Philpott Sheppard.[156] Samuel Thomson was the only one of the four to have been a shareholder in the company in 1883, with just a three per cent stake.[157] The business traded as Ibstock Colliery Company. William Philpott Sheppard had become managing partner by 1888.[158] A second pit opened on the site in 1890, 130 yd. from the first, and electric light was installed that year above and below ground.[159] Output increased to 550 tons daily at the No. 1 colliery and 500 tons daily from the No. 2 pit.[160] William Sheppard senior retired in 1896.[161] The remaining partnership was dissolved in 1899, when the business was transferred to a new limited company, Ibstock Collieries Ltd.[162] Robert Thomson was elected chairman, and Robert and William Philpott Sheppard were appointed joint managing directors.[163]

The colliery ordered its first coal-cutting machine in 1900.[164] In 1914, it employed 1,128 people underground and 215 on the surface.[165] Many of its miners joined the army during the First World War, when tunnelling skills were sought for the trenches.[166] The consequent labour shortage resulted in a heavy reliance on those too young or too old for military service. The colliery 'collared every lad they could on leaving school', and employed 44 boys under 14 years in 1916, when their oldest worker was 87.[167]

Daily output in 1918 was 1,100 tons, rather than the 1,300 tons the directors considered achievable, with absenteeism an issue.[168] The company was heavily dependent on the London market (Figure 9). Profits were initially seen after the First World War, but the colliery side of the business lost money almost every month in 1927.[169] The

152 TNA, BT 31/1892/7597.
153 *Leic. Chron.*, 19 Sept. 1874;
154 ROLLR, DE 4939/759.
155 *Leic. Jnl.*, 12 Apr. 1884; 4 July 1884; 18 July 1884; TNA, BT 31/1892/7597.
156 Cassell, *Dig It*, 16; TNA, RG 9/512/34/25; RG 13/2972/48/1.
157 TNA, BT 31/1892/7597.
158 *Kelly's Dir. of Leics. and Rutl.* (1888), 541.
159 *London Eve. Standard*, 26 Aug. 1873; *Leic. Jnl*, 12 Sept. 1879; *Colliery Guardian*, 18 Sept. 1896; *Leic. Chron.*, 7 June 1890; Kinder, 'Ibstock Colliery', 39–42; Cassell, *Dig It*, 16.
160 *Colliery Guardian*, 18 Sept. 1896.
161 *London Gaz.*, 23 June 1896, 3663.
162 Ibid., 3 Oct. 1899, 6033.
163 Company minute book (priv. colln), 13 Oct. 1899.
164 Ibid., 29 May 1900.
165 *Coalville Times*, 10 Mar. 1916.
166 C. Griffin, *The Leicestershire Miners*, II (Coalville, 1988), 125.
167 *Coalville Times*, 10 Mar. 1916.
168 Company minute book (priv. colln), 8 May 1918, 15 Aug. 1918, 25 Oct. 1918.
169 Ibid., mins 23 Feb. 1927 to 22 Feb. 1928.

Figure 9 *Ibstock Colliery No. 2 pit, showing coal in wagons destined for London. The properties in the image were owned by the colliery company.*

directors attributed the losses to poor London sales, due to an inability to compete on price, 'the Scottish and Northern Counties sending supplies by water by a very much cheaper rate than [Ibstock Colliery could send] by rail to London and Southern Ports'.[170] The company asked mining engineer A.R. Tomlinson to prepare a report on the colliery in 1928. He advised the directors that the pits should close as soon as possible, as they were losing money on every ton of coal sold.[171] The contracts of 140 miners had been terminated in advance of receiving the report, and in its aftermath another 600 workers were served with notice.[172] The remaining 300 men were retained until July 1929 for dismantling the colliery side of the business.[173] The brick, tile and pipe works continued to operate.[174]

After the establishment of the National Coal Board in 1947,[175] unworked sections of coal between adjoining collieries could be removed. The water was pumped from Ibstock pit in 1955, and the unworked coal was extracted by neighbouring collieries.[176]

Ellistown Colliery

The farmland which became Ellistown Colliery was purchased for £32,000 in 1873 by Joseph Joel Ellis, the proprietor of Nailstone colliery, 1.2 miles to the south-west.[177] Colonel Ellis, as he was known locally, had been born Joseph Joel in 1816, in Krotoszyn,

170 Ibid., 27 June 1928.
171 Ibid., 24 Oct. 1928.
172 *Nottingham Eve. Post*, 30 Aug. 1928; 31 Oct. 1928.
173 *Birmingham Daily Gaz.*, 10 Nov. 1928; *Nottingham Jnl*, 13 July 1929.
174 Below.
175 Coal Industry Nationalisation Act, 1946.
176 *Leic. Mercury*, 13 Jan. 1955.
177 ROLLR, DE 4939/589; *Leic. Daily Post*, 3 July 1873.

in modern Poland. He came to England in 1820.[178] In 1851 he was a jeweller and diamond merchant in Brompton (Middx),[179] and described himself as a banker in 1861.[180] He became a naturalised British citizen in 1855,[181] and took the surname Ellis, *c.*1863.[182] His title came from his commission as honorary colonel in the 1st Tower Hamlets Artillery, which he resigned in 1873.[183] Ellis appears to have had no connection with Leicestershire before he took a half-share in Nailstone colliery in 1867.[184] He sold his interest in Nailstone, *c.*1877.[185]

The site chosen for Ellistown Colliery adjoined the Leicester and Burton branch of the Midland Railway (originally the Leicester to Swannington line). Thomas Millership, manager of Nailstone colliery, was appointed general manager.[186]

Immediately beneath the surface clay, the red marls of the New Red Sandstone formation were 300 ft thick and held a vast quantity of water.[187] Whitwick Dolerite lay under the sandstone and above the coal.[188] When they began to sink the mine, 'they seemed to have tapped all the springs of the neighbourhood'. After pumping out the water they soon struck hard rock, 'almost as hard as a diamond, and on which the highest tempered tools could hardly make an impression'.[189] A 'few gentlemen interested in mining' watched the application of a McDermott drill to create a bore. Dynamite was inserted and blew out four feet of rock.[190] It took two years to reach Top Main coal at 768 ft.[191] The sinkings provided 68 ft of workable coal in 13 seams and ten beds of fireclay totalling 55 ft. The coal was dry, gas was rare, there were no geological faults and the strata dip was only 1 in 14.[192]

The business traded initially as Ellistown New Colliery, and from 1879 as Ellistown Collieries.[193] While Joseph Ellis was alive, he was the sole proprietor. Following further land purchases, in 1879 the colliery estate comprised 400 a. of freehold land and 154 a. of freehold minerals (where the surface land was owned by another party).[194] The shafts were close to the railway and were capable of raising 1,400 tons daily.[195] It was estimated that the Roaster seam alone contained enough coal to provide 200,000 tons annually for 21 years.[196] About 600 men were probably employed.[197] The colliery was initially worked

178 TNA, HO 1/68/2140.
179 TNA, HO 107/1469/324/37.
180 TNA, RG 9/21/19/36.
181 TNA, HO 1/68/2140.
182 *London Eve. Standard*, 19 Nov. 1863.
183 *Morning Post*, 29 Oct. 1873.
184 *Birmingham Jnl*, 23 Nov. 1867.
185 *Leic. Daily Post*, 3 Mar. 1877.
186 *Leic. Jnl.*, 4 July 1873; 5 Dec. 1873; *Leic. Chron.*, 12 Feb. 1876.
187 ROLLR, DE 490/16, p. 16.
188 C. Fox-Strangways, *The Geology of the Leicestershire and South Derbyshire Coalfields* (1907), 33–4.
189 *Leic. Chron.*, 12 Feb. 1876.
190 *Leic. Jnl*, 5 Dec. 1873.
191 *Leic. Chron.*, 12 Feb. 1876.
192 ROLLR, DE 490/16, pp. 5, 11–12, 16.
193 *Leic. Jnl*, 9 Feb. 1877; ROLLR, DE 4939/41–46.
194 ROLLR, DE 4939/352, pp. 1–2.
195 Ibid., pp. 2, 3.
196 Ibid., pp. 17–18.
197 Owen, *Leicestershire*, 238.

Figure 10 *Ellistown Colliery Rescue Brigade, c.1913, with breathing apparatus designed by Henry Fleuss.*

on the 'long wall' system.[198] A new system was introduced in 1888, by which all the men, not just the butties, were employed directly by the colliery.[199]

Ellis died in 1885, leaving the business to trustees, who ran it under the supervision of the High Court until 1935.[200] An undated valuation from the early 20th century shows that the colliery was raising 1,200 tons of coal daily. It held rights over nearly 900 a. of unworked coal in the Roaster seam, which yielded 7,500 tons per acre, and 964 a. in the Upper seam, yielding 6,500 tons per acre.[201] Further annual income of £340 was obtained through an agreement of 1893 to supply 400,000 gallons of water daily for 30 years to Leicester Corporation's Thornton Reservoir.[202]

From 1911, coal owners employing more than 250 men were required to establish brigades of five or more men with appropriate training, qualifications and equipment to rescue miners in the event of an underground accident or explosion.[203] Training was supplemented by regular competitions between collieries (Figure 10).[204] Four men from Ellistown Colliery, John Vernon, Lewis Noble, James Edwards and Walter Bourne,

198 Above.
199 *Leic. Daily Post*, 20 July, 27 July, 31 July, 2 Aug., 3 Aug., 30 Aug. 1888.
200 Principal Probate Registry, COW272384g; ROLLR, DE 4939/765.
201 ROLLR, DE 4939/365/1.
202 Ibid.; *Leic. Chron.*, 23 Dec. 1893; 30 Dec. 1893.
203 Mines Accident (Rescue and Aid) Act, 1910; ROLLR, DE 1177/15.
204 ROLLR, Misc 1383/1–36.

received awards from the Carnegie Hero Trust Fund for saving the life of William Bramley, a miner crushed by a roof fall in 1928.[205]

The court agreed in 1935 that two companies could be formed, one to buy and work the colliery, and the other to buy and run the attached brickworks.[206] Ellistown Colliery Ltd and Ellistown Brick, Pipe and Fireclay Works and Estates Ltd began operations in 1936.[207] By 1938, all the coal cutting and face conveying had been mechanised. This resulted in a doubling of output, and profit levels consistently higher than those at other local collieries.[208]

Deep seams, modern plant, sound management and hard work combined across many mines in the Leicestershire coalfield to produce some of the highest levels of output in the United Kingdom. Ellistown colliery was producing 2,000 tons per day in 1951, about two tons per man-shift, well above the national average of 24 cwt, although not the highest figure locally.[209] Pit head baths were provided in 1953.[210] Greater mechanisation was introduced from 1958.[211] Ellistown and Bagworth were linked by underground road in 1969, and the coal was conveyed to Nailstone coal preparation plant from 1971.[212]

By the 1980s, many of the pits in the Leicestershire coalfield were approaching exhaustion, and the inevitability of closure was one reason why the 1984 miners' strike was less divisive in Leicestershire than elsewhere.[213] Ellistown and Bagworth collieries merged in 1986.[214] Production in the Ellistown part of the mine ended in 1989, and at the Bagworth end in 1991.[215]

Clay

Three pottery kilns and a tile kiln were found during the excavation of the Roman settlement near the north-west parish boundary, which presumably used local clay.[216]

A furlong in Bufton Field was known as Claypitts Flat in 1690.[217] A deed of 1737 mentions a kiln 'in the common fields'.[218] This may be the clay pit and kiln found immediately to the south of the point where Pretoria Road becomes a bridle way, probably dating from the 18th century.[219] A plan of Thomas Paget's estate in 1775 shows Brick-kiln Close on the east side of Overton Road immediately to the north of the

205 *Coalville Times*, 5 Nov. 1928.
206 ROLLR, DE 4939/631, DE 4939/765.
207 ROLLR, DE 4939/765; DE 4939/771/4.
208 ROLLR, DE 4939/382.
209 *Coal*, Feb. 1952, 11.
210 D. Amos and N. Braber, *Coal Mining in the East Midlands* (Sheffield, 2017), 21.
211 M. Woodward, *A Coalville Miner's Story* (Stroud, 1993), 70–5.
212 Ibid., 76.
213 Griffin, *Leicestershire Miners*, III, 212–3.
214 Ibid., 1.
215 Amos and Braber, *Coal Mining*, 21–2.
216 Leics. and Rutl. HER, MLE 9016 (OS: SK 401116); MLE 4561 (OS: SK 406114); J. Lucas, 'A Romano-British settlement at Ravenstone', *Trans.* LAHS, 57 (1981), 104–7.
217 ROLLR, 1D 41/2/340.
218 ROLLR, DE 41/1/59, abstract of title, 1826.
219 Leics. and Rutl. HER, MLE 20941.

northernmost brook.[220] Brick Kiln Yard lay immediately to the south-east of that land in 1838, when another Brick Kiln Close and Yard lay in the angle between Chapel Street and Curzon Street.[221] Brick production was probably only on a very small scale. When Ibstock rectory was rebuilt and extended in 1789, the contract specified bricks from Ravenstone, Shackerstone or Snarestone,[222] and insufficient bricks could be obtained to build a boundary wall for the British School in 1850.[223] A brick yard containing an area of excavated ground stood on the south side of High Street in 1883, but only the depression in the ground survived in 1903.[224]

Ibstock Brick and Pipe Works

A 'valuable Brick Yard ... in full working' had opened at Ibstock colliery by 1837, with 'Beds of excellent Clay, for making Yellow Earthenware and Fire Bricks'.[225] This suggests that only the fireclay was extracted, but this changed from 1854 when Ibstock Colliery Company entered an agreement for Joseph Bradshaw to operate the brickyard. Bradshaw took responsibility for the entire process, from the extraction of the clay to loading the finished bricks into wagons. The colliery provided the clay mills, brick and tile moulds, pressing machines, tile machines and four kilns, while Bradshaw provided all other tools, sand for the moulds and labour. He was paid an agreed sum for every thousand bricks or tiles made, ranging from 11*s*. for common bricks to 40*s*. for eight-inch quarries.[226] This is the earliest reference to making common bricks.

A sale of 'Surplus Brickyard Stock' in 1879, which included 236,600 bricks and 106,100 other pieces, may indicate a review of the business. It was also a means of generating cash in a period when the miners were taking industrial action.[227] Even with this stock clearance, the brickworks only generated sales of £2,991 that year, while coal sales were over £27,000.[228] The 'entire stock' of over one million 'best common bricks' and over 55,000 other pieces was put up for sale in 1884, on the instruction of a creditor (probably William Whetstone).[229] The site was taken over by the partnership formed by Samuel and Robert Thomson and the two William Sheppards, trading as Ibstock Colliery Company. A broad range of clay products was produced in 1888, including facing bricks in three colours, copings, quarry-tiles, chimney-pots, roof tiles and a range of sanitary pipes (Figure 11).[230] Investment in this side of the business, *c*.1892, included the purchase of three new kilns and two new drying sheds.[231]

220 ROLLR, 109/30/95.
221 ROLLR, Ti/155/1.
222 Lincs. Arch., DIOC/MGA/7, estimate, 4 Feb. 1789.
223 TNA, ED 103/36/3.
224 OS Map 25", Leics. XXIII.15 (1883), (1903).
225 *Leic. Chron.*, 22 Apr. 1837.
226 ROLLR, DE 41/1/222.
227 *Leic. Jnl*, 29 Aug. 1879; *Leic. Chron.*, 28 Sept. 1879.
228 Cassell, *Dig It*, 16.
229 *Leic. Jnl*, 26 Sept. 1884.
230 *Kelly's Dir. of Leics. and Rutl.* (1888), 744
231 Cassell, *Dig It*, 19.

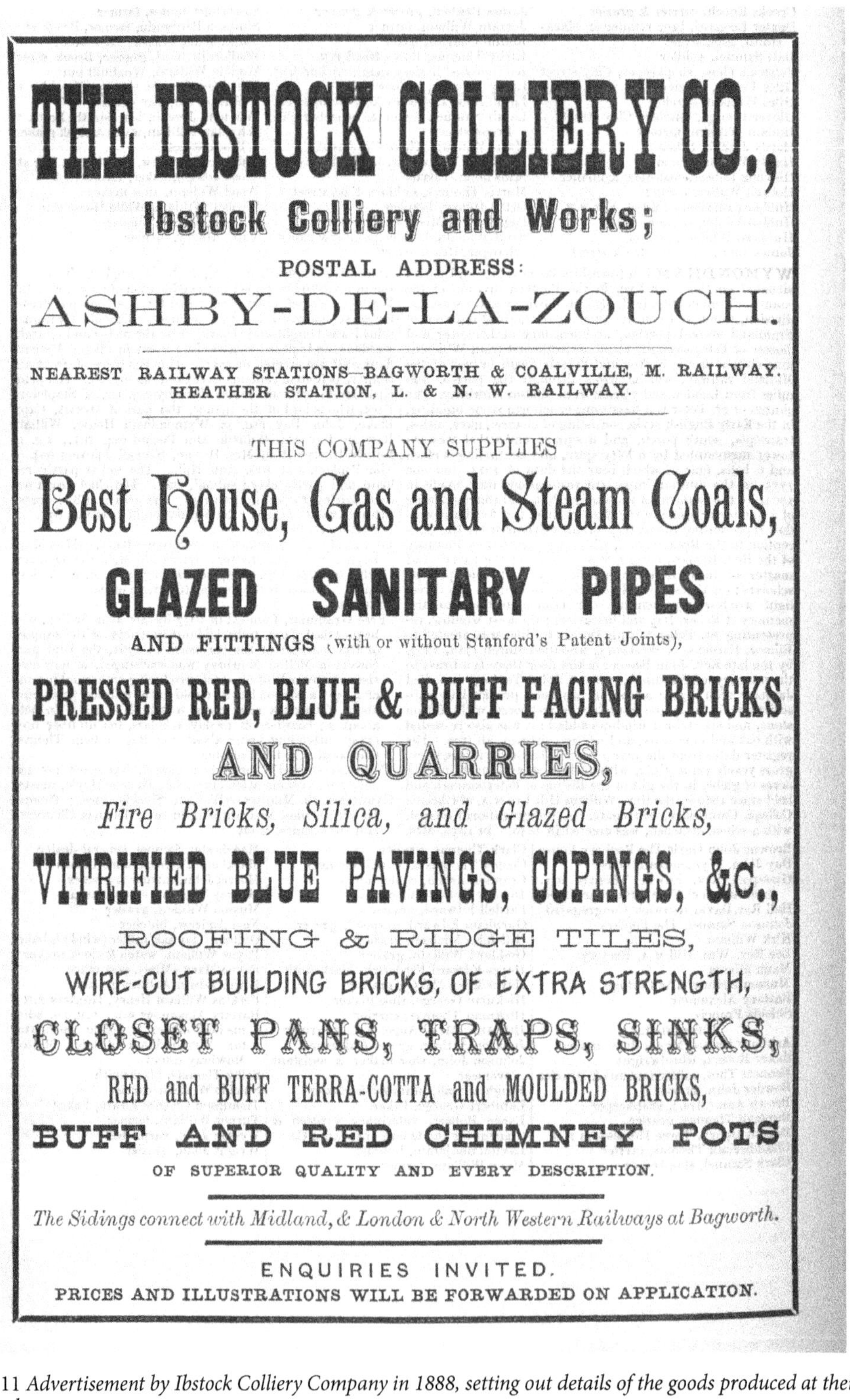

THE IBSTOCK COLLIERY CO.,

Ibstock Colliery and Works;

POSTAL ADDRESS:

ASHBY-DE-LA-ZOUCH.

NEAREST RAILWAY STATIONS—BAGWORTH & COALVILLE, M. RAILWAY.
HEATHER STATION, L. & N. W. RAILWAY.

THIS COMPANY SUPPLIES

Best House, Gas and Steam Coals,

GLAZED SANITARY PIPES

AND FITTINGS (with or without Stanford's Patent Joints),

PRESSED RED, BLUE & BUFF FACING BRICKS

AND QUARRIES,

Fire Bricks, Silica, and Glazed Bricks,

VITRIFIED BLUE PAVINGS, COPINGS, &c.,

ROOFING & RIDGE TILES,

WIRE-CUT BUILDING BRICKS, OF EXTRA STRENGTH,

CLOSET PANS, TRAPS, SINKS,

RED and BUFF TERRA-COTTA and MOULDED BRICKS,

BUFF AND RED CHIMNEY POTS

OF SUPERIOR QUALITY AND EVERY DESCRIPTION.

The Sidings connect with Midland, & London & North Western Railways at Bagworth.

ENQUIRIES INVITED.

PRICES AND ILLUSTRATIONS WILL BE FORWARDED ON APPLICATION.

Figure 11 *Advertisement by Ibstock Colliery Company in 1888, setting out details of the goods produced at their brickworks.*

The brickyard business was loss-making in 1914, as a shortage of labour meant break-even production levels could not be achieved.[232] It returned profits after the First World War, and continued after the colliery closed in 1929. A report of 1933 found that the company was producing three million bricks and five million tiles and pipes annually, but the plant was inefficient. The following year the company built one of the first tunnel kilns in Britain at the 'North Works' on the colliery site. Cars loaded with bricks passed through the tunnel, which was 297 ft long and reached 1,040 degrees Celsius in the centre. The new plant enabled the company to produce nine million bricks annually. The company changed its name in 1935 to Ibstock Brick and Tile Company Ltd.[233] A 20-chamber kiln was constructed on the 'South Works' in 1946, increasing annual capacity to 18 million bricks.[234] The railway track was removed in 1957.[235]

The directors had ambitions to increase sales beyond the local area, and expansion proceeded by the acquisition of brick producers in other parts of the United Kingdom, with funding partly provided by flotation on the stock exchange in 1963.[236] The pipeworks at Ibstock closed in 1965, with all attention then focused on bricks.[237]

The corporate history is of limited relevance to events in the parish, other than the opportunity it provided to local people for a career in the head office of an international company, or across different plants, companies and overseas subsidiaries.[238] The public company was acquired by the Irish materials group CRH in 1998 (which had been formed in 1970 through the merger of two Irish public companies, Cement Ltd and Roadstone Ltd). The CRH concrete products and roof tile business, Forticrete, was integrated into the Ibstock business.[239] The Ellistown brick factory and site was purchased in 1999, giving Ibstock one third of United Kingdom brick capacity. The company, with Forticrete, separated from CRH in 2015 and returned to the stock exchange in its own right as Ibstock plc.[240]

Ibstock plc was the leading clay-brick manufacturer in the United Kingdom in 2018, and a major manufacturer of concrete products for the building, roofing, fencing and rail markets.[241] Bricks and concrete products are made at the Ibstock site. A new factory (known as Eclipse) opened at Ibstock in 2018, capable of producing 100 million bricks annually, more than doubling annual production on this site to 190 million bricks.[242] The

232 Company minute book (priv. colln), min. 7 Jan. 1915.

233 Cassell, *Dig It*, 35–36; http://www.ibstock.com/history/ (accessed 25 Mar. 2017); *Rpt of the Monopolies and Mergers Commission London Brick plc and Ibstock Johnsen plc. A Report on the Proposed Merger* (Parl. Papers 1983–4 [Cmnd 9015]), p.15.

234 Cassell, *Dig It*, 42.

235 Cassell, *Dig It*, 51.

236 *The Times*, 4 Dec. 1963; *Report of the Monopolies and Mergers Commission*, p. 15.

237 Cassell, *Dig It*, 48.

238 *Rpt of the Monopolies and Mergers Commission; The Times*, 21 Oct. 1998, 26; 24 Oct. 1998, 28; http://www.ibstock.com/history/ (accessed 25 Mar. 2017); Cassell, *Dig It*, 134–149.

239 *The Times*, 22 Dec. 1998, 23; 15 Jan. 1999, 28; 19 Jan. 1999, 32; http://www.ibstock.com/history/ (accessed 25 Mar. 2017); https://www.crh.com/about-crh/our-history/ (accessed 23 Nov. 2019).

240 *Financial Times*, 29 Sept. 2015.

241 *Ibstock plc, Rpt and Accts* (2018), 16.

242 https://www.ibstockbrick.co.uk/news/brokenshire-opens-ibstock-brick-new-eclipse-factory-which-will-help-build-up-to-15000-new-homes-a-year/ (accessed 12 Apr. 2019).

total workforce on the Ibstock and Ellistown sites grew to 340, including head office staff. The majority of the bricks made were used within an 80-mile radius.[243]

It was estimated in 2003 that on-site clay reserves would be sufficient until 2038.[244] The quarry was set back from the roads and screened by trees, with fences and trees along the boundaries near footpaths. There is little wastage in brick production, but any non-usable clay was retained to restore quarried areas. The exhausted 'north quarry' was reinstated as pasture for livestock in 2015.[245]

Ellistown Brick and Pipe Works

Ten beds of fireclay with an aggregate thickness of 55 ft were found when Ellistown colliery was sunk from 1873, including two beds immediately above and below the Roaster coal seam.[246] Ellistown fireclay works opened in 1879.[247] It was capable of handling 100 tons of fireclay daily, suitable for fire bricks, furnace linings, quarry tiles and sanitary pipes. It had three downdraught kilns with a fourth nearly complete in 1879, each capable of holding 25,000 bricks or 12 tons of pipes, two oblong kilns to hold 30,000 bricks each and an 'experimental' kiln with a chimney in the centre, for 4,000 bricks. There were three drying sheds.[248]

The red marl immediately below the surface was suitable for making blue bricks, and a second works was established in 1879 for this purpose.[249] As blue bricks and sanitary pipes were relatively new products, the size of the market could not then be estimated, but demand was strong.[250] One valuer reported that the fireclay works could be increased 'to any amount ... as the amount of clay is so enormous', and the red marl could yield 96 million bricks per acre.[251] A company catalogue, undated but early 20th century, shows a large product range including moulded and ornamental bricks, cornices, copings, chimney pots, glazed sanitary pipes, ridge tiles and finials.[252] Many examples can be seen on local houses.

The brick and pipe business became a separate entity in 1936, when Ellistown Brick, Pipe & Fireclay Works & Estates Ltd was incorporated.[253] It was therefore unaffected by the vesting of the coal industry in 1947. The business was taken over by Hepworth Iron Co. Ltd in 1968, when the main business initially became pipe manufacture.[254] A large brick plant was built on the site between 1986 and 1988, to produce up to 55

243 www.leicesterbrickfactory.co.uk (accessed 16 Apr. 2017).

244 NWL Draft Local Plan, Background Paper 7: Brickworks and Pipeworks (undated), 6, https://www.nwleics.gov.uk/files/documents/background_paper_7_policy_ec4/BackgroundPaper7%20-%20Policy%20Ec4.pdf (accessed 30 Jan. 2019).

245 www.leicesterbrickfactory.co.uk (accessed 16 Apr. 2017).

246 ROLLR, DE 490/16, pp. 12–14.

247 *Leic. Jnl*, 21 Feb. 1879.

248 ROLLR, DE 490/16, pp. 14–15.

249 Ibid., p. 16.

250 ROLLR, DE 4939/352/1, p. 7.

251 ROLLR, DE 490/16, p. 19.

252 ROLLR, DE 4939/326.

253 ROLLR, DE 4939/11.

254 *The Times*, 26 Apr. 1968, 32.

million bricks annually.[255] The brick business was sold by Hepworth to the Ibstock brick company in 1999.[256] The pipeworks remained with Hepworth, who sold the pipe-factory in 2006 to F.P. McCann Ltd, the United Kingdom's largest producer of pre-cast concrete products.[257]

Some quarried land was restored from 2014.[258] Clay continued to be extracted from other parts of the site, with planning consent in place until 2042. In 2003, reserves were estimated to last until 2088.[259]

Stone

Bromsgrove Sandstone crops out around the margins of the coalfield,[260] including near Pickering Grange in Ibstock.[261] Stone from Ibstock was taken to Leicester in 1351–2, for work on the North Bridge.[262] Three fields were named Pit Close in 1838, two towards the southern parish boundary on the former monastic land, and one in the extreme east of the parish.[263] The geology at these locations suggests these were probably stone pits.[264]

Ironstone was found when Ellistown colliery was sunk,[265] and 200 tons were advertised for sale in 1880.[266] A lack of later references to ironstone suggests that extraction did not continue.

Manufacture

Textile Industries

William and Benjamin Thirlby traded from Ibstock as bobbin-twist lace manufacturers and machine makers from 1817 to 1827, with the business then continuing in William's sole name.[267] As trade declined, Benjamin became a hosier, and William started Ibstock

255 NWL DC, Permit with introductory note, no. I/37/3.6 (A)(2)(a) (2007), p. ii, https://www.nwleics.gov.uk/files/documents/ (accessed 30 Jan. 2019).

256 *The Times*, 3 July 1999, 26.

257 Leics. CC Development Control and Regulatory Board, 'Extension of concrete factory at Ellistown (2006) http://politics.leics.gov.uk/documents/s17280/E.Ellistown%20Concrete%20Plant.pdf; https://fpmccann.co.uk/about-us (accessed 4 Apr. 2019).

258 Ibstock plc, Sustainability Report, 2018, 24.

259 NWL Draft Local Plan, Background Paper 7: Brickworks and Pipeworks (undated), 6, 12, https://www.nwleics.gov.uk/files/documents/background_paper_7_policy_ec4/BackgroundPaper7%20-%20Policy%20Ec4.pdf (accessed 30 Jan. 2019).

260 Historic England, 'Strategic Stone Study: A Building Stone Atlas of Leicestershire' (2017), 15–16, file:///Z:/Downloads/Leicestershire_Building_Stone_Atlas.pdf (accessed 7 Mar. 2019).

261 http://mapapps.bgs.ac.uk/geologyofbritain/home.html (accessed 19 Feb. 2019).

262 M. Bateson (ed.), *Records of the Borough of Leicester*, II (1901), 78; *VCH Leics.* III, 43.

263 ROLLR, Ti/155/1; PP 454.

264 http://mapapps.bgs.ac.uk/geologyofbritain/home.html (accessed 19 Feb. 2019).

265 ROLLR, DE 4939/352, pp. 16–17.

266 *Sheffield Daily Telegraph*, 6 Apr. 1880.

267 *London Gaz.*, 29 Apr. 1817, 1039; 2 Sept. 1817, 1884; 2 Mar. 1827, 512.

colliery in 1825. By 1841 there were only two lace-makers in the village, and one lace-dealer.[268]

William Pemberton served an apprenticeship as a framework-knitter in Ibstock in the early 19th century before going to sea in the Napoleonic Wars. He said the trade was 'in great prosperity' when he returned home in 1815, and there had been 150 frames in the village.[269] Framework-knitting was the third most common occupation in Ibstock in 1841 (behind agriculture and mining), although it only employed 38 people, excluding family members who probably worked alongside.[270] There were between 47 and 59 frames in the village in 1844, mostly producing wrought hose (shaped during the knitting process), in cotton and in worsted (wool). Four people made gloves, which was higher-paid work.[271] The industry was then in decline, due to changes in fashion and technology.[272] By 1851, just nine men and four women were described as framework-knitters.[273]

There is no evidence for any other significant textile businesses in Ibstock until *c.*1927, when Ibstock Knitting Co. Ltd built a factory on Melbourne Road to produce elastic webbing.[274] The company described itself as a knitted fabric manufacturer in the 1950s, and its main products in 1970 were foundation garments and swimwear.[275] It had become a division of Clutsom-Penn International Ltd by 1977, part of the Courtaulds Group.[276] The business moved to Coalville, *c.*1980.[277]

Textile Spares made shuttles and looms for the narrow-fabrics trade. Founded in 1948 by five former loom manufacturers, the business was initially based in the former rectory stables, moving to Melbourne Road in 1954, when it changed its name to Midland Loom and Batten Co.[278] It had moved again to the former Wesleyan Reform Chapel on Reform Road by 1963.[279] The company was dissolved in 1977.[280]

Footwear

In Leicestershire, it was common for the upper parts of shoes to be stitched together ('closing') in a satellite factory, often in a village. Several shoe closing rooms have been based in Ibstock, providing female employment in a parish where women's work was

268 Census, 1841.
269 *Report on Framework Knitters, Appendix to Part I*, pp. 544–5; *Appendix to Part II* (Parl. Papers 1845 [C 641], xv), p. 692.
270 Census, 1841.
271 *Report on Framework Knitters, Appendix to Part I* (Parl. Papers 1845 [C 618], xv), pp. 542–6; Appendix to Part II (Parl. Papers 1845 [C 641], xv), pp. 688, 692–3; W Felkin, *A Census of, and Report upon, the Present Extent and Condition of the Framework Knitting Trade* (1844), 8–9, 18–19, 23–4, 26–7.
272 *VCH Leics.* III, 12–13.
273 Census, 1851.
274 OS Map 25", Leics. XXIII.11 (1929 edn); *Kelly's Dir. of Leics. and Rutl.* (1932).
275 *PO Telephone Dir. Leic. Area* (1956), 125; *Liverpool Echo*, 24 June 1970.
276 *PO Telecomm. Midlands Commercial Classified Dir.* (1977), 215; L. Briscoe, *The Textile and Clothing Industries of the United Kingdom* (Manchester, 1971), 172.
277 *PO Telephone Dir. Leic. Area* (1979), 334; *BT Telephone Dir. Leic. Area* (1982), 378.
278 *Leic. Mercury*, 11 Feb. 1955; *PO Telephone Dir. Leic. Area* (1956), 162.
279 *PO Telephone Dir. Leic. Area* (1963), 156.
280 *London Gaz.*, 29 Sept. 1977, 12293.

scarce.[281] George Ward Ltd of Barwell (ten miles south of Ibstock) opened closing rooms in Ibstock's former National School in 1947, where it employed up to 100 women.[282] The factory closed *c.*1980, but the premises were used in the late 1980s by Glovease Shoes Ltd.[283] The former town hall also became a closing room in the late 1940s.[284] George Green and Sons of Leicester had closing rooms in Melbourne Road in the 1960s.[285] British Shoe Corporation Ltd (a subsidiary of the retail conglomerate Sears) had closing rooms on Melbourne Road in the 1970s until *c.*1988,[286] when the company was gradually withdrawing from manufacture.[287]

Other Manufacturing

In the 1970s the parish council was 'most anxious to attract new industry' and advertised that 'sites with all services are available'.[288] A small industrial estate was created near Spring Road in 1974.[289] About ten businesses occupied the units in 2019, the largest of which was ATA Garryson Ltd, a manufacturer of speciality abrasives and precision engineering tools.[290]

Housebuilding

David Wilson Homes, one of Britain's largest housebuilders in the opening years of the 21st century, developed from the joinery business of Albert Wilson, which turned its focus to housebuilding in the 1960s, when Albert's son David joined the business. Then known as A.H. Wilson, the business was building around 150 homes annually in the early 1970s. It became Wilson Bowden Properties in 1973, and Wilson Bowden plc when it was floated on the Stock Exchange in 1987, with house-building and commercial property development divisions.[291] The company head office, on Leicester Road, Ibstock, provided the opportunity of office work with a major national company, as well as employment for skilled tradespeople.

Through organic growth, David Wilson Homes became one of Britain's top twenty housebuilders by volume in 1988, building 1,372 homes that year,[292] and came through the housing recession of the early 1990s unscathed.[293] By 2000, it had become one of

281 D. Holmes, Development of the boot and shoe industry in Leicester during the nineteenth century', *Trans. LAHS* (2009), 175–218.
282 *Ibstock Par. Mag.*, May 1946; oral history interview with director Tom Lucas, https://www.hinckleypastpresent.org/oralhistory-tomlucas.html (accessed 16 Mar. 2019).
283 *PO Telecomm. Midlands Commercial Classified Dir.* (1977), 170; *Yellow Pages Leicester Area* (1987), 408.
284 *Leic. Mercury*, 15 Dec. 1955.
285 ROLLR, L 711, Ibstock Village Survey (1963); *East Midlands South Classified Telephone Directory* (1965), 18.
286 *PO Telecomm. Midlands Commercial Classified Dir.* (1977), 169; *Yellow Pages Leicester Area* (1987), 408.
287 Ex inf. David Holmes, historian of the Leicester footwear industry.
288 Ibstock Parish Council, *Ibstock, Leicestershire: Official Guide* (Carshalton, undated, probably 1970s), 14.
289 *Ibstock Par. Mag.*, Apr. 1974, 16.
290 https://www.atagroup.co/ (accessed 10 Apr. 2019).
291 http://www.wilsonbowden.co.uk/history (accessed 13 Nov. 2018).
292 F. Wellings, *British Housebuilders: History and Analysis* (Oxford, 2006), 90.
293 Ibid., 98.

Britain's 'top ten' housebuilders by volume, with developments across the country.[294] In 2004 it employed, directly or indirectly, nearly 6,000 people.[295] It also operated a small plant hire company in Ibstock, which employed about 40 people in 2007.[296] The group was sold to the much larger housebuilder Barratt Developments plc in 2007.[297] The parties had agreed that the Barratt head office in Newcastle-upon-Tyne would be transferred to Bardon, three miles from Ibstock, preserving local jobs.[298] Barratt Developments plc, David Wilson Homes Ltd and Wilson Bowden Developments Ltd continued to be based at Bardon in 2019.[299]

The former David Wilson head office premises were sold back to the Wilson family. They became the headquarters of a new family company, Davidsons Developments Ltd, which began trading as Davidsons Homes in 2008.[300] The managing director was David Wilson's son James. The business sold its 1,000th home in 2015.[301] It had *c.*300 staff in 2019, a regional office in Northamptonshire, and was building on sites in Leicestershire, Northamptonshire, Warwickshire and Staffordshire.[302]

Retail and Services

Retail

The nearest historic market towns were Ashby-de-la-Zouch, six miles away, which gained its market charter in 1219, and Market Bosworth, five miles away, with a market charter from 1224.[303] Both held weekly markets in 1622,[304] but Bosworth's market was 'almost in disuse', *c.*1800.[305] Bagworth was also granted a market charter in 1270, but markets ceased to be held by 1622, and possibly long before then.[306]

Ibstock's position, surrounded by smaller villages, at a distance from a market town, and with no dominant landowner, placed it in a good position to attract traders prior to the growth of Coalville in the 19th century. Elias Goadby appeared in the hearth tax for the first time in 1664, with one hearth.[307] He was a mercer.[308] Samuel Goadby, probably

294 F. Wellings, *British Housebuilders: History and Analysis* (Oxford, 2006), 99–100.
295 Ibid., 100, 261; http://davidwilsonfoundation.com/History.aspx (accessed 13 Nov. 2018).
296 *Coalville Times*, 1 May 2007.
297 Barratt Developments plc, *Rpt and Accts* (2007); *The Times*, 5 Feb. 2007.
298 Ex inf. David Wilson.
299 https://www.barrattdevelopments.co.uk/contact-us/head-offices (accessed 3 June 2019).
300 Ex inf. David Wilson.
301 *Ibstock Community Voice*, Sept. 2015, 7.
302 Ex inf. David Wilson; *Leicester Mercury*, 24 Sept. 2018; https://davidsonsgroup.co.uk/ (accessed 13 Nov. 2018); https://www.eastmidlandsbusinesslink.co.uk/mag/property/local-housebuilders-northamptonshire-expansion-creates-whole-new-workforce/; (accessed 17 Sept. 2020).
303 S. Letters, 'Gaz. of Markets and Fairs', https://archives.history.ac.uk/gazetteer/gazweb2.html (accessed 2 Dec. 2019).
304 Burton, *Description*, 4.
305 Nichols, *History* III, 499.
306 Letters, 'Fairs and markets'; Burton, *Description*, 4.
307 TNA, E 179/251/4 pt 8, f. 225v.
308 R.H. Evans, 'Nonconformity in Leicestershire in 1669', *Trans LAHS* (1949), 108–9, 126–7.

his son, was also a mercer. His shop carried a large stock of cloth, groceries and other items at his death in 1705.[309] The range of goods compares well with those sold in other Leicestershire market towns, and presumably attracted customers from neighbouring villages.

In 1841, Ibstock had three bakers, two butchers, seven 'grocers and dealers in sundries', two drapers, six milliners and dressmakers and six tailors,[310] including two shops run by hosiers, where framework-knitters were forced to spend some of their earnings.[311]

Ibstock's 'Main Street', lined with houses by 1775, was renamed High Street between 1881 and 1891, a period when some residents wished to see Ibstock gain urban status.[312] Coalville was then growing quickly, and by 1901 had a population almost twice the size of Ibstock.[313] A weekly Friday market was established in Coalville in 1879, with a market hall for dairy products.[314] In 2019, Coalville market traded on Tuesdays, Fridays and Saturdays.[315]

Ibstock's shops in 1928 included seven butchers, three bakers, four grocers, two general stores, six drapers and clothes shops, a milliner, four shoe shops, a saddler, two hardware stores, an electrical store, a paint shop, five greengrocers, two newsagents, a wool shop, chemist, tobacconist, three fish and chip shops and six sweet shops.[316] Most were in High Street, but others were in Melbourne Road and Chapel Street. There were 103 shops in 1963, mostly in High Street and Chapel Street, many run by mining families.[317] The number of shops had substantially reduced by the early 21st century. In 2019 there was a large Co-operative supermarket on a major road junction, a few shops on Chapel Street and Melbourne Road, and a High Street with general stores, two pharmacies, an electrical retailer, Post Office, hardware store and a few specialist shops. There were also eight take-away food outlets, and several service businesses, including a solicitor, accountant, insurance office, beauty, hair and tanning salons. Ibstock Business Centre, on High Street, housed a photographer, online bookshop, a legal and financial services business, a café and the office of a community magazine.

Bus and Coach Businesses

Ibstock's sizeable population and position on the edge of a semi-urban area where most employment was on the fringes of the towns and villages made it well-suited for the early establishment of a bus company. William and Albert Brooks of Copson Street and Albert

309 ROLLR, PR/I/112/150.
310 *Pigot's Dir. of Leics.* (1841), 41–3.
311 *Report of the Royal Commission on the Condition of the Framework Knitters, Appendix to Part I* (Parl. Papers 1845 [C 618], xv), pp. 543, 545–6; *Pigot's Dir. of Leics.* (1841), 42–3; Census, 1841; above, Social history, social character.
312 TNA, RG 11/3135/64/11; RG 12/2507/68/7; below, Local government, local government from 1894.
313 VCH Leics. III, 185, 190.
314 *Leic. Chronicle*, 15 Mar. 1879; Ashby-de-la-Zouch *Gaz.*, 6 Dec. 1879.
315 https://www.nwleics.gov.uk/pages/coalville_market (accessed 24 Jan. 2020).
316 H. Crane, 'An Ibstock childhood from 1928', in J. Carswell (ed.), *Ibstock Lives* (Coalville, *c.*1991), 61–4.
317 ROLLR, L 711, Ibstock Village Survey (1963).

Hipwell of Leicester Road ran passenger services in converted army lorries after the First World War.[318]

By 1928, four bus operators were based in the village: Albert Hipwell trading as Green Bus Service, Hubert Bircher trading as Victory Buses, G. Rudin and Son, and Windridge Sons & Riley, who traded as Comfy Coaches.[319] Harry Fowkes of Chapel Street had begun trading as H.F. Bus Service by 1933.[320]

Midland Red (Birmingham Midland Motor Omnibus Company) acquired Bircher's bus business in 1932, and Fowkes's business in 1936.[321] Markfield bus proprietor Lawrence Brown acquired Hipwell's garage on Leicester Road in 1946, with 11 vehicles and all services.[322] Brown also purchased Rudin's six vehicles in 1954, taking over their services, but not their garage premises on Melbourne Road.[323] He incorporated the business that year as Browns Blue Coaches Ltd, with depots in Markfield and Ibstock.[324]

The Bircher family turned to haulage in 1932 after selling their bus business, but returned to buses after the haulage industry was nationalised in 1948, taking over the Windridge, Sons and Riley business and changing the operating name to 'Victory'.[325] Lawrence Brown purchased the business in 1956, agreeing to operate it as a separate business under the Victory name for two years.[326] It was absorbed into Browns Blue in 1958.[327]

Passenger numbers fell from the 1950s, as car ownership increased. Windridge, Sons and Riley and Bircher Bros. closed in 1962.[328] Browns Blue was acquired by Midland Red in 1963.[329] They closed the Ibstock depot in 1968.[330] A new company, Reliant Coaches Ltd, was set up in 1963 by three former Browns employees and was based in the former Windridge premises on Melbourne Road.[331] The business was sold to new management in 1998; it closed in 2007.[332]

318 L.S. Eggington, *Ibstock: A Story of her People* (Moira, 1984), 3, 23; above, Ibstock Parish, communications.
319 *Kelly's Dir. of Leics. and Rutl.* (1925), 116–7; (1928), 115–6.
320 *Kelly's Dir. of Leics. and Rutl.* (1936), 114.
321 P.L. Hardy, *Midland Red, Leicester and Leicestershire Route History* 1920–1929 (Leicester, 1972), 13, 14.
322 M. Gamble, *Brown's Blue: The Leicestershire Bus Company that took the Community to its Heart* (Enderby, 2012), 27–8, 198–9.
323 Ibid., 59–60, 205–6.
324 Ibid., 59.
325 Ibid. 71; Gamble, *Brown's Blue*, 71; C.S. Dunbar, 'Independent Still', in *Commercial Motor*, 4 May 1956; http://archive.commercialmotor.com/article/4th-may-1956/60/independent-still (accessed 5 Oct. 2018); Eggington, *Ibstock*, 13.
326 Ex inf. Mick Gamble.
327 Gamble, *Brown's Blue*, 71, 88, 207–9.
328 *London Gaz.*, 18 Jan. 1963, 633, 634.
329 Gamble, *Brown's Blue*, 102, 111–4; Dunbar, 'Independent Still'.
330 R.C. Anderson, *A History of the Midland Red* (Newton Abbot, 1984), 87.
331 Gamble, *Brown's Blue*, 138–40; *Commercial Motor*, 5 July 1963, at http://archive.commercialmotor.com/article/5th-july-1963/74/planning (accessed 5 Oct. 2018).
332 Gamble, *Brown's Blue*, 140–1.

Social Character

Before 1400

INGULF, IBSTOCK'S LORD IN 1086, was not a great magnate. He had two categories of tenant beneath him, almost equal in number: ten sokemen (free peasants) 'with' 11 bordars (owing services to their lord), who may have worked for the sokemen.[1] Of the 58 places listed in Sparkenhoe hundred, Ibstock was the only one where more than ten people were enumerated but had no villans.[2] In contrast, Bagworth had 24 villans among 35 recorded people.[3] Ibstock's unusual social structure may reflect an earlier role, as a specialist dairy farm within a large estate around Bagworth.[4]

In 1279 there were 33 unfree peasants (*servi*) owing services and 11 free tenants,[5] but it cannot be assumed that the latter were descendants of the sokemen, as there had been major changes in society and peasant status in the intervening period.[6]

After the division of Ibstock manor between co-heirs in the 13th century, there may have been little disparity in wealth between the lords and their more affluent tenants. Fifteen residents were assessed for tax of between 9*d*. and 10*s*. in 1327. The 3*s*. assessment of the two lords, Robert Garshall and Emma Verdun, was only slightly more than the median of 2*s*. 9*d*.[7] A different picture appears in 1332, when Robert Garshall, along with William Sutton, headed the list of 12 assessments, at 10*s*. each. Reginald Bertram and Thomas of Reigate were each assessed at 8*s*. Although still lords, the Verdun name does not appear, suggesting they were no longer resident.[8]

No manorial lord was resident in 1379, but three men were of sufficient rank or estate to be assessed for more than the standard poll tax of 4*d*.[9] Reginald Bertram, described as a petty franklin, paid 2*s*. Franklins were wealthy freeholders below the rank of knight,

1 *Domesday*, 649; S.P.J. Harvey, 'Evidence for settlement study: Domesday Book', in P.H. Sawyer (ed.), *Medieval Settlement: Continuity and Change* (1976), 197–9.
2 *VCH Leics*. III, 161–2.
3 *Domesday*, 649.
4 Above, Ibstock Parish, landscape.
5 Nichols, *History* IV, 749–50.
6 C. Lewis, P Mitchell-Fox and C. Dyer, *Village, Hamlet and Field: Changing Medieval Settlements in Central England* (Bollington, 2001 edn), 149–153.
7 W.G.D. Fletcher, 'The earliest Leicestershire lay subsidy', *Assoc. Archit. Soc. Rep. & Papers*, 19 (1887–8), 280.
8 TNA, E 179/133/2, rot. 8d.
9 Fenwick, *Poll Taxes*, 586–7.

who may have held *c.*150 a. of land.[10] John Dalinger, also assessed at 2*s*., was described as a landholder (*terr' tenens*), probably a leaseholder or a tenant at will, perhaps with a similar amount of land as Bertram. Reginald Huet, assessed at 12*d*., was a leaseholder (*ferm*'), perhaps farming the demesne land of one of the manors.[11] The Bertrams, Dalingers and Huets were probably the leading families in the village: Bertram had one of the highest tax assessments in 1332, Roger Huet and John 'Dollyng' (probably Dalinger) had been Ibstock's tax collectors in 1377,[12] and Roger Huet was the 'collector' of rents for the manorial lords in 1384.[13]

1400–1650

With no resident lords or major landowners living in the parish, four families rose to prominence in the 15th and 16th centuries: Clare, Paget, Pickering and Watts. Henry Watts was the rent collector for Sir Humphrey Stafford (d. 1486) in the 1470s.[14] Thomas Pickering was assessed for tax of 20*s*. in 1524, 54 per cent of Ibstock's total, on goods worth £20.[15] Thomas, John and Margaret Pickering were granted a 50-year lease of the grange in 1530,[16] which may have replaced an earlier lease, perhaps to Thomas alone. The next highest assessments in 1524 were William Bery for 2*s*. 6*d*, and Thomas White and Robert Tatewell for 2*s*. 2*d*. Cornish Watts, Richard Watts and Thomas Paget were assessed for 18*d*. (the median assessment), 12*d*. and 12*d* respectively.[17] The taxation of 1543 was headed by a broad band of 11 residents who were assessed on goods worth £5 or more. The highest of the 21 assessments were for Thomas Pickering, John Pickering and Cornish Watts, each with goods worth £10 and Robert Tatewell and Thomas Clare, each with goods valued at £8. Widow Alice Paget had goods worth £5.[18] In 1621, Thomas Paget was one of just four residents who was assessed for tax on land, although of a lower value than Nicholas Clare's goods.[19]

From 1650

The sale of the manor in 1654 by the non-resident William Stafford to Samuel Bracebridge and Thomas Clare, and its subsequent partition, may have changed social relationships within the village, as Clare was a resident.[20] Clare and Bracebridge apparently regulated the manor with a light touch, and by the later 17th century manor courts were not being held.[21] Thomas Clare's landholding was divided between his two

10 R.H. Hilton, *The English Peasantry in the Later Middle Ages* (Oxford, 1975), 26.
11 Fenwick, *Poll Taxes*, 586–7.
12 Fenwick, *Poll Taxes*, 511.
13 TNA, SC 6/908/17.
14 Staffs. RO, D 641/1/2/262–3.
15 TNA, E 179/134/323, part 2, m. 15.
16 TNA, SC 6/HenVIII/1825, m. 20.
17 TNA, E 179/134/323, part 2, m. 15.
18 TNA, E 179/134/323 pt 8, m. 1d; E 179/134/323 pt 5, rot 2.
19 TNA, E 179/134/286, rot 6d.
20 Above, Landownership, Ibstock manor.
21 Below, Local government, manor courts and the management of the open fields.

sons in 1668.[22] The Bracebridge portion was divided by sale from 1707, and the purchase of seven yardlands (but not the manor) by Sir John Astley in 1737 introduced a more socially-prominent landowner to the parish, with a substantial estate in neighbouring Nailstone and Odstone. Francis Dugdale Astley appears to have assumed for himself some of the rights of the lord of Ibstock manor by 1775.[23]

The hearth taxes of the later 17th century (which do not appear to include Pickering Grange farmhouse) show no large mansion, and a steady gradation from the wealthiest to the poorest inhabitants. Thomas Clare was one of two people assessed on five hearths in 1662 (the other being Thomas Carver), seven people had four hearths (including Thomas Paget), three had two hearths, and the remaining 27 taxpayers had a single hearth.[24] Around one third of residents in 1670, 23 of 65 households, were too poor to be taxed.[25]

The Paget family were building a substantial landholding across the parish. They inter-married with the Clares in 1639 and 1775.[26] The Pagets were Protestant Dissenters,[27] and their position as major landowners would have helped to foster a culture of religious toleration. Ibstock's early Dissenters include several of the 'better off' residents, with houses or outbuildings large enough for meetings.[28] This may have encouraged other religious Dissenters to move to the village.

Thomas Paget (d. 1818) had wide social contacts through his membership of Leicester Unitarian chapel, his association with noted stock-breeder Robert Bakewell and as a partner in a Leicester bank.[29] His son Thomas (d. 1862) lived in Humberstone Hall, Leicester, and was a Leicester banker, MP for Leicestershire in 1831–2 and mayor of Leicester in 1836–7.[30] He provided a plot of land for Ibstock's British School, giving parents the option of a non-denominational education for their children.[31] His son, Thomas Tertius Paget (d. 1892), succeeded his father as senior partner in the bank, became a partner and injected personal cash into Ibstock colliery in the 1870s, and gave land for Ibstock's cemetery in 1881.[32] Thomas Guy Frederick Paget, the great-grandson of the Leicester mayor, was Ibstock's largest landowner in 1910, when he owned 770 a. in the parish.[33]

Poor law records do not survive to show the impact on the poor of the enclosure of the final open fields in 1775. Only 16 people were allotted more than 4 a. Those with small allotments may have sold their land, and cottagers would have lost access to open

22 ROLLR, Wills, Leicester archdeaconry and Vicar General's court, 1668/91; above, Landownership, Ibstock manor.
23 Above, Landownership, Ibstock manor.
24 TNA, E 179/134/322 rot 2d.
25 *VCH Leics.* III, 172.
26 ROLLR, DE 1717/1, 7; above, Landownership, Ibstock manor.
27 Below, Religious History, Protestant nonconfomity.
28 Ibid.
29 M. Dawes and C.N. Ward-Perkins, *Country Banks of England and Wales* (2000), II, 323–4; *Hist. Parl. Commons* 1820–32, VI, 213.
30 Dawes and Ward-Perkins, *Country Banks*, II, 323–4, 326; *Hist. Parl. Commons* 1820–32, VI, 213.
31 Below, education.
32 Dawes and Ward-Perkins, *Country Banks*, II, 326; ROLLR, 1D 43/29/4; ROLLR, DE 4565/7, 11 Aug. 1881.
33 ROLLR, DE 2072/176.

field grazing, but most of Ibstock's *c.*400 inhabitants may have been little affected, as most had no grazing rights, and other common resources would have been thinly stretched among so many.

Framework knitting provided a source of income for those with no land, and Spencer Madan, Ibstock's rector between 1786 and 1836, contributed to a county-wide fund to enable families to buy knitting frames.[34] By 1801 Ibstock was becoming a manufacturing village, with 105 of its 379 households chiefly employed in manufacture or trade (28 per cent).[35] The industry peaked *c.*1815,[36] and some may have had little choice but to work for Ibstock hosiers Joseph Newbold and Benjamin Thirlby. Hosiers owned the frames, delivered the yarn, collected the finished goods, took them to Leicester and paid the craftsman a net sum after deducting frame rent and material costs.[37] Newbold was also a grocer, and Thirlby was a grocer, butcher and draper.[38] Until at least 1844, they paid their knitters partly in cash and partly through credit which had to be spent in the hosier's shop.[39] Thirlby also served as overseer of the poor, an elected position which he exploited in his own favour by insisting that framework-knitters took work at any price before poor relief was granted.[40] Their firm financial grip may help to explain why Ibstock's framework-knitters received the lowest clear weekly earnings across 27 towns and villages in the East Midlands in 1844, at 4*s.* per frame.[41]

The several ministers of religion helped to shape the culture of the village. Ibstock's rectors established the first Sunday school and the first weekday school of a significant size. Several of them worked tirelessly to extend the school buildings as the population continually increased, ensuring the Anglican Church remained the predominant influence on school life until 1906. This was a remarkable achievement, given the extent of Nonconformity in the village, but the existence of four chapels in the 19th century divided the Nonconformist interest and absorbed funds when these buildings also needed to be extended. The churches and chapels encouraged many of the clubs and societies which flourished in the village, providing an alternative to the public house.

Coal prices were volatile, through seasonal demand and increased supply when new mines opened. Owners tried to turn a profit by reducing miners' earnings when prices were low. Two-thirds of all male residents aged 14 and over worked in the mines in 1881.[42] Committees were formed during strikes to alleviate hardship. Thomas Hextall, a resident, former builder and county councillor, was treasurer of the Ibstock Relief Committee in 1893, when industrial action continued for 14 weeks. Collections were made by Ibstock's brass bands and in the churches and chapels.[43] The committee also

34 W. Jackson, *An Address to the Framework-Knitters of the Town and County of Leicester* (Leicester, 1833).
35 Census, 1801; above, Economic history, manufacture.
36 *VCH Leics.* III, 3–8.
37 *VCH Leics.* III, 8–9.
38 *Rpt of the Royal Commission on the Condition of the Framework Knitters, Appendix to Part I* (Parl. Papers 1845 [C 618], xv), pp. 542–6; *Pigot's Dir. of Leics.* (1841), 42–3; Census, 1841; above, Economic history, manufacturing.
39 *Royal Commission Framework Knitters,* p. 543; *VCH Leics.* III, 10.
40 *Royal Commission Framework Knitters,* pp. 545, 546.
41 *Rpt on Framework Knitters* (Parl. Papers 1845 [C 609], xv), p. 53; above, Economic History, manufacturing.
42 Census, 1881 (data from https://icem.data-archive.ac.uk/, accessed 4 Mar. 2019).
43 *Leic. Chron.*, 18 Nov. 1893.

obtained donations from the owners of the Ibstock, Ellistown, Heather and Nailstone collieries, who wished to ensure the miners' children did not suffer.[44] In one week, the fund distributed 1,000 loaves and a variety of dried foodstuffs, and free breakfasts were provided for school children.[45]

The miners' strike of 1984–5 was one of the most divisive nationally, but less so in Leicestershire. The county's coalmines were nearly exhausted when it began, and concerns were voiced that the pits would flood and potentially not reopen if work stopped.[46] There was also unease about the strike being called without a national ballot. Of the *c.*2,500 miners employed in Leicestershire, fewer than 40 men, spread across six pits, joined the strike, including two men at Ellistown colliery. The strikers were nicknamed the 'Dirty Thirty', a soubriquet they were happy to accept.[47] The effect of the strike in Ibstock was therefore modest economically and socially, in contrast to its impact and legacy in other mining areas.

Following the closure of the mines across the Leicestershire coalfield between 1983 and 1991, North West Leicestershire District Council encouraged new businesses to locate within Coalville Urban Area and along the corridor of the Leicester to Burton railway line.[48] Hoping to stimulate the local economy and improve village facilities, a not-for-profit company, Ibstock Community Enterprises, was set up in 1996 by a group of local business owners and others keen 'to make Ibstock a better place'.[49] With the assistance of grants from public bodies and local industries, the former National School on High Street was renovated and reopened as units for office and retail businesses, and the former Palace cinema was restored and reopened as a community centre. A wide range of weekly, monthly and occasional events were held in the Palace in 2019,[50] helping to foster a sense of community and an opportunity to socialise or be entertained without having to travel to a local town.

Communal Life

Friendly Societies

A sermon was preached to the two friendly societies of the parish in 1811, on what was clearly an annual occasion,[51] although only one (unnamed) society was officially recorded in 1803 and in 1813, with 134 members at the latter date.[52] The Framework

44 *Leic. Chron.*, 23 Sept. 1893.
45 *Leic. Chron.*, 16 Sept. 1893; 23 Sept. 1893; School Log Book, 1890–1910, pp. 64, 66 (at St Denys school).
46 C. Griffin, *The Leicestershire Miners*, 1945–1988 (Coalville, 1989), 212–3; *Coalville Times*, 30 Mar. 1984.
47 D. Bell, *Memories of the Leicestershire Coalfields* (Newbury, 2007), 102–9; D. Bell, *The Dirty Thirty: Heroes of the Miners' Strike* (Nottingham, 2011).
48 'North West Leicestershire Local Plan, 1991–2006', 113–15, 119–20.
49 *Ibstock Community Voice*, Feb. 2019, 28.
50 The Palace Community Centre, Forthcoming Events (flyer), Apr. 2019.
51 S. Madan, *A Sermon preached to the two Friendly Societies assembled in the Parish Church of Ibstock on Whit-Monday, June 3, 1811* (Birmingham, 1812).
52 *Returns on the Expense and Maintenance of the Poor* (Parl. Papers 1803–4 (175), xiii), 262–3; *Returns relative to the Expense and Maintenance of the Poor* (Parl. Papers 1818 (82) xix), pp. 230–1.

Knitters' Friendly Society was established in 1820,[53] and Ibstock's overseers contributed subscriptions totalling £35 10*s*. between 1820 and 1822.[54] Male workers contributed 6*d*. weekly and received 6*s*. weekly when unemployed, with half the subscription and benefits applying to women and youths.[55]

There were two main friendly societies in the village by the 1870s, affiliated to the major orders. The Earl Howe Lodge (Manchester Unity) was established in 1839.[56] The Hope and Persevere Lodge (Nottinghamshire Independent Order of Oddfellows) was formed in 1869.[57] Both continued beyond the First World War.[58] A 'Female Friendly Society' met in the Baptist Sunday school rooms, but was dissolved in 1888.[59] The Lily of the Valley society for women was registered in 1882, and was dissolved in 1909.[60]

Social Activities of the Churches and Chapels

St Denys's parish church offered weekly Bible classes, choir practices, mothers' meetings, a fortnightly clothing club and a monthly communicants' meeting in 1886.[61] It provided a separate afternoon children's activity on the day of the annual friendly societies' parade and sermon, sometimes with games and swings in a farmer's field.[62] A branch of the Church of England Men's Society was formed in 1908, and two weekday evening 'recreation clubs' began for those who attended Sunday school.[63] The Church Lad's Brigade, formed in 1909, offered an ambulance squad, a signallers' squad and a bugle band, and a cadet branch was formed in 1912 for younger boys.[64] Groups provided by the Nonconformist churches are less well documented, but the Wesleyan Reform church had a sewing club in 1888.[65] Sports teams and brass bands were also formed by the churches.[66]

Each church had social groups attached to it in the 1970s. St Denys's church had a Mother's Union, Ladies' Fellowship and Men's Fellowship groups. The Baptist Church had a Men's Club, a Ladies' Bright Hour, a Christian Fellowship Club, a table tennis club and choir practices. The Methodist church had a Men's Fellowship group and a Women's Bright Hour. Ibstock Wesleyan Reform church had a Ladies' Meeting and separate clubs for boys and girls.[67]

In 2019, the Baptists had regular Saturday coffee mornings, a ladies' group which met weekly, a monthly men's breakfast and a music group which supported worship.[68] The

53 W. Felkin, *History of the Machine-Wrought Hosiery and Lace Manufactures* (1867; Newton Abbot, 1967), 443.
54 ROLLR, DE 390/7.
55 Felkin, *History*, 443.
56 *Leic. Mercury*, 26 June 1939.
57 *Leic. Jnl*, 10 June 1870.
58 *Leic. Mercury*, 26 June 1939; *Leic. Daily Post*, 25 Nov. 1919.
59 *London Gaz.*, 31 July 1888, 4133.
60 Staffs. RO, D 15/9/9; *London Gaz.*, 23 Feb. 1909, 1479.
61 Northants. RO, X922, Ibstock Incumbents.
62 *Ibstock Par. Mag.*, Aug. 1899; Aug. 1905.
63 *Ibstock Par. Mag.*, Nov. 1908, Dec. 1908.
64 *Ibstock Par. Mag.*, Aug. 1909, Sept. 1909, Nov. 1912.
65 *Leic. Chron.*, 29 Dec. 1888.
66 Below.
67 Ibstock Parish Council, *Ibstock, Leicestershire: Official Guide* (Carshalton, undated, 1970s), 9–10.
68 Notice outside church, extant March 2019.

Wesleyan Reform church had a monthly coffee morning.[69] The Methodist church had a monthly indoor cake stall and 'time of fellowship', and a parent and toddler group.[70] St Denys's church had a parent and toddler group, a Saturday morning indoor market stall and a monthly 'chat and craft' afternoon.[71]

Libraries

A lending library had opened by 1881.[72] There were 700 volumes in 1885 when the library was open four times weekly.[73] In 1895 the parish council arranged a poll to decide whether the parish should adopt the Public Libraries Act. The majority of those who voted were in favour of a free public library, but a parish meeting refused to provide £36 for this purpose.[74] A free library had opened by 1912.[75]

There was a branch of the county library service on High Street in 1963.[76] This moved to Ibstock Community College shortly afterwards, but closed in 2016 when Leicestershire County Council restructured its library services. A new community library staffed by volunteers opened initially in Ibstock Business Centre. It reopened in 2019 in the junior school 'mobile' classroom on two afternoons and Saturday mornings weekly.[77]

Village Groups and Societies

A Hampden Club was formed in 1817 (a political organisation campaigning for parliamentary reform), which met in the Baptist chapel.[78] Ibstock and District Floral Society was formed in 1880.[79] It may have merged with the Agricultural and Horticultural Society, whose 16th annual show, funfair and sports day in 1913 was a major event with many competitors.[80] The Ibstock in Bloom team achieved silver awards in the East Midlands division for their floral displays around the village in four consecutive years, 2009 to 2012.[81] A debating society was formed 1904, and continued until the start of the Second World War.[82] A Homing Pigeon Society formed in 1907 and raced 1,500 birds in 1939. An Ibstock club was part of the Warwickshire Federation

69 Notice outside church, extant Mar. 2019.
70 http://www.nfemc.org.uk/churches/ibstock (accessed 25 May 2019).
71 https://ibstockstdenys.weebly.com/regular-events.html (accessed 25 May 2019).
72 *Kelly's Dir. of Leics. and Rutl.* (1881), 537.
73 *Ibstock Par. Mag.*, 1885.
74 *Leic. Chron.*, 23 Nov. 1895, 21 Dec. 1895.
75 *Kelly's Dir. of Leics. and Rutl.* (1912), 108.
76 ROLLR, L 711, 'Ibstock Village Survey Rpt' (1963).
77 *Ibstock Community Voice*, May 2016, 13; https://ibstocklibrary.weebly.com/about-us.html (accessed 9 Apr. 2019).
78 *Leic. Chron.*, 15 Feb. 1817.
79 *Leic. Jnl*, 13 Aug. 1880.
80 *Leic. Daily Post*, 8 Sept. 1913.
81 Plaques on Ibstock Business Centre, extant 2019.
82 L.S. Eggington, *Ibstock: A Story of her People* (Moira, 1984), 19; Armson, *Ibstock*, 14; Memories of S. Wallace, in J. Carswell (ed), *Ibstock Lives* (Coalville, *c.*1991), 27.

of Racing Pigeon Clubs in 2019.[83] Guides, Brownies and Scouts were formed in 1930.[84] Rainbows, Brownies, Guides and Rangers, and Scouts, Cubs and Beavers met in Ibstock in 2019.[85] Ibstock has never had a Women's Institute, but a Townswomen's Guild was formed in Ibstock in 1948, when the government was encouraging the movement to expand. It continued to meet in 2018.[86] Ibstock Historical Society was formed in 1982, and continued to meet regularly in 2019.[87]

Bands and Parades

St Denys's brass band and the Excelsior brass band, the latter started by Sam Vickers, choirmaster at the Primitive Methodist chapel, both played carols in the streets in December 1888.[88] Ibstock Town Band, under bandmaster James Cooper, had formed by 1894.[89] Ibstock United Band was formed by George Underwood and his son James in 1898. They engaged a professional music director in 1912, and won many medals and cups in the 1920s and 1930s. A grant from the Coal Industries Social Welfare Organisation enabled the band to replace their instruments in 1956, when they changed their name to Desford Colliery Band.[90] They won the national championships four times in the 1980s and 1990s, but the connection with Ibstock was severed.[91] Ibstock Brick Brass Band, which competed and gave concerts in 2019, was founded in 1971 as Coalville Band, and is named after its sponsors.[92]

The bands played a prominent role in the social life of the parish. They performed on stages at events such as the annual horticultural show,[93] played on the street to raise money for mining families during strikes and lock-outs,[94] and led annual friendly society and church parades.[95] Each of Ibstock's churches, schools, several village groups, Ibstock colliery and the Excelsior and Ibstock United bands took part in a parade and gala held in 1913 which raised £75 for Leicester Royal Infirmary (Figure 12).[96] This was a well-supported cause in the village, and £1,000 was raised in 1943 to endow a bed in the hospital.[97]

83 *Leic. Chron.*, 11 Jan. 1908; *Coalville Times*, 13 Aug. 1926; Leic. Daily Mercury, 2 Oct. 1939; http://warwickshirefederation.org.uk/member-clubs/clubs/ (accessed 23 Oct. 2019).

84 *Ibstock Par. Mag.*, May 1930, Aug. 1930, Nov. 1930.

85 https://scouts.org.uk/groups?loc=le67%206jd (accessed 23 Oct. 2019); information from Stacey Paling, County Administrator, Girlguiding Leicestershire, Oct. 2019.

86 www.the-tg.com/history.aspx; https://www.the-tg.com/Guild/ibstock-central-evening/230.aspx (accessed 23 Oct. 2019); *Ibstock Par. Mag.*, Jan. 1948; information from Janet Beniston, Ibstock Townswomen's Guild.

87 *Ibstock Historical Society Yearbook* (Ibstock, 1987), 1.

88 *Leic. Chron.*, 29 Dec. 1888; Eggington, *Ibstock*, 3.

89 *Leic. Chron.*, 29 Sept. 1894.

90 Eggington, *Ibstock*, 1–3; D. Bell, *Memories of the Leicestershire Coalfields* (Newbury, 2007), 72.

91 Desford Colliery Band, http://www.desfordcollieryband.co.uk/history.htm (accessed 14 Aug. 2018).

92 https://www.ibstockbrickbrass.com/history/ (accessed 15 Dec. 2019).

93 *Leic. Daily Post*, 8 Sept. 1913.

94 *Leic. Chron.*, 18 Nov. 1893.

95 *Leic. Chron.*, 11 June 1892.

96 *Leic. Daily Post*, 15 Sept. 1913; 2 Oct. 1913.

97 ROLLR, DE 3451/3.

Figure 12 *Parade passing along Ibstock High Street in 1913 as part of a Gala Day in aid of Leicester Royal Infirmary.*

Carnivals and parades continued. Those between the 1930s and 1950s regularly included the Red Garries Carnival Band, who wore distinctive red gingham outfits and played drums, piano accordions and bazookas (cheap conical wind instruments, popular in mining and other working-class areas).[98] Regular parades with floats continued to be held through Ibstock's streets into the 1980s, with another in 2000 for the millennium.[99]

Cinema and Travelling Entertainment

From at least 1890, and probably earlier, schoolchildren were given a holiday in October to attend the annual Wakes.[100] By then it was a large funfair, but it probably originated as a hiring fair for servants. It was sometimes held in a field opposite the Crown (at the junction between High Street and Hinckley Road) and sometimes behind the Ram (at the northern end of High Street).[101]

Travelling entertainers visited occasionally, including a 'Wild Beast Show' in 1890, Wombwell's Menagerie in 1892 and circuses in 1896 and 1911.[102] The 'renowned

98 Memories of F. Gregory, in Carswell (ed.), *Ibstock Lives*, 38; T. Brown, 'Into battle with the bazooka bands', *Direct Action*, 4 (1963), 6–7, at https://www.katesharpleylibrary.net/tqjrrr (accessed 23 Oct. 2019).

99 Ibstock Historical Society photograph colln and inf. Paula Gretton.

100 School Log Book, 1890–1910, pp. 12, 21, 90; II, 213 (at St Denys school).

101 Memories of F. Bradley and D. Middleton, in Carswell (ed.), *Ibstock Lives*, 18, 32.

102 School Log Book, 1890–1910, pp. 12, 39, 139; II, 48, 50 (at St Denys school).

Figure 13 *Ibstock's former cinema, The Palace, in 2018.*

mesmerist and illusionist' Dr Lynn visited in 1882.[103] Billy Holloway's portable 'Empire Theatre' visited in the late 19th and early 20th century, and staged variety performances in the yard behind the Ram.[104]

The Palace cinema was built on land adjacent to the Ram and opened in 1912. There were 650 seats, with a choice of plush upholstery in the balcony at 9*d.* or tip-up tiered seating downstairs for 4*d.*[105] It was one of *c.*3,500 cinemas opening across Britain between 1910 and 1914.[106] The number of seats had reduced to 450 by 1955.[107] Cinema audiences reduced from the 1960s as television ownership increased, and weekly bingo evenings were introduced, *c.*1963.[108] The last film was shown in 1970.[109] Bingo continued until 1986, when the building closed. It was purchased by the parish council in 1995,[110] and let to the newly-formed Palace Arts Centre Ltd in 2000.[111] After grant-funded restoration by Ibstock Community Enterprises, it reopened in 2006 as a community venue (Figure 13), and hosted a wide range of meetings and events each week in 2019.[112]

103 *Leic. Chron.*, 25 Nov. 1882.
104 *Stage*, 15 Jan. 1903, 24; Armson, *Ibstock*, 16; Eggington, *Ibstock*, 8.
105 *Coalville Times*, 3 Jan. 1913; ROLLR, DE 3608/1912/604.
106 R. Gray, *Cinemas in Britain: One Hundred Years of Cinema Architecture* (1996), 18, 22–3.
107 *Kinematograph yearbook* (1955): ex inf. C. Polden, archivist, Cinema Theatre Association Archive, London.
108 J. and B. Vaughan, *Presenting the Palace Past: Patrons' Reminiscences of Ibstock Palace Cinema* (Ibstock, 2001), 34, 45.
109 Ibid., 42.
110 Ibid., 20–1.
111 Ibid., 21.
112 'The Palace Community Centre, Ibstock: the story so far', http://www.thepalaceibstock.co.uk/storysofar.html (accessed 21 Nov. 2018); The Palace Community Centre, Forthcoming Events (flyer), Apr. 2019.

Inns and Clubs

Four inns were recorded in 1827: the Crown, Golden Lion, Ram and Swan.[113] Four were also listed in 1863: the Boot, Crown, Ram and Royal Oak.[114] As the village expanded, three more opened: the Waggon & Horses by 1876,[115] and the Hastings Arms and the Whimsey by the 1890s.[116] The impact of Nonconformity may account for Ibstock's low ratio of one public house to every 467 people in 1881, against one to 289 in Barrow-upon-Soar and one to 281 in Earl Shilton, places with similar population levels.[117] There were still seven public houses open in 1963, but only four continued to trade in 2019: the Boot (Gladstone Street), Ram (High Street), Wagon & Horses (Curzon Street) and Whimsey (High Street).[118]

The former Wesleyan Reform Chapel on Reform Road became a Liberal Club and Institute in 1912, offering a billiards room and a galleried hall for meetings and reading.[119] It later became a TocH club, but had been converted to a factory by 1963. Ibstock Working Men's Club and Institute was built on Central Avenue in 1919, and is said to have cost £5,000.[120] Renamed Ibstock Central in 2016, it offered darts and pool, a large function room and a children's indoor play area.[121] The Royal British Legion opened a club house on High Street in 1956, which closed in 1984.[122] The Miners' Welfare pavilion opened in 1929 and initially served no alcohol.[123] It had a licensed bar and games room in 2019.

Allotments, Recreation and Sports

Allotments

Market Bosworth RSA purchased 41 a. of land in Ibstock in 1889, east of Copson and Orchard Streets, which was mostly laid out as allotments.[124] By 1901, other allotments had been created to the east of Grange Road, in the Penistone Street area, on both sides of Pretoria Road, the west side of Ellistown Terrace Road and to the south of Battram Road.[125] Later additions include plots behind Chapel Street, behind Melbourne Road and off Station Road. A substantial number of the Pretoria Road allotments had been given up by 1963, and the land returned to agriculture.[126] The only remaining allotments in 2019 were on the south side of Pretoria Road and off Station Road. There was also a

113 ROLLR, QS 36/2/10.
114 W. White, *Hist., Gaz. and Dir. of Leics. and Rutl.* (Sheffield, 1863), 678.
115 *PO Dir. of Leics. and Rutl.* (1876), 372–3.
116 *Kelly's Dir. of Leics. and Rutl.* (1895), 94; *Leic. Chron.*, 4 Dec. 1897.
117 *VCH Leics.* III, 180–203; *Kelly's Dir. of Leic. and Rutl.* (1881), 486, 515–6, 537, 718.
118 ROLLR, L 711, 'Ibstock Village Survey Rpt' (1963).
119 *Leic. Daily Post*, 30 Sept. 1912.
120 *Nottingham Jnl*, 26 Aug. 1919.
121 *Ibstock Community Voice*, Feb. 2016, 15.
122 *Coalville Times*, 26 Oct. 1984.
123 ROLLR, DE 1177/31, min. 804.
124 *Leic. Chron.*, 6 Aug. 1898; OS Map 25", Leics. XXIII.15 (1903 edn).
125 OS Map 25", Leics XXIII.11 (1903 edn); XXIII.15 (1903 edn); XXIII.16 (1903 edn).
126 ROLLR, L 711, 'Ibstock Village Survey Rpt' (1963).

community garden connected to Ibstock Community College, with an orchard and plots for growing vegetables.[127]

Sports Grounds

Ibstock's sports grounds have included a large ground behind the Hastings Arms, at the junction of Ashby Road, Leicester Road and Chapel Street,[128] smaller grounds behind the Ram and Royal Oak, a ground off Melbourne Road,[129] another at Ibstock brickworks,[130] and another provided on Ashby Road from the early 1970s.[131]

The most significant sports facilities were provided as a result of the Mining Industry Act of 1920. This required colliery owners to set aside 1*d*. for every ton of output over the following five years, to create a fund which was to be spent on recreation facilities, better living conditions and mining education for coalminers.[132] The Leicestershire District Miners' Welfare Committee collected information about the number of miners in each village, and after estimating the likely size of the fund after five years, a figure of £5 for each resident miner became a rule of thumb when considering applications for grants.[133] One application from Ibstock sought a grant of £4,500 towards the purchase of 7 a. of land off Leicester Road for football, cricket, tennis and bowls, with a pavilion for indoor games and a library. The parish council agreed to inject cash towards the cost, and cover ongoing maintenance costs.[134] The committee agreed to support a grant of £3,737 for the outdoor facilities, and accepted a further application in 1928 for an additional £1,300 to provide a pavilion.[135] The grounds opened in 1929.[136]

An extension by the 1950s provided a children's playground.[137] Facilities were also added for other ball games. A skateboard park was added by the parish council in 2018, to replace one off Melbourne Road.[138] The football pitch passed grading standards to host Step 6 football, and in the 2018–19 season it was used by Hinckley AFC (Midland League Division 1) and Sunday league side Sporting Dynamo.[139]

The Miners' Welfare committee also supported a grant of £850 for a tennis court, bowling green and institute for indoor recreation for Battram and Ellistown.[140] Building commenced in 1927 on a site adjacent to Battram school (Map 6).[141] When

127 http://www.ibstockcollege.leics.sch.uk/news/could-you-volunteer-for-community-garden- (accessed 15 Dec. 2019).
128 OS Map 6", Leics. XXIII.SE (1904 edn); 1:2500 SK 4010 (1980 edn).
129 OS Map 1:2500, SK 4010 (1960 edn).
130 OS Map 1:2500, SK 4111 (1960 edn).
131 OS Map 1:2500, SK 4010 (1973 edn).
132 10 & 11 Geo. V, c. 50.
133 ROLLR, DE 1177/30, pp. 12–28.
134 ROLLR, DE 1177/30, pp. 27–8, 31–2.
135 ROLLR, DE 1177/30, p. 126; DE 1177/31, min. 375.
136 ROLLR, DE 1177/31, min. 507.
137 Ibstock Parish Council, *Official Guide to the parish of Ibstock, Leicestershire* (Croydon, undated, *c*.1950), 6.
138 *Ibstock Community Voice*, Nov. 2018, 12.
139 http://nonleague.pitchero.com/headlines/hinckley-play-ibstock-welfare/ (accessed 26 Oct. 2018); http://footygrounds.blogspot.com/2017/05/ibstock-united-welfare-ground.html (accessed 26 Oct. 2018); https://www.facebook.com/sporting.dynamofc (accessed 26 Nov. 2018).
140 ROLLR, DE 1777/30, pp. 168–9, 200.
141 ROLLR, DE 1777/30, p. 266.

the committee visited the completed facilities in 1930, they considered it to be one of the most used and best managed institutes it had funded.[142] Meetings were held in 1979 between the district council and representatives for the miners because it was expected the site would be lost due to subsidence after planned undermining of the ground.[143] Battram Bowls Club relocated in 1982 to Victoria Road, Ellistown, where they remained for ten years on a site owned by British Coal. That land was then sold for industrial development, and the club moved to Ellistown Terrace Road, where they remained in 2019.[144]

Team Sports

Sport was 'an integral part of Nonconformist life' in the 1920s and 1930s, which aimed at keeping young men 'within the orbit of the church'.[145] Ibstock's chapels and churches encouraged team sports, and other more inclusive teams were also formed.

Ibstock Albion played in the Leicestershire Football Association in 1895.[146] Ibstock United had formed by 1902.[147] Other teams over the years included Ibstock Ivanhoe, Ibstock Villa, Ibstock Swifts, Ibstock St Denys, Ibstock Primitive, Ibstock Baptist, Ibstock Colliery, Ibstock Brickworks and Ibstock Penistone Rovers. The latter was formed in the 1920s.[148] The club became founder members of the Central Midlands League in 1983, but folded in 1986.[149] Ibstock Welfare FC played in the Leicestershire Senior League from 1986.[150] They merged in 2005 with Ibstock Youth, which had formed in 1979, and the combined club adopted the earlier Ibstock United name.[151] The senior team merged with Ellistown FC in 2013 to form Ellistown and Ibstock United. They played at Ellistown Terrace Road in 2019.[152] Ibstock United's Junior and Youth Clubs remained separate, and had 26 teams in 2018, for players from five years upwards, playing on the Ashby Road ground.[153] Sunday league team Sporting Dynamo formed in 1998 and played in 2019 at the Welfare ground.[154]

142 ROLLR, DE 1777/31, min. 710.
143 *Ibstock Par. Mag.*, July 1979, 6.
144 *Ibstock Community Voice*, Aug. 2016, 4.
145 H. McLeod, 'Thews and sinews': nonconformity and sport', in D. Bebbington and T. Larsen (eds), Modern Christianity and Cultural Aspirations (2003), 30, 35.
146 *Leic. Chron.*, 7 Sept., 24 Oct. 1896; *Loughborough Echo*, 16 Jan. 1914; 'Leicestershire Senior League 1894–1950' at www.nonleaguematters.co.uk/nlmnet/Regs_2_M/Leicy1894.html (accessed 23 Oct. 2018).
147 *Leic. Chron.*, 13 Sept. 1902.
148 S.W. Wallace, *Sports Societies in Ibstock during the Present Century* (Ibstock, 1983), 5–6; Carswell (ed.), *Ibstock Lives*, 90; 'Leicestershire Senior League 1894–1950' at www.nonleaguematters.co.uk/nlmnet/Regs_2_M/Leicy1894.html (accessed 23 Oct. 2018); 'Football Club History Database', http://www.fchd.info (accessed 26 Nov. 2018).
149 'Football Club History Database', http://www.fchd.info (accessed 26 Nov. 2018); 'Leicestershire Senior League 1894–1950' at www.nonleaguematters.co.uk/nlmnet/Regs_2_M/Leicy1894.html (accessed 23 Oct. 2018); Carswell (ed.), *Ibstock Lives*, 90.
150 'Football Club History Database', http://www.fchd.info (accessed 26 Nov. 2018).
151 Ibid.
152 Ibid; http://eastmidlandscountiesleague.pitchero.com/archive2670-club-info/119649 (accessed 26 Nov. 2018); *Ibstock Community Voice*, Aug. 2016, 4.
153 http://www.ibstockunited.co.uk/teams/ (accessed 26 Nov. 2018).
154 *Ibstock Community Voice*, Oct. 2016, 7.

There was a cricket team in Ibstock in 1857.[155] Ibstock Colliery Cricket Club was founded in 1885.[156] Other cricket clubs included Ibstock Baptist, Ibstock Free Church, Ibstock Primitive, Ibstock Wesleyan Reform, Ibstock Ivanhoe, Ibstock Brickworks and Ibstock Liberals.[157] Ibstock Town CC were champions of the Coalville and District League in 1909. The team moved to Melbourne Road in 1953, and bought the land in 1964.[158] In 2018 they had senior, ladies' and five junior teams.[159]

A mixed hockey club was formed shortly after the First World War, which played matches on a field off Overton Road. Another club was formed in the late 1920s, which continued until the Second World War.[160]

Ibstock Town Welfare Bowls Club was formed in 1929 and played on the green at the Miners' Welfare site. Renamed Ibstock Bowling Club, it continued to play matches in 2019.[161] Battram Bowls Club played at Battram Miners' Welfare Ground between 1930 and 1982, then Victoria Road until 1992, then Ellistown Terrace Road, where they continue to meet in 2019.

Other Sports

Boxing was popular with participants and spectators. Evening gym classes held in Battram School in the 1930s included boxing lessons.[162] A building in the yard of the Whimsey Inn was converted into a gymnasium in the 1920s, and a boxing club and tournaments were held there.[163] Organised amateur boxing has also been held at the Boot Inn (Gladstone Street) and Ram Inn (High Street).[164] Occasional matches continued to be played in Ibstock until the 1970s.[165]

A tennis club was formed in Ibstock before the First World War. It restarted between the wars on a field along Hinckley Road, where three grass courts were laid out. Three hard courts on the Welfare grounds proved very popular from 1929, and a fourth court was added.[166]

Tennis and badminton courts at Ibstock Community College opened in 1964 and were available to the public. A badminton club was formed.[167] An indoor swimming pool opened in the college in 1974, partially funded by Leicestershire County Council,

155 *Leic. Jnl*, 24 July 1857.
156 *Ibstock Par. Mag.*, 1885.
157 Wallace, *Sports Societies*, 8.
158 Ibid., 7–8; http://www.ibstocktowncc.co.uk/history/default.aspx (accessed 26 Nov. 2018).
159 http://www.ibstocktowncc.co.uk/history/default.aspx (accessed 26 Nov. 2018).
160 Wallace, *Sports Societies*, 3.
161 Ibid., 4; https://www.ibstockbowlsclub.co.uk/about-us (accessed 26 Nov. 2018); *Ibstock Community Voice*, Oct. 2016, 14.
162 Memories of Edith Roberts, whose father ran the gym classes, in Carswell and Roberts (eds), *Getting the Coal*, 114.
163 Wallace, *Sports Societies*, 9; memories of Sim Woolley, former professional boxer, in J. Carswell and T. Roberts (eds), *Getting the Coal: Impressions of the Twentieth-century Mining Community* (Coalville, 1992), 114; Coalville Times, 27 Feb. 1959, obituary of J.E. Black.
164 Eggington, *Ibstock*, 19; memories of C. Tompkin, V Gimson and S. Barrs, Ibstock Historical Society Facebook, 23 Oct. 2019.
165 Memories of K. Pallett, Ibstock Historical Society Facebook (23 Oct. 2019).
166 Wallace, *Sports Societies*, 1
167 Ibstock Parish Council, *Ibstock*, 15.

and remained popular in 2019.[168] A floodlit outdoor sports pitch was also available at the College for hourly bookings in 2019.[169]

Education

Sunday Schools

There was an Anglican Sunday school by 1788.[170] Sunday schools were also opened by the General Baptists in 1820,[171] Wesleyan Methodists in 1827,[172] Primitive Methodists in 1870,[173] and the Wesleyan Reform chapel by 1880. Although the Anglican Sunday school was the best attended in 1880, with 180 members, they were far outnumbered by the 430 people who attended the Sunday schools of the Nonconformist churches: 140 at the Baptist school, 120 at the Primitive Methodist school, 90 at the Wesleyan Reform school and 80 at the Wesleyan Methodist school.[174]

Day Schools before 1818

Gilbert Caulton was licensed to teach at a school in Ibstock in 1662, and George Turner was licensed to serve in 'the 'office of schoolmaster' in Ibstock in 1680, wording which suggests a parish school had been established.[175] In 1712, Ibstock's rector John Laughton was paying for a number of poor children to be taught in a school.[176] This was held in a cottage owned by Job Varnham, which was purchased by Thomas Clare, who devised it in his will of 1731 for the schoolmaster to live in rent free forever, in exchange for 'teaching two poor boys to write and read' and keeping it in repair.[177] Other paying pupils would have been essential. The school appeared to flourish. Charles Houghton, who died in 1790, was schoolmaster for over 31 years.[178]

Spencer Madan, Ibstock's rector, was paying for an additional six poor children to be taught in 1789.[179] The schoolmaster was only required to teach reading, writing

168 *Coalville Times*, 25 Oct. 1974.
169 http://www.ibstockcollege.leics.sch.uk/leisure-facilities (accessed 23 Oct. 2019).
170 S. Madan, *An Address to the Inhabitants of the Parish of Ibstock ... and a Sermon preached to the two Friendly Societies assembled in the Parish Church of Ibstock on Whit-Monday, June 3, 1811* (Birmingham, 1812), 6.
171 ROLLR, N/B/150/2, 30 Jan. 1820, 27 Feb. 1820; *Education Enquiry* (Parl. Papers 1835 (62), xlii), p. 488.
172 *Education Enquiry*, p. 488.
173 *Leic. Chron.*, 21 Aug. 1880.
174 Ibid.
175 ROLLR, 1D 41/34/2, ff. 4v, 46.
176 J. Broad (ed.), *Bishop Wake's Summary of Visitation Returns from the Diocese of Lincoln 1705–15* (Oxford, 2012), II, 879; [Society for Promoting Christian Knowledge] *An Account of the Charity Schools in Great Britain and Ireland* (1713), 37.
177 TNA, PROB 11/663/63.
178 Nichols, *History* IV, 755.
179 Lincs. Arch., DIOC/MGA/7, certificate of value of living.

and arithmetic.[180] The school had 50 poor pupils in 1811, supported 'by charitable contributions'.[181] The building was 'very dilapidated' in 1818.[182]

Day Schools, 1818–70

Land on High Street measuring 256 sq. yd. was purchased by Spencer Madan in 1818 for a new weekday and Sunday school, to be affiliated to the National Society for Promoting the Education of the Poor in the Principles of the Established Church.[183] He contracted with Robert Keightley to build a schoolroom and master's house for £304, and collected donations towards the cost.[184] The school opened later that year.[185] The earlier school building was demolished.[186]

By 1833, the National School (as it was known) was teaching 80 boys and 50 girls, possibly including some who only attended on Sundays.[187] Spencer Madan provided an annual personal donation of between £40 and £50, and collected donations from others.[188] There were 70 weekday pupils in 1846.[189]

There were also three dame schools in Ibstock in 1818, which may have been short-lived.[190] By 1833, three small infant schools existed, in addition to the National School, at least two of which had been established within the previous decade, teaching 23 boys and 13 girls in total.[191] Some poorer parents could little afford schooling, and it was claimed in 1844 that the children of Ibstock's framework-knitters started seaming hosiery on two days each week from the age of five.[192]

Thomas Paget (d. 1862) gave a plot of land on Melbourne Road *c.*1845 for a British School to be built to provide non-denominational teaching. The land was conveyed to ten trustees including Paget. Seven of the other nine were Ibstock residents: John Jackson Burbery, William Rowell, Joseph Smith and Thomas Ward (all farmers), John Dean (builder), Thomas Farmer (cooper) and John Messenger (saddler); the others were from Heather and Measham.[193] A subscription and a government grant of £81 covered building costs and training for a teacher at the British School's teacher training establishment in London. The school opened in 1847, with places for 100 children.[194]

180 *Leic. Herald*, 12 May 1792.
181 Nichols, *History* IV, 751.
182 *Digest of Parochial Returns to Select Committee on Educ. of the Poor* (Parl. Papers 1819 (224), ix), p. 455.
183 ROLLR, DE 41/1/59, abstract of title to land formerly owned by John and Joseph Storer; PR/T/1818/173.
184 ROLLR, DE 390/60, contract; CERC, NS/7/1/6813, letter 5 Mar. 1920; extracts from trust deed of 1818; TNA, ED 21/10307, note, Apr. 1915.
185 CERC, NS/7/1/6813, letter 25 Oct. 1876; TNA, ED 21/10307, note, Apr. 1915.
186 ROLLR, DE 390/7, 21 July 1821, 25 Aug. 1821; *Report of the Charity Commissioners* (Parl. Papers 1839 [163], xv), p. 179.
187 CERC, NS/7/7/1/2, p. 275.
188 *Education Enquiry*, p. 488; CERC, CC/OF/NB19/93B.
189 Northants. RO, Box X920, Ibstock.
190 *Digest of Parochial Returns*, p. 455.
191 *Education Enquiry*, p. 488.
192 *Royal Commission Framework Knitters*, pp. 543–4.
193 TNA, ED 103/36/3; ROLLR, PR/T/1850/176; DE 462/3 (1860) (wills of Samuel and Elizabeth Weston).
194 *Leics. Mercury*, 25 Sept. 1847.

Figure 14 *Former National School on the junction of High Street and Grange Road. Embedded in the front of the building are two state tablets inscribed 'National 1818' and 'School 1818'.*

The schoolroom floor sloped upwards towards the back of the room, as advocated for British Schools by Joseph Lancaster in 1811.[195] An additional classroom was added in 1852.[196] There were 120 pupils in 1863.[197]

Education from 1870

The Board of Education required 300 school places in 1870.[198] The British School had 126 places, and the National School (Figure 14) was enlarged in 1872, to provide 210 places.[199] The British School closed in 1873 through 'lack of funds'.[200] Fearing the imposition of a non-denominational board school for all pupils, the managers of the National School added two classrooms, increasing capacity to 380.[201] Local people voiced their concerns over church control, but the National School's managers rejected a petition that they should be elected.[202] The Baptist church opened a day school in 1881, but it closed in 1882.[203]

195 ROLLR, DE 630 MA/E/BG/155/3; M. Seaborne, *The English School, its Architecture and Organization, 1370–1870* (1971), 137.
196 *Leic. Chron.*, 23 July 1853; TNA, ED 103/36/3; ROLLR, DE 630 MA/E/BG/155/2.
197 W. White, *Hist., Gaz. and Dir. of Leics. and Rutl.* (Sheffield, 1863), p. 677.
198 TNA, ED 2/274.
199 W. White, *Hist., Gaz. and Dir. of Leics. and Rutl.* (Sheffield, 1877), 249.
200 TNA, ED 2/274; CERC, NS/7/1/6813, letter 1 May 1876.
201 CERC, NS/7/1/6813, letters, 1 May 1876, 19 Oct. 1876; TNA ED 2/274.
202 *Leic. Chron.*, 17 Nov. 1883; 22 Dec. 1883.
203 ROLLR, N/B/155/1, minutes 20 Mar. 1881; 14 June 1881; 26 Sept. 1881; 20 Mar. 1882.

Figure 15 *Architect's drawing of the south elevation of the proposed school at Battram.*

Ibstock's rectors and curates ensured the Anglican Church maintained its monopoly over weekday education by raising money for new classrooms almost on a continuous basis between 1872 and 1902. A new classroom in 1891 increased capacity at the National School to 420 places, which were soon filled.[204] With no further room for expansion, the school managers purchased land on what became Grange Road, where a new school was built for 250 infants. It opened in 1895, and the younger children transferred to the new building.[205] The total cost of £1,075 was funded by donations and debt, including gifts of £100 from Ibstock Colliery and £100 from Ellistown Colliery.[206]

The infant and junior schools were again full in 1902, when the Board of Education required a further 240 places to be provided.[207] With borrowing still outstanding on the infant school, the school managers decided they could go no further.[208] The Leicestershire (County Council) Education Department, which was empowered to provide schools under the 1902 Education Act, opened temporary schools for 120 boys in Ibstock Town Hall (the former British School) in 1904,[209] and for 65 children in Battram Wesleyan Reform Chapel in 1905.[210] It also purchased land on Melbourne Road for a permanent school, and instructed Leicester architect William Cowdell to draw up plans for seven classrooms to accommodate 100 infants and 236 older children.[211] Its modest size did not threaten the existence of the church schools, but gave parents

204 School Log Book, 1890–1910, pp. 25, 55, 57 (at St Denys school); *Kelly's Dir. of Leic. and Rutl.* (1895), 94.

205 School Log Book, 1890–1910, p. 111 (at St Denys school); *Kelly's Dir. of Leic. and Rutl.* (1895), 94.

206 CERC, NS/7/1/6813, retrospective grant application 1904; ROLLR, DE 4939/724, letters 8 May, 10 May, 2 July and 9 July 1894.

207 CERC, NS/7/1/6813, grant application, 1903.

208 CERC, NS/7/1/6813, letters 23 Feb. 1903, 20 Mar. 1903, 10 Mar. 1904, 17 June 1904.

209 TNA, ED 21/10309; School Log Book, 1890–1910, p. 354 (at St Denys school).

210 TNA, ED 2/274; ROLLR, E/MB/B/155/1, 5 Jan., 2 Feb. 1905; ROLLR, DE 5174/1, p. 1.

211 ROLLR, DE 3806/Market Bosworth/1906/248; TNA, ED 21/10308.

a choice for children of all ages. The temporary school in the Town Hall closed in December 1906,[212] and the new school opened in January 1907.[213]

The council also instructed Coalville architects Goddard and Wain to provide plans for a permanent school in Battram, for 60 infants and 150 older children (Figure 15).[214] This opened in 1907 on Wood Road, and the temporary school in the chapel closed.[215]

The new Melbourne Road school quickly filled, and further plans were drawn in 1910 for two large classrooms to be added, to provide an additional 112 places.[216]

The National School on High Street was described by a school inspector in 1914 as 'one of the worst places for a fairly large school that I have seen for years'. Four classes were taught in one room, separated only by low screens; heating, lighting and ventilation were poor; the lavatories were just seats over a channel flushed by a pump and the yards were too small for physical exercise. The managers accepted the deficiencies, but could not afford to rebuild and were 'not prepared to spend any money on patching it up'.[217] The National Society's own surveyor visited in 1922. He found a hole in the roof and a ceiling at risk of falling on the children, but he could not recommend the cost of repairing such a poor-quality building.[218]

The raising of the school leaving age to 14 from 1918 created a need for more school places and specialist rooms for science and practical lessons for older children. This provided an opportunity to reorganise Ibstock's schools and close the High Street building, although it was reopened in 1939–40 for teaching evacuees.[219] Ibstock Senior School was built and opened on Central Avenue in 1925. From then, all Ibstock children would attend the Church of England infant school on Grange Road from the age of five, all would transfer at the age of seven to the council school on Melbourne Road,[220] and then to the senior council school at age ten or 11, where they would be joined by children of a similar age from neighbouring villages.[221] Grammar schools at Ashby-de-la-Zouch, Market Bosworth and Coalville provided the option of a more academic education, with scholarships available to those who passed the examination.[222] The arrangement saved the council the cost of providing all the school places, and gave the church an ongoing and clearly defined role to educate Ibstock's infants.

Under the provisions of the 1944 Education Act, Ibstock senior school became a secondary modern school. Even with the use of the neighbouring former Mining and Technical Centre,[223] the facilities were too small, but funding restrictions delayed further building. Meanwhile, the 'Leicestershire Plan' to introduce comprehensive education across the county was gradually being rolled out, under which children would change

212 TNA, ED 21/10309.
213 TNA, ED 21/10308; ROLLR, E/LB/155/5, pp. 1–2.
214 ROLLR, DE 3806/Market Bosworth/1907/307.
215 *Leic. Daily Post*, 17 Dec. 1907; ROLLR, DE 5174/1, p. 45.
216 ROLLR, DE 3806/Market Bosworth/1907/307; TNA, ED 21/10308, certificate, Apr. 1911.
217 TNA, ED 21/10307, minute, Oct. 1914.
218 CERC, NS/7/1/6813, report and letter, 6 Feb. 1922; TNA, ED 21/33504, minute, Dec. 1921.
219 TNA, ED 21/33504, note, Dec. 1921; ED 21/33506, particulars of building.
220 ROLLR, E/LB/155/5, p. 142.
221 TNA, ED 21/33504, letter, Aug. 1925; ED 21/33505.
222 ROLLR, E/LB/155/5, p. 69; TNA, ED 21/33504, letter, Aug. 1925.
223 Below.

schools at ages 11 and 14.[224] Building began on land adjacent to the secondary modern school in 1962, and a new scheme of management was sealed that year for the senior school to become a high school and community college (a type of school with facilities which can also be used by the wider population) for children aged between 11 and 14.[225] The school became fully comprehensive in 1967, when all Ibstock children attended from age 11. They transferred at 14 to an upper school at either Coalville or Ashby-de-la-Zouch (with an exception for those leaving at 15, until the school leaving age was raised to 16 in 1972). The school gained 'academy' status in 2012 (state funded but independent of local authority control) and had 539 pupils on the roll in 2019.[226]

Land immediately behind the junior school was purchased by the county council in 1962 for a new infant school.[227] The government agreed to finance 100 places, and was deaf to pleas that there were already 99 pupils at Grange Road, and new housing estates were being built. There were 160 pupils at Grange Road infant school when St Denys Church of England Voluntary Controlled Infant School opened in 1975, some of whom had to be accommodated in two temporary classrooms in the grounds.[228] An extension in 2016 created permanent places for 280 children.[229] There were 188 pupils at the infant school in 2014 and 213 pupils at the junior school in 2016.[230]

Battram county primary school closed in 1981, due to subsidence. The 38 children on the roll transferred to primary schools in Ellistown and Nailstone.[231]

Technical and Adult Education

A Mining and Technical Centre was built near the senior school and opened in 1925, partly funded by £700 from the Miners' Welfare Fund. Certificate courses on mining topics were held in the evening for those who had left school.[232] During the day it was used by the Senior School for woodwork, metalwork and science.[233] The building was taken over by the Senior School after Ibstock colliery closed in 1929, as the mining centres at Coalville and Bagworth were more convenient for those employed at other collieries.

Between 1983 and 2003, and probably beyond those dates, Ibstock Community College offered a range of evening classes, including typing, keep fit and basic computer skills.[234] The nearest adult learning classes offered by any provider in 2019 were in Coalville.[235]

224 A.N. Fairburn, 'Introduction', in A.N. Fairburn (ed.), *The Leicestershire Plan* (1980), 1–9.
225 ROLLR, DE 3627/154, mins 26 Sept. 1962, Nov. 1962; 16 Jan. 1963.
226 https://reports.ofsted.gov.uk/provider/23/138721 (accessed 23 Oct. 2019).
227 ROLLR, DE 3627/74, letter from Deputy Director, 23 Feb. 1965; minute of meeting, 10 June 1970; DE 3627/75 (plans).
228 *Coalville Times*, 27 Dec. 1974.
229 *Ibstock Community Voice*, Jan. 2016, 13.
230 https://files.api.ofsted.gov.uk/v1/file/2441278; http://www.ibstockjuniorschool.co.uk/parents/ofsted-report-1 (accessed 10 Apr. 2019).
231 ROLLR, DE 5174/3 (school log, closed record).
232 Eggington, *Ibstock*, 1.
233 Memories of G. Moore, in Carswell (ed.), *Ibstock Lives*, 49. TNA, ED 21/33506, letter June 1924.
234 ROLLR, 374, Ephemera.
235 *Go Learn! Leicestershire Adult Learning Service* (Sept. 2019); https://enrolonline.wea.org.uk/Online/CourseSearchResults.aspx?Page=1 (accessed 23 Oct. 2019).

Social Welfare

Charities for the Poor

There were five charitable bequests of £10 for Ibstock's poor, established by Thomas Clare in 1714, Joseph Jennings in 1741, Thomas Copson in 1744, Mary Clare in 1745 and Elizabeth Kemp in 1747.[236] The bequests from Jennings and Copson were used to buy loaves, but Jennings' bequest had been lost through insolvency by 1786.[237] The capital from Mary Clare's bequest had reduced to £2 10*s*. in 1816.[238] Inflation eroded their value, and none of these charities, nor any successor, was registered with the Charity Commission in 2018.[239]

Poor Relief

Surviving parish apprenticeship records for the years between 1704 and 1710 and 1756 and 1834 (inclusive), identify six girls and 42 boys who were apprenticed, some as young as eight years, with the peak decade in the 1790s (13 children).[240] All but four of the children were sent to other parishes, where they would gain a new legal settlement, 36 within Leicestershire, and eight in Derbyshire, Staffordshire, Warwickshire and Worcestershire.[241] Framework-knitting accounted for 28 of the apprenticeships, including all but two between 1791 and 1815.[242]

Overseers' accounts survive from 1819 to 1828, and vestry minutes between 1834 and 1837 provide detailed information about cases.[243] The parish provided some work for the unemployed, including mending roads and repairing and rethatching the parish houses. The 'houserow' system was adopted when there was no parish work, where the ratepayers in turn agreed to provide work at a set daily wage, which was supplemented from the poor rates.[244] Relief was strictly controlled, and inhabitants were expected to find alternative sources of income. William Holmes was denied relief in 1834, as it was understood he was being paid by the 'union' (probably the Framework Knitters' Friendly Society).[245] Richard Perry was ordered to work for William Jackson, Ellen Foreman for Mr Bradley, and Sam Asker was told to find work 'at the coal pits'.[246] Nathan Perry's wife was told to work at stone picking. She was refused relief when she became a widow, and told to find employment.[247] William Revell's widow was told to take a lodger.[248] No relief

236 *Returns of Charitable Donations* (Parl. Papers 1816 (511) xvi), pp. 658–9; board extant in church, 2018.
237 *Report of the Charity Commissioners*, p. 179; ROLLR, Wills, 1741 (Jennings); ROLLR, Wills, 1743 (Copson).
238 *Report of the Charity Commissioners*, p. 179; ROLLR, Wills, 1745; Returns of Charitable Donations (Parl. Papers 1816 (511) xvi), pp. 658–9.
239 https://www.gov.uk/find-charity-information (accessed 28 Feb. 2018).
240 ROLLR, DE 390/27/1–55.
241 Ibid.
242 ROLLR, DE 390/27/15, 17–19; Ibstock parish registers.
243 ROLLR, DE 390/7–8; DE 4565/7; below, Local Government, parish government.
244 ROLLR, DE 390/7.
245 ROLLR, DE 4565/7, 20 Mar. 1834.
246 ROLLR, DE 4565/7, 20 Mar. 1834, 3 Apr. 1834, 1 May 1834.
247 ROLLR, DE 4565/7, 17 Feb. 1834, 26 Nov. 1835.
248 ROLLR, DE 4565/7, 1 May 1834.

was paid to anyone who kept a dog.[249] Local practitioners were contracted to provide medical services to the poor on annual contracts.[250]

The parish owned a number of houses which were occupied by paupers.[251] It may have acquired another in 1835 when John Foreman was told he would not be provided with relief until he conveyed his house to the parish.[252] Paupers could be moved from house to house, for example in 1834 when Richard Foreman was moved to the house occupied by Benjamin Ball, who was moved to Powerill's house.[253]

Ibstock became part of Market Bosworth Poor Law Union from 1834, and a workhouse was built in Market Bosworth.[254] In theory, relief was only provided in the workhouse, but this was not practical on occasions, including miners' strikes. The union would not pay relief to strikers, but would not allow dependants to starve, and also faced requests from brickyard workers, who were unable to work without coal for the kilns. Guardians' minutes survive for the miners' strike and lock-out of 1926, which began at the end of April and continued until November.[255] The number of people receiving poor relief outside the workhouse rose rapidly from an average of 237 before the lock out, to a peak of 1,839 in July, including 1,009 children.[256] Relief was mostly provided by loans of a fixed sum for a wife and each child, repayable when the lock-out ended.[257] The attitudes of the guardians hardened from July, and they resolved to end relief on 20 August.[258] In November, a resolution was agreed delaying repayment of the loans until after Christmas.[259]

249 ROLLR, DE 4565/7, 29 May 1834.
250 For example, ROLLR, DE 390/7, 29 Mar. 1822; DE 390/8, 27 Mar. 1824, 27 Nov. 1824.
251 ROLLR, DE 4565/7, 10 June 1853; DE 8666.
252 ROLLR, DE 4565/7, 17 Sept. 1835.
253 ROLLR, DE 4565/7, 4 Mar. 1834.
254 TNA, MH 12/6566; below, Local Government, Poor Law Union.
255 ROLLR, G/9/8a/4; *Nottingham Evening Post*, 14 May 1926, 24 Nov. 1926.
256 ROLLR, G/9/8a/4, pp. 215–42.
257 *Coalville Times*, 11 June 1926.
258 ROLLR, G/9/8a/4, p. 231.
259 Ibid, p. 244.

A CHURCH HAD BEEN BUILT in Ibstock by the 1170s. It was completely rebuilt in the early 14th century. Surviving records from 1176 to 1558 consistently show that the church was dedicated to St Helen.[1] One of the bells cast *c.*1500 beseeches 'St Elena' to pray for us.[2] The church was rededicated to St Denis (here spelled Denys), probably in the 18th century.

An attractive income from glebe land and tithes, coupled with an advowson held in episcopal hands from 1531, resulted in the presentation of some well-educated clergy, most notably William Laud (later archbishop of Canterbury) in 1617. Laud and several of Ibstock's other rectors did not reside in the parish.

Differing views on church governance and infant baptism took root in the parish from 1646, and 'many' dissenting groups were meeting in 1669. Nonconformity grew in the 19th century, when there were Baptist, Wesleyan Methodist, Wesleyan Reform and Primitive Methodist congregations. Weekly worship continued to be held in 2019 in St Denys parish church and in Baptist, Methodist and Wesleyan Reform churches in the village.

Church Origins and Parochial Organisation

A generous endowment of five yardlands suggests Ibstock's church may have been an early foundation. The first documentary evidence for the church is from the 1170s, when Garendon abbey agreed a composition with the rector for its tithes.[3] Ibstock church had two chapelries by 1220, one in Hugglescote and another in Donington-le-Heath, served three times weekly from Ibstock.[4]

Christchurch, Coalville was built in the north of the ecclesiastical parish between 1836 and 1840,[5] requiring the approval of the Church Commissioners because fewer than 300 people lived within one mile of the site.[6] Ibstock's rector Spencer Madan had

1 Nichols, *History* III, 819; *Cal. Papal Reg. Papal Letters*, X, 1455–64, 601; wills include ROLLR, Will Reg. 1515–26/281; Will Reg. 1526–33/72v; W & I 1540/37; W & I 1557/415–6; W & I 1558 A-F/146; W & I 1558 G-O/160.

2 T. North, *Church Bells of Leicestershire* (Leicester, 1876), 193; G. Dawson, National Bell Register at http://georgedawson.homestead.com/nbr.html (accessed 24 May 2018); bell extant and seen by author, 2019.

3 Nichols, *History* III, 819, 821.

4 W.P.W. Phillimore (ed.), *Rotuli Hugonis de Welles, Episcopi Lincolniensis, A.D. MCCIX–MCCXXXV*, I (Lincoln Rec. Soc. 3, 1912), 247.

5 *Leic. Chron.*, 23 July 1836; *British Magazine*, 1840, 472; *Return of Parishes Divided and Districts Assigned to Churches under the Church Building Acts, 1818–56* (Parl. Papers, 1861 (557) xlviii), p. 50.

6 1 & 2 Will. IV, c. 38.

contributed to the building fund, but his successor, Charles Goddard, was dismayed at the thought of an evangelical Anglican church being planted within his parish, and suspected that those behind the scheme were driven by a desire to 'take uninhabited lands from the parish to ground a building speculation'.[7] Christchurch was a perpetual curacy which could not be held with any other benefice, and a 'particular district' was assigned to it, which was carved from Hugglescote chapelry in Ibstock, Swannington chapelry in Whitwick, Whitwick itself and Snibston chapelry in Packington.[8]

Hugglescote and Donington became a separate ecclesiastical parish in 1865,[9] and the living was divided following the resignation of Ibstock's rector John Bennett in 1889.[10] An Anglican church was built in Whitehill (later Ellistown), within Hugglescote and Donington parish, in 1896.[11] The 'consolidated chapelry of St Christopher, Ellistown' was created around this new church. Its boundaries included the village of Battram and the houses near Ellistown colliery, within Ibstock parish.[12]

Ibstock benefice was extended in 1978 to include St John's church in Heather (a medieval foundation).[13]

Parishes in Leicestershire were transferred from Lincoln to Peterborough diocese in 1837, and from Peterborough to the re-founded Leicester diocese in 1926.[14]

Advowson

Presentations to the living were made by manorial lords Robert of Garshall and Roland of Verdun jointly in 1220,[15] and Robert of Verdun held the advowson in 1279.[16] The patronage had been acquired by the Hastings overlords by 1313, and passed with the overlordship.[17] Juliana, the daughter of Sir Thomas Leybourne and widow of John, Lord Hastings (d. 1325), held the advowson in dower when she married her second husband Sir Thomas Blount, and was granted livery in 1325.[18] Blount was named as patron when Fanton Marsopini of the diocese of Florence was presented as rector in 1326, although Pope John XXII is believed to have used his power of presentation in this instance.[19]

7 *Leic. Chron.*, 23 July 1836; Lincs Arch., COR.B.5/5/17/6–11 (emphasis original).
8 *Return of Parishes Divided and Districts Assigned to Churches under the Church Building Acts, 1818–56* (Parl. Papers, 1861 (557) xlviii), p. 50; Youngs, *Admin. Units*, II, 224. Youngs records Coalville as an ecclesiastical parish from 1840, but this is an oversimplification of the legal status.
9 *Return of Benefices and Parishes United and Disunited by Orders in Council* (Parl. Papers, 1872, (227) xlvi), p. 21; Youngs, *Admin. Units*, II, 228.
10 *Leic. Chron.*, 3 Aug. 1889.
11 *Leic. Chron.*, 31 Aug. 1895; 2 May 1896; Pevsner, *Leics. and Rutl.*, 150.
12 *London Gaz.*, 30 June 1896, 3789–90.
13 *Leic. Dioc. Dir.* (1977), 79; ibid. (1978), 122.
14 *London Gaz.*, 12 Sept. 1837, 2397–8; 12 Nov. 1926, 7321–2.
15 W.P.W. Phillimore (ed.), *Rotuli Hugonis de Welles, Episcopi Lincolniensis, A.D. MCCIX-MCCXXXV*, II (Lincoln Rec. Soc. 6, 1913), 280.
16 Nichols, *History* I, cxv.
17 *Cal. Inq. p.m.* V, p. 236; above, Landownership, Ibstock manor.
18 *Cal. Inq. p.m.* VI, pp. 385, 389–90; *Cal. Close* 1323–7, 433–4; *Complete Peerage*, VI, 350.
19 N. Bennett (ed.), *The Registers of Bishop Henry Burghersh 1320–1342*, I (Lincoln Rec. Soc. 87, 1999), 116; A. Deeley, 'Papal provision and royal rights of patronage in the early fourteenth century', *Eng. Hist. Review* (1928), 498, 518. Although the article mentions Ibstock, no relevant source is cited containing specific grounds for this collation by the pope.

After Juliana's death in 1367, the advowson passed to her grandson John, 2nd earl of Pembroke (d. 1375),[20] and then probably to his son, also John, who died without issue in 1389.[21] It became detached from the overlordship at an unknown date between 1375 and 1476. The advowson was held by Edward Nevill, Lord Bergavenny, at his death in 1476.[22] His wife Elizabeth (daughter of Richard Beauchamp, 1st earl of Worcester) was the second cousin once removed of John, 3rd earl of Pembroke (d. 1389), through their common ancestor Roger Mortimer, earl of March (d. 1330).[23] The advowson was presumably inherited in 1476 by George, Lord Bergavenny (d. 1492).[24] His son George gave the advowson in 1531 to John Fisher, bishop of Rochester and his successors.[25]

The advowson came into the hands of Henry VIII by the attainder of Bishop John Fisher in 1534,[26] but was restored to the bishops of Rochester by 1551.[27] The patronage fell to parliament upon the abolition of the episcopate in 1646, but was restored to the bishops of Rochester after 1660.[28] It was transferred by the bishop of Rochester to the bishop of Peterborough in 1852,[29] and to the bishop of Leicester in 1927.[30] Following the addition of Heather to the benefice in 1978, joint patronage was agreed between the bishop and the patron of Heather, the Martyrs Memorial and Church of England Trust.[31]

Church Endowment

In the 17th century, the glebe contained three yardlands in Ibstock and two yardlands in Hugglescote and Donington (*c*.150 a.).[32] The rector would also have benefited from tithes across the ecclesiastical parish of *c*.4,000 a.

By 1170, the abbot of Garendon, a Cistercian house, had agreed a composition of two marks annually (£1 6*s*. 8*d*.) in lieu of tithes, which had increased to three marks by 1176.[33] This was a period when the Cistercian order's freedom from tithes was being challenged.[34] The benefice was assessed at 13 marks (£8 13*s*. 4*d*.) for tax in the early 12th

20 *Cal. Inq. p.m.* XIV, p. 157.
21 *Complete Peerage* X, 395.
22 Ibid., [J. Caley and J. Bayley, eds,] *Calendarium inquisitionum post mortem sive escaetarum* ... IV, 379.
23 *Complete Peerage* I, 28.
24 Ibid.
25 Register of Bishop John Fisher, 1504–35, ff. 161–161v, in *Church Authority and Power in Medieval and Early Modern Britain: The Episcopal Registers*, Part 8 (Brighton, 1987).
26 *L&P Hen VIII*, VII, 523; *ODNB*, s.v. Fisher, John [St John Fisher] (*c*.1469–1535) accessed 9 May 2018.
27 C.W. Foster (ed.), *Lincoln Episcopal Records in the time of Thomas Cooper, Bishop of Lincoln 1571 to 1584* (Lincoln Rec. Soc. 2, 1912), 249.
28 Lincs. Arch., DIOC/PD/1666/21.
29 Northants. RO, ML 1116, p. 184.
30 *London Gaz.*, 23 Dec. 1927, 8232.
31 *Leic. Dioc. Dir.* (1979), 87.
32 ROLLR, 1D 41/2/340 (Ibstock, 1690); Lincs. Arch., DIOC/TER/8 (Hugglescote and Donington, 1625).
33 Nichols, *History* III, 819.
34 G. Constable, *Monastic Tithes from their Origins to the Twelfth Century* (Cambridge, 1964), 241–2, 270–81, 299–306.

century, the fifth highest assessment in Sparkenhoe deanery.[35] This increased to 35 marks (£23 6*s.* 8*d.*) in 1291.[36] A valuation of £19 8*s.* 11¼*d.* was recorded in 1535.[37] The annual value in 1706 was said to be £200.[38]

The open fields in Ibstock and in Hugglescote and Donington were enclosed by two parliamentary awards of 1775. The rector was allotted 83 a. for his glebe and 199 a. in lieu of tithes in Ibstock, and 74 a. for the glebe and 76 a. in lieu of tithes in Hugglescote and Donington.[39] Tithes remained payable on earlier enclosures. Rector Spencer Madan certified the gross annual value of his living to be £454 in 1789,[40] from which he paid stipends of £120 to his curate in Ibstock, and £60 to his curate for Hugglescote and Donington.[41] The residual tithes in Ibstock, Hugglescote and Donington were converted to tithe rent charges totalling £527 in 1837.[42] The annual income had increased to £1,408 by 1889, when the living was divided. Ibstock's new rector, Samuel Flood, received an apportionment of £958, and £450 was awarded to Hugglescote's first vicar, Henry Broughton.[43]

Rectory House

The rectory house comprised six bays in 1690, with seven bays of barns, two bays of stables, a cow house, garden and orchard.[44] The house was later extended to eight bays, all timber-framed.[45] It was 'in a very decay'd State' by 1789, when rector Spencer Madan arranged for it to be taken down and rebuilt in brick, for £484.[46] The new house faced west, with servants' quarters to the north.[47]

The house contained four living rooms, 14 bedrooms, three kitchens, a pantry, larder and dairy in 1922, with a coach-house, stables and other outbuildings.[48] Too large for modern clerical living, the property was divided in 1954. The northern portion was sold (and given a separate identity as Lockers End), with the remainder retained for Ibstock's rectors.[49] The coach-house and stables were converted into a church hall, which opened in 1958.[50] The rector moved to a new house built on Hinckley Road in 1997, and the old house was sold.[51]

35 Phillimore (ed.), *Rotuli Hugonis de Welles*, 279.
36 *Tax. Eccl.*, 64.
37 *Valor Eccl.* IV, 180.
38 J. Broad (ed.), *Bishop Wake's Summary of Visitation Returns from the Diocese of Lincoln 1705–15* (Oxford, 2012), 879.
39 ROLLR, DE 8666; DE 144/7 (EN/A/150/1).
40 Lincs. Arch., DIOC/MGA/7.
41 CERC, CC/OF/NB19/93B.
42 ROLLR, Ti/150/1; Ti/151/1; TNA, IR 18/4506.
43 *Peterborough Dioc. Calendar* (1890), 47.
44 ROLLR, 1D 41/2/340.
45 Lincs. Arch., DIOC/TER BUNDLE/LEICS/IBSTOCK (undated, *c.*1705).
46 Lincs. Arch., DIOC/MGA/7.
47 Ibid.; ROLLR, DE 390/5.
48 CERC, CC/OF/NB19/93B.
49 ROLLR, DE 1717/44/1–29; NHLE, no. 1177344, Lockers End, The Rectory, accessed 11 Apr. 2017.
50 ROLLR, DE 1717/93–4.
51 Date plaque on gable wall, extant 2019.

Religious Life

Religious Life before 1547

Following a dispute in 1281, it was held that the rector had no right to cut rushes or grass (*cirpos vel herbam*) for the floors of his church or parsonage from the meadow belonging to Garendon abbey.[52] The disagreement, which may relate to dissatisfaction over tithe retention by the abbey, continued or re-emerged in 1332, when rector Fanton Marsopini was said to have mowed the abbot's grass and carried away the hay,[53] although it was more likely to have been his curate. Marsopini had become chancellor and prebendary of Finglas, Dublin, in 1324 in exchange for his positions as canon and prebendary of Athens.[54] His presentation to the rectory of Ibstock in 1326 was accompanied by a series of episcopal licences to study from 1326 to 1332, which required him to appoint a curate.[55] He would rarely, if ever, have visited Ibstock. Other rectors who may have been non-resident include Thomas Wells in 1405, who was also the rector of Lydgate (Suff.), Richard More, who was licensed for two years' non-residence in 1416, and Geoffrey Fayreclogh, who received papal dispensation in 1461 to hold another benefice alongside Ibstock.[56]

The church had three chaplains in addition to the rector in 1377.[57] In 1526, William Watson was rector, Roger Semper was paid an annual stipend of £4 13*s.* 4*d.* by the rector, presumably as curate, and John Pennyngton also served, and was probably paid by a chantry.[58]

A lady chapel is mentioned in the 1534 wills of Henry Byrte and Richard Chawner.[59] This may have been at the east end of the south aisle, where there is an early-14th-century piscina. This chapel appears to have increased in importance in the later medieval period, as the window in the south wall has been cut, perhaps to take a sedilia. There was an aumbry in the east wall. A chapel at the east end of the north aisle presumably had a raised sanctuary, as its piscina is 5 ft above the modern floor level.

Henry Dodely bequeathed 2*s.* and a sheep in 1533 towards the cost of making a rood loft. No hint of the loft or a rood staircase remains.[60] Land was given for a sepulchre light, and three selions of land were given for a light which shone before an image of St Sithe.[61]

52 *Ab. Placitor*, 201.
53 *Cal. Pat.* 1330–1334, 389; Constable, *Monastic Tithes*, 241–2, 270–81, 299–306.
54 *Cal. Papal Reg.* II, 237.
55 N. Bennett (ed.), *The Registers of Bishop Henry Burghersh 1320–1342*, III (Lincoln Rec. Soc. 101, 2011), 39, 40, 41, 48; L.E. Boyle, 'The constitution "*Cum ex eo*" of Boniface VIII: education of parochial clergy', *Medieval Studies*, 24 (1962), 271–3.
56 *Cal. Papal Reg.* VI, 27–8; Ibid, XI, 601; M. Archer (ed.), *The Register of Bishop Philip Repingdon, 1405–1419*, III (Lincoln Rec. Soc. 74, 1982), 152.
57 A.K. McHardy (ed.), *Clerical Poll Taxes of the Diocese of Lincoln 1377–1381* (Lincoln Rec. Soc. 81, 1992), 19.
58 H Salter (ed.) *A Subsidy collected in the Diocese of Lincoln in 1526* (Oxford, 1909), 104.
59 ROLLR, Will Reg. 1526–33, f. 72.
60 ROLLR, Will Reg. 1515–26, f. 210.
61 *Cal. Pat.* 1572–75, 324–40; *Cal Pat.* 1569–72, 275–6; TNA, C 66/1077, m 40.

St Sithe (or Zita), was a pious servant and housekeeper from Italy, who was popular across England by the late medieval period, especially among women.[62]

The windows of the medieval church contained 17 images of coats of arms, including Beaumont (perhaps a tribute to Robert, who held the manor in 1086), Verdun, Garshall, Hastings, Clinton and Stafford (all holders of the advowson), Valence (Isabel Valence had married John Hastings, who d. 1313) and the arms of England. Four of these windows had been broken by 1622.[63] The remainder were extant in 1811, but had been lost by 1975, when a new scheme was planned.[64]

The Parish Church and its Congregation after 1547

Lands given for lights and chantries were sold between 1568 and 1585.[65]

William Laud, archbishop of Canterbury from 1633, was presented as Ibstock's rector in 1617 by his former tutor, Bishop John Buckeridge (of Rochester). Laud was also rector of two other parishes, president of St John's College, Oxford, prebendary of Buckden, archdeacon of Huntingdon and dean of Gloucester.[66] His curate in Ibstock was John Pickering.[67] Laud was permitted to remain rector of Ibstock when he was appointed bishop of St Davids in 1621. He visited rarely, but preached in Ibstock in 1624, recording in his diary that he 'set things in order there'.[68] His meaning is unclear, but he is unlikely to have appointed a curate who did not share his churchmanship. A locally-held belief that Laud blocked up the chancel windows is untrue.[69] Laud resigned as rector in 1626.[70] He was succeeded by Richard Bayley, who was also presented by Buckeridge,[71] and therefore probably shared Laud's views on ceremonies. Bayley may also have been non-resident, as Pickering continued to sign the registers as curate until 1628.[72]

The church had three bells in 1630.[73] Curiously, when two new bells were cast by Thomas Hancox of Walsall (Staff.) in 1632, one was inscribed, '+ *Somrosa Polsata Monde Maria Vocata*' [*Sum Rosa Pulsata Mundi Maria Vocata*], 'I when rung am called Mary, the rose of the world' (Figure 16). This bell also included a seal, identical to one on a bell cast by Hancox for St Andrew's, Droitwich (Worcs.) the previous year, where the casting clearly depicts the Virgin and child.[74] The tone and weight of this bell indicates

62 S. Sutcliffe, 'The cult of St Sitha in England: an introduction', *Nottingham Medieval Studies*, XXXVII (1993), 83–9.

63 Burton, *Description* (1777 edn), 131.

64 Nichols, *History* IV, facing 752, 754; *Ibstock Par. Mag.*, May 1976.

65 *Cal. Pat.* 1566–69, 226; 1569–72, 275–6; TNA, C 66/1077, m 40; *Cal Pat.* 1572–75, 324–40; *Cal Pat. 27 Eliz. I* (L&I Soc. vol. 293), 111.

66 W. Laud, *The Diary of the Most Reverend Father in God, William Laud* (1694), 3; *ODNB*, s.v. 'Laud, William (1573–1645), archbishop of Canterbury' (accessed 31 July 2017).

67 ROLLR, DE 1717/1.

68 Laud, *Diary*, 3.

69 Several church guides; below.

70 Laud, *Diary*, 29–30.

71 Nichols, *History* IV, 753.

72 ROLLR, DE 1717/1.

73 ROLLR, 1D 41/18/6, f. 6v.

74 Ibstock bell seen by author; H.B. Walters, *Church Bells of Worcestershire* (Worcester, 1901), 32.

Figure 16 *Part of the Marian inscription on the fifth bell of Ibstock's peal of six.*

that it replaced an earlier bell, which presumably also bore this inscription and seal.[75] It is unlikely that Hancox would have added this detail without the explicit agreement of the rector and churchwardens.

John Lufton had become rector by 1636. He was described by Archbishop Laud as a 'hot man', possibly referring to his temperament when he was called to account for non-residence.[76] Lufton sat on the commission of array in 1642, accepting contributions to the Royalist cause from fellow clergy.[77] That year he also attempted to prevent Ibstock's constable, Thomas Clare, responding to parliament's warrant to send Ibstock's trained band of men to Leicester.[78] Lufton left his parish shortly afterwards for the Royalist headquarters at Oxford.[79] The living was sequestered by parliament. Job Grey,

75 John Taylor archives, 1897 and 1905. The author is very grateful to Chris Pickford, archivist, Loughborough Bellfoundry Trust, for this information and details of similar inscriptions and castings.

76 *Cal. SP Dom.* 1636–7, 80; *VCH Leics.* I, 381n.

77 *Walker Revised*, ed. A.G. Matthews, 233, 240 (entries for Thomas Cleaveland and William Parkes).

78 *LJ* 5, 132, 195; *VCH Leics.* I, 381; *Walker Revised*, ed. A.G. Matthews, 240.

79 J. Walker, *An Attempt towards Recovering an account of the Numbers and Sufferings of the Clergy of the Church of England* (1714), 295; *VCH Leics.* I, 381n.

brother of Henry Grey, earl of Kent (d. 1651), was initially presented but soon withdrew, and William Sheffield was appointed in 1646.[80]

The nature of Sunday services in the parish probably changed radically under Sheffield. He was an eloquent and persuasive preacher. He debated publicly with Samuel Oates, a Baptist, for over three hours at Leicester castle in 1649, until Oates ran out of arguments.[81] Sheffield signed a loyal address to Richard Cromwell in 1658,[82] and was one of 38 Leicestershire Puritan ministers who subscribed to a loyal address to parliament in 1659.[83] He left Ibstock in 1660, and was suspended from office in any part of the diocese in 1662.[84] Bishop Robert Sanderson found no surplice or book of canons in the church at his 1662 visitation, and the font had been removed.[85] The font standing in the church in 2019 is octagonal, on an octagonal pedestal and base, mounted on a modern circular base. It is a simple ribbed design, without ornament. It might post-date the Restoration, but its size and shape are consistent with the 14th-century,[86] so the possibility that it was removed from the church in the 1640s and kept safely elsewhere cannot be discounted. The bowl is almost identical to that of the old font in Nailstone church.[87]

Most of Ibstock's rectors appointed after the Restoration were graduates. John Laughton, inducted in 1699, held services twice each Sunday in 1718 and catechised the children each spring. He complained that attendance at communion, held four times annually, was 'much neglected', with just 50 people receiving at Easter, although 200 communicants lived in the village.[88]

The dedication to St Denys (Denis), the first bishop of Paris, was recorded in 1742,[89] and this continued to be the dedication in 2019.

A brief was issued in 1772, enabling the church to raise money to take down and rebuild the north aisle, re-roof the nave and make other repairs to the body of the church and its steeple. The total cost, quoted by master builders John Wyatt and John Mills, was £1,021 5*s.* 6*d.*[90] Any essential work had been completed by 1778, when the archdeacon found no faults at his visitation.[91]

Spencer Madan, 'a first-rate preacher', was instituted to Ibstock rectory in 1786, and remained rector until his death in 1836.[92] He was also rector of St Philip's church in Birmingham from 1787. From 1790 he played a prominent role in political life in Birmingham, where he 'chiefly' resided, publicly denouncing religious dissent and the

80 *LJ* 9, 567–8; 570–3; 10, 353–4.
81 *ODNB*, s.v. Oates, Samuel (bap. 1614, d. 1683) accessed 2 May 2018; Nichols, *History* IV 753n.
82 *Calamy Revised*, ed. A.G. Matthews, 436.
83 W Dugdale, *A Short View of the Late Troubles in England* (1681), 471–3.
84 *Calamy Revised*, ed. A.G. Matthews, 436.
85 A.P. Moore, 'The primary visitation of Robert Sanderson, Bishop of Lincoln, in 1662, for the Archdeaconry of Leicester', *Antiquary* (1909), 386.
86 F. Bond, *Fonts and Font Covers* (1908), 227–40, 265–74.
87 Extant 2019.
88 Nichols, *History* IV, 753; J. Broad (ed.), *Bishop Wake's Summary of Visitation Returns from the Diocese of Lincoln 1705-15* (Oxford, 2012), 879; Lincs. Arch., Gibson 4, pp. 707–8; Gibson 12, pp. 759–60.
89 J. Ecton, *Thesaurus Rerum Ecclesiasticarum* (1742), 327.
90 CERC, CLARKE/2/4/26.
91 ROLLR, 1D 41/18/21, f. 28v.
92 J. Throsby, *Supplementary Volume to the Leicestershire Views, containing a series of Excursions in Leicestershire* (1790), 476; J. Taylor, *Sermon on the Death of Spencer Madan* (Ashby-de-la-Zouch, 1836).

Figure 17 *Ibstock church in 1836, looking east from the west gallery. The painting is by the rector's daughter, Mary Judith Madan.*

radical views which were driving the French Revolution.[93] In 1788 he castigated his parishioners in Ibstock, some for not attending services and others for 'lolling on a seat, and looking about the Church' instead of kneeling for prayers.[94]

The chancel was 'under repair' in 1790.[95] A letter of 1838 from Madan's successor Charles Goddard to Bishop John Kaye records 'living witnesses' who could remember four windows in the chancel with painted glass in the upper sections being blocked up during Madan's incumbency, and the 'lancet window' at the east end being replaced by a window 'suited to a Methodist chapel'.[96] The chancel roof was probably raised in this period by adding courses of bricks (visible externally in 2019), perhaps to admit the east window, and a plaster ceiling and 'chancel arch' were added (Figure 17). As rector, Madan would have financed these changes himself. He also enlarged an existing west gallery,

93 *ODNB*, s.v. Madan, Spencer (1758–1836), Church of England clergyman, accessed 12 July 2013; Madan, Spencer (1729–1813), accessed 30 July 2017; Cornwallis, Frederick (1713–83), accessed 30 July 2017; Throsby, *Supplementary Volume*, 476.

94 S. Madan, *An Address to the Inhabitants of the Parish of Ibstock (Members of the Church of England)*, (Birmingham, 1812), 9–10.

95 Throsby, *Supplementary Volume*, 477.

96 Lincs. Arch., COR.B. 5/5/5/9/5, f. 2.

Figure 18 *The north wall of the chancel before restoration.*

replaced the nave seating, which parishioners claimed was insufficient for those without private pews, and probably installed the double-decker pulpit.[97]

Goddard was archdeacon of Lincoln in addition to his position as rector of Ibstock.[98] He appears to have been resident in Ibstock, or at least a very frequent visitor, as he regularly signed the vestry minutes.[99] Following Goddard's death, John Bennett was instituted as rector in 1849.[100] Average Sunday attendance in 1851, when the population was 1,188, was 250 in the morning and 90 in the afternoon.[101] Bennett moved to continental Europe shortly afterwards, leaving the duties to a curate with an annual stipend of £100.[102] Services were described as 'cold and lifeless' in 1875, and poorly attended.[103] Bennett returned in 1878.[104]

97 Madan, *Address*, 31–32; ROLLR, 1D 41/18/22, f. 38; G.K. Brandwood, *Bringing them to their Knees: Church-building and Restoration in Leicestershire and Rutland*, 1800–1914 (Leicester, 2002), 5. The painting was presented to the church by Spencer Madan's granddaughter, Mary Madan, in 1923: *Ibstock Par. Mag.*, Apr. 1923. It hung on the church wall in 2019.

98 TNA, PROB 11/2073/82; https://theclergydatabase.org.uk/jsp/search/index.jsp (accessed 10 Nov. 2019).

99 ROLLR, DE 4565/7.

100 TNA, PROB 11/2073/82; Northants. RO, ML 601.

101 TNA, HO 129/413/50; *VCH Leics.*, III, 190.

102 CERC, NS/7/1/6813, letter 1 May 1876; *Leic. Chron.*, 8 Dec. 1883. The country is not recorded.

103 *Leic. Chron.*, 6 Mar. 1875.

104 Northants RO, ML 597.

Figure 19 *The north and east walls of the chancel during restoration, revealing an aumbry and one of the medieval windows which had been covered over when Spencer Madan was rector (1786–1836).*

The church and chancel had become ruinous during Bennett's absence.[105] The walls of the north aisle had perished, the roof was leaking and the plaster chancel arch had fallen.[106] Leicester architects Goddard and Paget, and contractors Thrall and Payne, were appointed to restore the building, and work commenced in 1884.[107] The north aisle was rebuilt and a new chancel arch created. A new entrance was made on the north, with a porch, and the south doorway was blocked.[108] The west gallery was removed, and the pews were replaced by benches for 315 adults and children.[109] The total cost was £2,000.[110] The rector was pleased to note that 'so many more have availed themselves of the services' now the seating was free.[111] Morning congregations of 150 people and evening attendances of 300 were seen in 1886.[112]

The borrowing for the restoration had been repaid by 1890, and new rector Samuel Flood turned his attention to the chancel.[113] It had been intended to demolish and rebuild

105 Northants RO, ML 1120, pp. 38–40; *Leic. Chron.*, 6 Mar. 1875; 8 Dec. 1883.

106 Lambeth Palace Libr., ICBS 8915, f. 1; *Leic. Chron.*, 31 May 1884.

107 *Leic. Chron.*, 31 May 1884; 13 June 1885. Leicester architect Alfred Henry Paget (1848–1909) was not directly related to the Paget family of Ibstock.

108 *Leic. Chron.*, 31 May 1884; 13 June 1885.

109 Lambeth Palace Libr., ICBS 8915, ff. 7, 23v, 24v; ICBS MB 24, p. 239; *Leic. Chron.*, 13 June 1885.

110 *Leic. Chron.*, 13 June 1885.

111 *Ibstock Par. Mag.*, Sept. 1885.

112 Northants. RO, X922.

113 *Leic. Chron.*, 6 Dec. 1890.

this in 1884, but upon removing the plaster, four Gothic and two 'low-side' windows were uncovered on the north and south sides, causing a change of plan (Figures 18 and 19).[114] The fabric was restored in 1897–8, an organ chamber was added on the south, and a new two-manual organ was installed. A wide gabled vestry was also built outside the original south doorway.[115] Stained glass for the new east window was added by Mrs Frances Paget in 1899 in memory of her husband Thomas Guy Paget, who had died in 1894.[116] He was the grandson of Thomas Paget (d. 1862) and father of Thomas Guy Frederick Paget (d. 1952).

A new treble bell was added for Queen Victoria's diamond jubilee in 1897, the gift of Ibstock veterinary surgeon Edward Perry, and the five bells were further augmented to six in 1905.[117]

An altar and reredos at the east end of the north aisle was dedicated to the fallen of the First World War. Carved by William Sabine, the woodwork and handicraft teacher at the senior school, the design incorporates 72 carved poppies, one for each Ibstock life lost.[118] A stained glass memorial window above, by Heaton, Butler and Bayne of Covent Garden, depicts the sacrifice of Christ in the centre of the three lights, with a soldier kneeling by the cross. Figures in the left pane include a soldier and nurse, with miners, widows and children in the right-hand pane. A further memorial tablet commemorates the fallen of the Second World War.

The east window in the south aisle is in memory of medical practitioner Walter James Meldrum (d. 1971), with roses referencing the prizes he won for his exhibits at the Chelsea Flower Show.[119] Douglas Mee had expressed a wish that the coats of arms which had been recorded in the windows in 1622 should be added to the plain glass in the church. Following his death in 1975, his widow gave a window in his memory depicting the Leicestershire County Council arms and the arms of the Mee family.[120] The church sought further donations for other windows. The scheme was finally completed in 1983, when a total of 30 coats of arms had been added.[121]

Six Sunday services were held each month in 2018, two of which were communion services.[122]

Church Architecture

The body of the church is almost square and comprises a nave of three bays with a clerestory above, with north and south aisles. To the east is a long chancel, two-thirds of the length of the nave, and to the west, a tower in three stages, topped with a pierced

114 *Leic. Chron.*, 31 May 1884; 19 Feb. 1898.
115 *Leic. Chron.*, 19 Feb. 1898.
116 *Ibstock Par. Mag.*, May 1899.
117 Inscription on bells, seen by author in 2017; photograph of 1905 in church in 2018.
118 *Ibstock Parish Magazine,* July, Sept., Oct., 1938, Apr. 1939, Mar. 1978.
119 H. Crane, 'An Ibstock childhood from 1928', in J. Carswell (ed.), *Ibstock Lives* (Coalville, *c.*1991), 61; inscription on window, extant in 2018.
120 *Ibstock Parish Magazine*, May 1976.
121 *Ibstock Parish Magazine*, Mar. 1983, July 1983.
122 https://www.achurchnearyou.com/church/5331/service-and-events/events-regular/ (accessed 27 May 2018).

parapet and surmounted by a recessed spire. There is a porch to the north and a wide vestry to the south (Figure 2).[123] The church is almost all of the early 14th century, and is built of Bromsgrove Sandstone, which crops out around the edges of the coalfield.[124] A stone stoup survives outside the original south door (within the vestry of 1898).

The two arcades differ slightly, with hexagonal piers on the south, and octagonal piers on the north. The windows are a mix of Y, curvilinear and reticulated tracery.[125] The clerestory was added in the late 15th or early 16th century, and the two low side windows in the chancel (one north and one south) are also probably from the late medieval period. A kitchen area in the south aisle and toilet in the former vestry were added in 2013.[126]

Protestant Nonconformity

Early Dissent

Puritan views appear to have taken hold among some in the parish from 1646, and continued after William Sheffield left the living in 1660. Elias Goadby (a mercer) and Joseph Taylor (wheelwright) were presented to the archdeaconry court in 1668 for refusing to have their children baptised.[127]

Curate John Shakespeare reported in 1669 that 'many' conventicles (illegal religious meetings) were held in Ibstock, in the houses of Goadby, Taylor, John Erpe (a smith) and John Husband, attended by about 40 Presbyterians, and others holding 'all sorts' of beliefs. The ten 'most substantial' residents taking part were Erpe, Goadby, Taylor, Thomas Erpe, a tailor, yeomen Thomas Copson and Thomas Paget, three husbandmen, John Belcher, John Paybody and James Swinfield, and Samuel Barnes, whose occupation was not recorded.[128] Paget and Copson were two of the wealthiest men in the parish, paying tax on five and four hearths respectively in 1670.[129] Four former Anglican clergymen who had resigned or been ejected from their livings following the Restoration visited to lead the worship: William Smith (Packington), Matthew Clarke (Narborough), John Shuttlewood (Ravenstone) and Richard Drayton (Shangton).[130]

During a brief period of religious toleration in 1672, the houses of Thomas Paget, Joseph Taylor and John Husband were licenced to hold Presbyterian meetings, and those of Elias Goadby and Richard Batts were also licensed, with no denominational label attached.[131] Some Dissenters occasionally conformed, Thomas Paget and John Husband,

123 Above, Ibstock Parish, settlement.

124 Pevsner, 184; NHLE, no. 1074370, Church of St Denys and Paget tombs in churchyard, accessed 11 Apr. 2017; Brit. Geol. Surv., Strategic Stone Study, Leicestershire, 15, http://mapapps.bgs.ac.uk/buildingStone/BuildingStone.html (accessed 29 July 2017).

125 Pevsner, 184; NHLE, no. 1074370, Church of St Denys and Paget tombs in churchyard, accessed 11 Apr. 2017.

126 Prospect Archaeology, 'The Church of St Denys, Ibstock, Leicestershire' (2013).

127 R.H. Evans, 'Nonconformity in Leicestershire in 1669', *Trans LAHS*, XXV, (1949), 108–9.

128 Ibid., 126–7.

129 Ibid., 105–6, 126–7; TNA, E 179/251/5.

130 Evans, 'Nonconformity', 127.

131 *Cal. SP Dom.*, vol. XIII, May–Sept. 1672, pp. 238, 463, 678.

for example, were recorded as being in church in 1666 to hear rector Charles Bridgeman read the 39 Articles,[132] but it is stretching to believe the assertion of Ibstock's curate J. Grascombe in 1676 that only five women and eight men in the village were 'wilful abstainers from the Lord's table', and no one was 'wholly absent' from church services.[133]

The number of nonconformists faded in the decades which followed the 1689 Act of Toleration, as the ministers across the region who had lost their livings in 1662, and their followers, became older and died. In 1709, rector John Laughton reported that there were about 20 Presbyterians 'of all kinds' in Ibstock, about six per cent of the population. In 1718 and 1721, just three or four of Ibstock's 60 families were said to attend Presbyterian meetings. There were then no licensed meeting houses in the village.[134]

Baptists

Hugglescote Baptist chapel was established in 1798 from the chapel at Barton-in-the-Beans, and stood at the centre of a defined territory of *c.*35 sq. miles, which stretched from Coleorton Moor in the north-west to Stanton-under-Bardon in the south-east.[135] In that year Joseph Newbold (hosier and grocer), Edward Barrass, George Dean and Thomas Revel were granted a licence for worship in Samuel Pickering's house in Ibstock.[136]

The members of Hugglescote chapel agreed in 1812 that a branch chapel should be built in Ibstock.[137] Land then on the northern fringe of the village (which became Chapel Street) was purchased in 1814, and conveyed to eleven trustees: Joseph Newbold, Edward Barrass, George Dean, John Bott, John Dean, Joseph Green, William Green, John Newberry, Samuel Pickering, William Pollard and B. Sperry.[138] The building was completed and licensed for worship later that year, upon application by Thomas Orton (the Hugglescote minister), John Dean, Samuel Massey and Samuel Pickering.[139] About 150 people worshipped there in 1829.[140] The chapel had been enlarged by 1841 and provided 284 seats, 264 of which were freely available.[141] It also had a graveyard.[142] The two services on Sunday 30 March 1851 were attended by 70 people in the afternoon and 171 in the evening.[143] Fund raising efforts enabled a new chapel to be added alongside, which opened in 1857, following which the original chapel was converted for use by the Sunday school (Figure 20).[144]

132 ROLLR, DE 1717/2.
133 A. Whiteman, *The Compton Census of 1676: A Critical Edition* (1986), 332n.
134 Broad (ed.), *Bishop Wake's Summary*, 879; Lincs. Arch., Gibson 4, p. 706; Gibson 12, p. 758.
135 T. Cook, *The Barton Centenary* (Leicester, 1845), 18; A. Taylor, *The History of the English General Baptists*, II (London, 1818), 452; ROLLR, N/B/150/1.
136 ROLLR, 1D 41/44/91.
137 ROLLR, N/B/150/2, 9 Feb. 1812, 8 Mar. 1812, 28 June 1812.
138 ROLLR, N/B/150/2, 3 Apr. 1814, 1 May 1814, 8 June 1814.
139 ROLLR, 1D 41/44/276.
140 ROLLR, QS 95/2/1/166.
141 *Leic. Chron.*, 25 Sept. 1841; TNA, HO 129/413/51.
142 *Leics. Merc.* 22 Oct. 1853.
143 TNA, HO 129/413/51.
144 *Leics. Merc.*, 8 Aug. 1857; 20 Mar. 1858; *Leic. Jnl*, 13 Feb. 1858; 26 Mar. 1858; W. White, *Hist. Gaz. & Dir. of Leics.* (Sheffield, 1863), 677.

Figure 20 *Ibstock Baptist Church, Chapel Street. The building on the right is the original chapel, built in 1814, which was the first purpose-built nonconformist chapel in Ibstock. It was converted to Sunday School rooms when the later chapel (left) was built in 1856.*

It was agreed in 1877 that Ibstock would have a minister of its own, and the chapel formally split from Hugglescote, with 56 named members forming the Ibstock church.[145] An extension was added to the chapel in 1878 to provide 600 sittings.[146] Membership rose rapidly, from 68 in 1881 to 150 in 1898, outstripping the rate of increase in the population.[147] In 1908, the Sunday school classrooms were enlarged, and a new gallery and baptistry were constructed within the church, at a cost of *c*.£1,200.[148]

Following the departure of minister J. Robertson in 1975, Ibstock church returned to a joint pastorate with Hugglescote, although each church retained its own diaconate.[149] Disagreements in the 1990s, when there was no minister, led to the resignation of the entire Ibstock diaconate, but with the support of lay ministers and a Baptist church in Loughborough, the congregation began to grow again in the early years of the 21st century.[150]

145 ROLLR, N/B/150/2, 2 July 1877, 29 July 1877, Nov. 1877.
146 *Kelly's Dir. of Leics. and Rutl.* (1936) p. 113.
147 G.T. Rimmington, 'Baptist membership in rural Leicestershire, 1881–1914', *Baptist Quarterly*, 37 (1998), 393.
148 ROLLR, DE 3806/Market Bosworth/1908/381; *Leic. Chron.*, 21 Nov. 1908.
149 R.M. Scott, *Ibstock Baptist Church: A Short History* (Ibstock, 1978), 16.
150 Information from Roy Monks, minister 2012–18.

Wesleyan Methodists and Ibstock Methodist Church

Richard Chandler's house was registered for religious meetings in 1819.[151] A piece of land was purchased on Melbourne Road in 1823 and conveyed into in the names of 13 trustees for a Wesleyan church: farmer Richard Chandler, shoemaker Richard Lawrence, saddler John Messenger and gardener Joseph Walker, all of Ibstock, and nine men from Ashby, Heather, Measham, Odstone, Packington and Swannington.[152] A chapel was built, and in 1829 attracted congregations of 100 people.[153] The building was enlarged, *c.*1840, to accommodate 145 people.[154] Afternoon and evening services in 1851 were attended by 90 and 120 people respectively.[155] By building around and then demolishing the old walls, a larger church to seat 300 people was erected on the same site in 1891. The architect was Arthur Wakerley of Leicester, and the builder was James Crane of Ibstock. The total cost was £755.[156]

The Wesleyan and Primitive Methodist churches merged nationally in 1932. This congregation became known as Melbourne Road Methodist church, and was in the Ashby-de-la-Zouch (St John's) circuit.[157] They combined with the Curzon Street Methodist Church in 1964 (a Primitive Methodist church until 1932). The Melbourne Road congregation and building were then known as Ibstock Methodist Church.[158] Weekly services were held in 2019.[159]

Primitive Methodists

'Ranters', a derogatory name for Primitive Methodists, first met in Ibstock, *c.*1820. They were 'grossly insulted' by some residents, leading to a legal action which resulted in heavy expenses. No further meetings are recorded in Ibstock until 1841, when a camp meeting was 'well attended'.[160] A group began to meet regularly in the 1860s in the house of Mr J. Loydall.[161] Land was purchased in Curzon Street and the foundation stones for a Primitive Methodist chapel, to seat nearly 250 people, were laid in 1867.[162] The architect was James Kerridge of Wisbech (Cambs.).[163] Donations for bricks ranged from 1*s.* to £1, with gifts of £5 from MP Thomas Tertius Paget and £20 from Joseph Whetstone of Ibstock Colliery.[164] It was the closest chapel to Ibstock colliery and to the homes of many colliery and brickworks employees.

151 ROLLR, 1D 41/44/403.
152 ROLLR, N/M/73/44.
153 TNA, HO 129/413/52; ROLLR, QS 95/2/1/166.
154 *Leic. Chron.*, 25 Sept. 1841; TNA, HO 129/413/52.
155 TNA, HO 129/413/52.
156 *Leic. Chron.*, 14 Nov. 1891.
157 *Methodist Church Buildings, Statistical Returns* (Manchester, 1940), 110.
158 ROLLR, N/M/73/57, 19 Feb. 1964.
159 http://www.nfemc.org.uk/churches/ibstock (accessed 28 Dec. 2019).
160 *Leic. Chron.*, 28 Aug. 1841.
161 *Leic. Chron.*, 14 Mar. 1868.
162 *Leic. Mail*, 19 Oct. 1867.
163 *Leic. Chron.*, 14 Mar. 1868.
164 *Leic. Chron.*, 19 Oct. 1867; 14 Mar. 1868

When the Primitive and Wesleyan Methodist churches merged in 1932, it was decided that both the churches in Ibstock should remain open.[165] The churches were 900 m. apart, and it would inconvenience many if their congregations were to meet in a single place. The Primitive Methodist chapel became known as Curzon Street Methodist Church,[166] and was in the Coalville Methodist circuit.[167] Thirteen new trustees were appointed in 1938, most of whom lived in Curzon Street or the immediate vicinity: Joseph James Sparrow and Walter Bourne (respectively the manager and foreman at Ibstock brickworks), George Sparrow (pit deputy), Charles Deacon (miner), George Underwood (former miner), Albert Atkins and William Bourne (both employed in the footwear industry), George Wilson (boot repairer), Bernard Wilson and George Handy (both labourers), Mrs Allen Peat, Mrs Florence Wilson and Miss Frances Baker.[168]

Following the merging of the Curzon Street and Melbourne Road congregations at Melbourne Road in 1964, the Curzon Street building was sold.[169]

A Primitive Methodist chapel was built at the end of West Ellistown Terrace, near Ellistown colliery, in 1883–4 (Figure 5).[170] Isidore Ellis, director of Ellistown Colliery, left a bequest of £50 to this church in 1930.[171] It became a Methodist church in 1932. The building was demolished in the later 20th century, due to subsidence.[172]

Wesleyan Reform Methodists

Reformers broke away from the Wesleyan Methodist Church from 1849, believing the laity should have a greater involvement in church governance. Expulsions and resignations were at their height in 1851.[173] A group of between 25 and 40 people left Ibstock Wesleyan church in January 1851, to begin meeting for worship on Sunday afternoons under the leadership of Thomas Farmer, a cooper.[174] They purchased a piece of land on Narrow Lane (later Reform Road), which they reputedly bought for £1 from farmer Richard Thirlby.[175] The trustees included a cooper (probably Thomas Farmer), a cordwainer and a tallow chandler.[176] A chapel was built on the site in 1855, at a cost of £120.[177]

The church had 68 members in 1881, increasing to 119 in 1911, when a larger chapel was built on Melbourne Road.[178] Henry and Mary Holmes and Robert Beeson, described as 'founders' of the chapel in one account, may have been the prime movers in finding

165 ROLLR, N/M/73/57, 6 July 1938.
166 Ibid.
167 *Methodist Church Buildings*, 111.
168 ROLLR, N/M/73/57, 6 July 1938.
169 ROLLR, N/M/73/57, 19 Feb. 1964.
170 OS 6" Leics XXIII SE (1904); *Leic. Chron.*, 8 Sept. 1883; 30 Aug. 1884.
171 *Nottingham Eve. Post*, 26 Aug. 1930.
172 Above, Ibstock Parish, settlement.
173 K.D.M. Snell and P.S. Ell, *Rival Jerusalems: The Geography of Victorian Religion* (Cambridge, 2002), 147.
174 TNA, HO 129/413/53; HO 107/2083/420.
175 L.S. Eggington, *Ibstock: A Story of her People* (Moira, 1984), 6, 18; Mr Eggington saw the receipt for the land purchase.
176 A. Armson, *Ibstock: The Story of a Leicestershire Village* (Ibstock, 1938), 18.
177 W. White, *Hist. Gaz. and Dir. of Leics. and Rutl.* (Sheffield, 1863), 677.
178 G.T. Rimmington, 'The Wesleyan Reform Union in Leicestershire during the twentieth century', *Leicestershire Historian* (2012), 28; ROLLR, DE 3806/1911/549.

the site, fundraising and appointing the architect and builders.[179] The Wesleyan Reform church was very strong across the Leicestershire coalfield area and both Holmes and Beeson were miners.[180] A hall adjoining the side of the new church was originally used as a Sunday School. A larger schoolroom was built to the rear in 1925, facing Central Avenue.[181]

The Wesleyan Reform Church did not join the Union of Methodist churches in 1932. In 2018, Ibstock was one of four Wesleyan Reform churches in the Ashby circuit.[182]

Plans were approved in 1903 for a Wesleyan Reform chapel to be built in Battram. It was a simple building with benches either side of a central aisle, and a small gallery.[183] It had seven members in 1924, and 16 in 1935, in a period when membership of most of the other Wesleyan Reform chapels in the Ashby circuit was reducing.[184] The chapel is believed to have closed in the late 1980s. The property was purchased for conversion to a house, but demolished due to subsidence, *c.*1992.[185]

Salvation Army

The 'Deliverer Cavalry Corps' of the Salvation Army announced their intention to 'bombard' Ibstock in 1887 and began regular Sunday evening services.[186] A Salvation Army Hall had been built near the Welfare sports ground by 1929.[187] They had a band and provided a musical instrument and teaching for any boys who wanted to join.[188] The corps was listed in a directory of 1941,[189] but disbanded shortly afterwards.[190]

179 Eggington, *Ibstock*, 3, 6, 18.
180 Rimmington, 'Wesleyan Reform'; TNA, RG 10/3241/72; RG 11/3135/113v.
181 ROLLR, DE 3806/Market Bosworth/1911/549; Plaque on building, extant 2019.
182 Rimmington, 'Wesleyan Reform', 29–30; http://www.thewru.com/circuits-churches/ (accessed 27 May 2018).
183 ROLLR, DE 3806/ Market Bosworth/1903/77.
184 Rimmington, 'Wesleyan Reform', 29.
185 Ex inf. Vera Harding, owner of the building when it was demolished.
186 *Leic. Chron.*, 20 Aug. 1887.
187 OS Map 25", Leics. XXIII.11 (1929).
188 Memories of E. Gibson, in J. Carswell (ed.), *Ibstock Lives* (Coalville, *c.*1991), 58.
189 *Kelly's Dir. Leics. and Rutl.* (1941), 111.
190 Memories of E. Gibson, in Carswell (ed.), *Ibstock Lives*, 58.

Manor Courts and Managing the Open Fields

BERTRAM OF IBSTOCK HELD A messuage and land in Ibstock in 1301 from Thomas Garshall by homage, fealty and doing suit at Thomas's court 'from three weeks to three weeks'.[1] No manor court rolls survive from any period. Nothing is known about the nature of peasant tenure or the services owed to the lord, and there are no surviving records of the enfranchisement of copyholders.

The sale of 'the manors of Ibstock and Overton' by William Stafford in 1654 included the 'courts baron, courts leet [and] view of frankpledge'.[2] On the division of the manor between Samuel Bracebridge and Thomas Clare (d. 1668) later that year, each received 'a moiety or half of ... the courts baron and courts leet and view of frankpledge', which were to be kept in both names.[3]

It is not known whether Bracebridge and Clare ever held any courts. It appears none had been held for some time in 1697, when a number of inhabitants held 'severall meetings and debates' to discuss how best to minimise the 'great losses and inconveyiencyes' they were suffering through trespass and the overgrazing of the open fields and commons.[4] It followed a period of substantial population growth and the enclosure of part of the open fields.[5] The meeting agreed a set of 35 articles to run for 15 years. These were signed by 24 inhabitants, including the rector, Thomas Clare (gentleman, d. 1714, probably the lord of one moiety of the manor), Thomas Paget (gentleman, and possibly a major landowner by this date), seven yeomen, ten husbandmen, a wheelwright, a butcher, widow Frances Jennings (probably a freeholder) and a labourer. Two field masters were to be appointed annually, responsible for ensuring the by-laws were enforced. All occupiers of half a yardland or more were required to serve as field master, with the appointment made each year on a house-by-house basis. The field masters appointed two pinders each year to look after the fields on a daily basis.[6] Two trustees from outside the manor, Thomas Roby of Donington-le-Heath and John Boley of Loughborough, were appointed to collect the fines and divide them between the field masters, the pinders and the poor of Ibstock in proportions laid out within the individual articles. Three of the articles also provided payment to an informer.[7]

1 G.F. Farnham, *Medieval Village Notes*, III (Leicester, 1933), 4, citing TNA, CP 40/139, m. 87.
2 ROLLR, DE 355/39a.
3 ROLLR, DE 365/21.
4 ROLLR, DE 390/56.
5 Above, Ibstock Parish, population; Economic History, agriculture.
6 ROLLR, DE 390/56.
7 Ibid.; above, Economic history, agriculture.

The articles lapsed in 1712, and were replaced by new articles in 1717, 'made for the town of Ibstock' by the jury at the court held for the neighbouring manor of Nailstone.[8] This suggests that no manor court could be summoned for Ibstock, possibly due to uncertainty over the identity of the holder of the Clare moiety. No connection has been found between Nailstone manor and Ibstock in 1717. The new articles were mostly concerned with seasonal restrictions on common grazing, and were signed by four jurors: Harrington Power, Thomas Kemp, Job Varnham and Thomas Carver. Power was the lord of one moiety of the manor, and the others had signed the agreement of 1697.[9]

Parish Government

The Vestry

Vestry minutes survive from 1824 to 1890.[10] Meetings were held fortnightly between 1834 and 1837, to agree poor relief.[11] Outside these years the vestry appears to have been open and met at irregular intervals, whenever the needs of the parish warranted a meeting. Two overseers for the poor, two surveyors of the roads and a headborough were elected annually, and one churchwarden was elected annually from 1838.[12] Constables, and the assessors and collectors of national taxes, may have served for several years, as elections were recorded infrequently, perhaps only when the office changed hands. Their number increased as the village grew, for example, three constables and two assessors were elected in 1871, and ten constables with six assessors in 1881.[13] The constables' duties included conducting a 'strict inspection' of public houses, to prevent card-playing and reduce drunkenness 'by enforcing the existing laws'.[14] The parish had a small lock-up or 'round house' where petty criminals could be held for a short period. This was 'violently pulled down' in 1835, for reasons which are not recorded. It was rebuilt in 1836 behind 'some parish houses' known as Sand Pit Row.[15] Sand Pit close was by the junction between Melbourne Road and what became Station Road, and Sand Pit Row was probably one of two rows of buildings erected opposite between 1775 and 1838.[16]

Five ratepayers, including two directors of the gas company, requested a meeting of ratepayers in 1877, as required under the Lighting and Watching Act of 1833, to propose installing gas lighting in the parish.[17] Consent was required from two-thirds of the ratepayers who voted.[18] A poll of parish ratepayers was requested, and 276 ratepayers were in favour, with 42 against.[19] Some controversy developed and the vote was taken

8 ROLLR, DE 390/58.
9 Ibid.; DE 390/56.
10 ROLLR, DE 4565/7.
11 Above, Social history, social welfare.
12 ROLLR, DE 4565/7.
13 Ibid., 23 Feb. 1871; 24 Feb. 1881.
14 Ibid, 26 Nov. 1835; 12 Apr. 1838.
15 Ibid., 10 Dec. 1835; 21 Jan. 1836.
16 ROLLR, DE 8666; Ti/155/1.
17 ROLLR, DE 4565/7, 30 Aug. 1877.
18 3 & 4 Wm IV, c. 90.
19 ROLLR, DE 4565/7, 20 Sept. 1877.

again at another meeting in 1880, when nine of the twelve ratepayers present gave their agreement.[20] A contract for street lighting was signed in 1881.[21]

Poor Law Administration before 1836

Annual expenditure on the poor fluctuated widely, but the increase from £434 in 1803 to £700 in 1829 (61 per cent) is not out of line with the experience elsewhere.[22] Most of this can probably be accounted for by the decline of the framework-knitting industry after 1815.

Nichols recorded that there were 30 people in a workhouse at Ibstock in 1776,[23] but the parliamentary return he cited stated that the workhouse was in Hugglescote and Donington. This building may have been shared with Ibstock, or Ibstock's payment of £7 12*s.* that year for 'workhouses and habitations for the poor' may relate to Ibstock's own parish houses.[24] Any arrangement to share a workhouse would presumably have ceased in 1787, when Ibstock's overseers borrowed £100 from Henry Rowell to purchase the 'Hemp House' from Leonard Palmer and convert it into 'a workhouse for the use of the parish'.[25] Known as the 'house of industry' in 1817, this building contained ten residents in 1803, who earned £2 18*s.* towards their keep.[26] The overseers' accounts between 1820 and 1825 show purchases of hurds (the waste from flax or hemp), and wages paid for spinning, weaving, warping and making bobbin-net lace.[27] The tithe award of 1838 listed a 'workhouse close', but this was a close of 4 a. behind the High Street plots, stretching down to the brook, 300 m. to its south, with no direct access.[28] There was no building on this site and its position suggests it is unlikely to be the site of a workhouse, but this land may have been used to grow flax, hemp or food for the workhouse residents.

A vestry met fortnightly between 1834 and 1836 to decide the nature and amount of poor relief to be given on a case-by-case basis.[29] This suggests the parish was mirroring the Sturges Bourne Act of 1819, which enabled a parish to establish a select vestry 'for the concerns of the Poor' of between five and 20 'Substantial Householders or Occupiers' chosen in an open vestry meeting. The approval of the county magistrates was required to adopt the Act, but no approval can be traced for Ibstock. Ibstock's apparent select

20 Ibid., 19 Aug, 1880; 2 Sept. 1880.
21 *Leic. Chron.*, 15 Jan. 1881.
22 *Report from Committee appointed to Inspect the Returns made by the Overseers of the Poor* (Parl. Papers 1776–7), p. 385; *Returns on the Expense and Maintenance of the Poor* (Parl. Papers 1803–4 (175), xiii), pp. 262–3; *Returns Relative to the Expense and Maintenance of the Poor* (Parl. Papers 1818 (82) xix), pp. 230–31; *Select Committee on Poor Rate returns* (Parl. Papers 1825 (334), iv), p. 119; M. Blaug, 'The myth of the old poor law and the making of the new', *Journal of Economic History* (1963), 164.
23 Nichols, *History* IV, 751.
24 *Report on Overseers of the Poor*, p. 385.
25 TNA, MH 12/6566/1837, abstract of title; MH 12/6566/1838, f. 240.
26 *Leic. Chron.*, 29 Mar. 1817; *Returns on the Expense and Maintenance of the Poor* (Parl. Papers 1803–4 (175), xiii), pp. 262–3.
27 ROLLR, DE 390/7–8.
28 ROLLR, Ti/155/1.
29 59 Geo. III, c. 12; S.A. Shave, *Pauper Policies: Poor Law Practice in England, 1780–1850* (Manchester, 2017), 113–4; above, Social history, social welfare.

vestry had 20 members, although they did not all attend each meeting.[30] The fortnightly meetings ended in 1836.

Poor Law Union

Ibstock became part of the Poor Law union centred around Market Bosworth, five miles to its south, in 1836. Only three of the 28 townships in the union in 1836 had any significant industry: Ibstock (framework-knitting and mining), Markfield (quarrying) and Ratby (framework-knitting). The remainder were rural settlements that were almost entirely dependent on agriculture. Ibstock was one of five townships represented by two guardians.[31]

The Union workhouse opened in Market Bosworth in 1837, and Ibstock's parish workhouse was auctioned in 1839. The proceeds of £283 were used to clear the outstanding mortgage and reduce Ibstock's share of the cost of building the Union workhouse.[32]

Rural Sanitary Authority

Ibstock was the most populous of the settlements within the jurisdiction of Market Bosworth Rural Sanitary Authority (RSA), which was established in 1872.[33] Ibstock was developing the character of a town, and by the 1880s it suffered from overcrowding, inadequate sewerage provision, polluted water and the rapid spread of infectious diseases. Dr John Turner, the district medical officer, reported in 1890 that the privies and ashpits in Meadow Row were full and there was no clean drinking water, two privies shared by eight houses in Deacons Lane were full to overflowing, and there were not enough privies at the National School for the number of children.[34] The soil was so polluted in Chapel Street, he advised that cleaning the wells and pump, or sinking a new well, would only be a short-term solution.[35] A committee was established, and recommended laying drains (basic sewers) and converting privies to pail closets, which would be emptied weekly.[36] This could not have been fully implemented as there was a complaint in 1892 that the wells of newly-built cottages (in an unspecified location) had been polluted by sewage seeping through the ground, which was attributed to the lack of drains for the older houses further uphill.[37]

Figures for serious diseases across the RSA's area emphasise how far Ibstock differed from the remainder of the district. In the third quarter of 1894, 90 cases of smallpox, scarlet fever and typhoid were notified across the district, 87 of which were within Ibstock.[38] When the first three smallpox cases were notified in 1894, Dr Turner commandeered the former British School as a temporary isolation hospital, and engaged

30 ROLLR, DE 4565/7, 17 Mar. 1836.
31 TNA, MH 12/6566/1836, memorandum 16 Jan. 1836.
32 ROLLR, DE 4565/7, 26 June 1837; TNA, MH 6566/1839, statement on sale.
33 *VCH Leics*. III, 179–203.
34 ROLLR, DE 3640/159, pp. 361–2.
35 *Leic. Chron*., 29 Mar. 1890.
36 ROLLR, DE 3640/159, p. 364.
37 *Leic. Chron*., 3 Dec. 1892; 10 Dec. 1892.
38 ROLLR, DE 3640/160, p. 173.

two nurses.[39] When more cases were confirmed, he recommended that a 12-bed isolation hospital was built away from the village. A site was found between Pretoria Road and Ibstock colliery, and a tender for £65 was accepted by the RSA for a wooden building on brick foundations.[40] It opened within two weeks.[41]

Rural sanitary authorities could agree to the formation of parochial committees containing members of the RSA board and parish ratepayers nominated at a vestry meeting.[42] Ten ratepayers were nominated to a parochial committee for Ibstock in 1890, without seeking the prior agreement of the RSA. Retrospective approval was given through the chairman's casting vote. The parochial committee met monthly, but had no power beyond making recommendations to the full board, to be voted upon by all members.[43] The work of the RSA was absorbed into Market Bosworth Rural District Council in 1894.

Burial Board

A committee of three churchmen and three Nonconformists was formed in 1880, with the rector at its head, to discuss the provision of a cemetery for Ibstock.[44] A site on Pegg's Lane (later Pretoria Road) was given by Thomas Tertius Paget MP.[45] Eleven men stood at the first election for eight seats on the board. John Bennett (rector), Richard Thomas (doctor), John Cart (farmer), William Thirlby (farmer), William Rowell (farmer), Thomas Bailey (postmaster), John Dormer (plumber) and Thomas Hextall (builder and carpenter) were elected.[46] It is not known how many of them were Nonconformists. The vestry approved construction costs of £1,000, to include a chapel, lodge and wall with entrance gates.[47] The cemetery opened in 1883.[48] The work of the board was absorbed into the parish council from 1894.

Local Government after 1894

Parish Council

A belief that Ibstock's pressing public health issues were not being taken seriously enough may help to account for the interest shown in elections to the first parish council in 1894. Voters in Battram and Ellistown wanted the parish to be divided into wards, but this

39 Ibid., pp. 150–2.
40 Ibid., p. 154.
41 Ibid., pp. 158, 162, 164–5, 173.
42 Public Health Act, 1875.
43 *Leic. Chron.*, 29 Mar. 1890; 26 Apr. 1890; 24 May 1890.
44 *London Gaz.*, 6 Sept. 1881, 4593–4; 1 Nov. 1881, 5346–7; *Leic. Chron.*, 24 Jan. 1880; ROLLR, DE 4565/7, 15 Jan. 1880.
45 ROLLR, DE 4565/7, 11 Aug. 1881.
46 Ibid., 13 Dec. 1881
47 *Leic. Chron.*, 25 Feb. 1882; ROLLR, DE 4565/7, 23 Feb. 1882.
48 ROLLR, DE 8444/2.

was declined, to minimise election expenses.[49] Ten seats were available.[50] The Liberals were keen to field ten candidates, and with 19 people wishing to stand under the Liberal banner, they held their own preliminary ballot to decide who would be nominated.[51] The Conservatives also had ten candidates. Four other candidates stood, including Radicals.[52] Eight Liberals and two Conservatives were elected.[53]

The parish council purchased land beyond the brook behind Orchard and Copson Streets in 1897 to provide a recreation ground to mark Queen Victoria's diamond jubilee.[54] The council's desire to adopt the Baths and Washhouses Act in 1898, to provide a 'bathing tank' to benefit miners who lacked adequate washing facilities at home, had to be delayed as the site relied on water from the brook, which was contaminated by sewage.[55] That problem was resolved when the sewage works opened in 1898.[56] 'Public baths' fed by the brook opened on the recreation ground in 1899. There was no roof and the water was unheated, but 1,922 people had paid for admission by the end of the first 'season'.[57] As seen elsewhere, the baths appear to have become a leisure facility, either through changed plans, or by use, perhaps because the admission fee proved a barrier to the poorest families.[58] The parish council closed the baths in 1913, but the reason is not recorded.[59] No alternative facility was provided, and in 1917 two miners were prosecuted and fined 7*s.* 6*d.* each for preparing to bathe within 200 yd. of a footpath.[60]

The parish council purchased the former British School for £6 in 1897, to provide a non-denominational venue for parish council meetings, social activities and coroners' inquests.[61] Demonstrating the urban ambitions of some residents, the building was named the 'Town Hall'.[62]

The desire for urban status was driven by a combination of local pride, petty jealousies and the desire of Liberal and Radical voices to defeat Conservative views. Ibstock's residents had seen the creation of Coalville civil parish in 1894 from parts of the four civil parishes of Hugglescote and Donington, Whitwick, Swannington, and Ravenstone with Snibston.[63] This was followed by the formation of Coalville Urban District Council in 1895.[64] At a meeting of Ibstock parish council in 1899, Thomas Hextall, Ibstock's first county councillor, moved that they should apply to the county council for Ibstock to be constituted an urban district. It was pointed out that the costs to

49 *Leic. Chron.*, 30 June 1894.
50 *Leic. Jnl*, 30 Nov. 1894.
51 *Leic. Chron.*, 24 Nov. 1894.
52 *Leic. Chron.*, 15 Dec. 1894.
53 *Leic. Jnl*, 21 Dec. 1894.
54 *Leic. Chron.*, 24 Apr. 1897.
55 *Leic. Chron.*, 13 Aug. 1898.
56 *Leic. Chron.*, 30 July 1898.
57 *Leic. Chron.*, 15 July 1899, 23 Sept. 1899; 24 Mar. 1900; S.W. Wallace, *Sports Societies in Ibstock during the Present Century* (Ibstock, 1983), 9.
58 S. Sheard, 'Profit is a dirty word: the development of public baths and wash-houses in Britain, 1847–1915', *Social History of Medicine* (2000), 76–8.
59 *Melton Mowbray Merc.*, 3 July 1913; 17 Sept. 1913.
60 *Leic. Daily Post*, 21 June 1917.
61 *Leic. Chron.*, 13 Nov. 1897; 18 Dec. 1897; 19 Mar. 1898; 18 Mar. 1899.
62 *Leic. Chron.*, 18 Feb. 1899; 18 Mar. 1899.
63 Youngs, *Admin. Units.* II, 224; *Leic. Chron.*, 21 July 1894.
64 *Leic. Chron.*, 19 Jan. 1895.

obtain the expert evidence and legal advice required could be substantial, and a decision was deferred for three months.[65] The topic was still debated without resolution in 1913.[66] It then faded from residents' concerns.

The parish was divided into three wards and had 13 elected councillors in 2019. The council managed the cemetery, churchyard, recreation grounds and the allotments,[67] and had three committees, for planning, employment, and parks and play areas.[68] Through the application of agreed contributions from property developments in Ibstock, in the early 21st century the parish council provided a skate[board]-park and 'play ball' park, additional equipment for the recreational facilities on Leicester Road and at the Welfare sports ground, and improvements to the 'under-5s' play area off Melbourne Road.[69]

District Council

Ibstock became part of Market Bosworth Rural District Council (RDC) in 1894.[70] The village elected five of the council's 40 members, with the first members being Samuel Bridget (miner, Liberal), Thomas Hextall JP (retired builder and carpenter, Liberal), Joseph Palmer (innkeeper, Liberal), William Philpott Sheppard (colliery proprietor, Conservative) and William Thirlby (farmer, Conservative).[71] The parochial committee also continued, and made recommendations to the RDC on public health issues, including housing. This committee was independent of the parish council.

The RDC resolved to purchase land in 1896 for an isolation hospital to serve the needs of the whole district.[72] Ibstock already had an isolation hospital, provided by the RSA in 1894.[73] Ibstock's councillors were reluctant to receive infectious children from other villages, but accepted that the hospital needed to be near a centre of population. Thomas Hextall suggested that a small iron building with eight beds could be erected in a corner of 'the allotment field' to the south of Pretoria Road, mid-way between the (later) public baths and Ibstock Grange.[74] A plan and tender were accepted for £230,[75] and the hospital was open by 1899.[76] It closed in 1932, and the site became Redholme Bungalow Farm.[77]

The RDC began to lay sewers in 1898, provided a sewage treatment plant that year near the confluence of the brooks,[78] and arranged to lease a piece of land to treat Battram's sewage in 1930.[79]

65 *Leic. Chron.*, 18 Feb. 1899.
66 *Leic. Chron.*, 20 Sept. 1913.
67 Chairman's Letter, *Ibstock Community Voice*, July 2018, 10.
68 https://www.ibstockparishcouncil.org.uk/the-council.html (accessed 8 Nov. 2019).
69 Chairman's Letter, *Ibstock Community Voice*, Oct. 2018, 12.
70 56 & 57 Vict., c. 73.
71 ROLLR, DE 3640/160, pp. 196–7; *Leic. Chron.*, 8 Dec. 1894; *Leic. Jnl*, 21 Dec. 1894.
72 ROLLR, DE 3640/160, p. 341.
73 Above, Rural Sanitary Authority.
74 *Leic. Chron.*, 1 and 8 Jan. 1898.
75 *Leic. Chron.*, 19 Feb. 1898.
76 ROLLR, DE 3640/161, pp. 134, 152, 165, 190, 205, 381.
77 ROLLR, DE 3640/170, p. 205.
78 *Leic. Chron.*, 30 July 1898.
79 ROLLR, DE 3640/170, parochial committee, p. 1.

The first council houses were built in Ibstock from 1921, but the RDC struggled to obtain the funding needed to reduce overcrowding and replace homes that were considered 'unfit' for habitation.[80] It arranged for piped water to be supplied to all of Ibstock's houses in 1932, through an arrangement with Coalville Urban District Council, which was negotiating for the supply and treatment of water pumped from Ellistown colliery.[81]

Under the local government reforms of the 1970s, the Boundary Commission proposed to merge Hinckley Urban District and Market Bosworth Rural District in west Leicestershire to create the new district of Hinckley and Bosworth, and to create a new district in the north-west of the county containing the parishes in the rural districts of Ashby-de-la-Zouch and Castle Donington, and the urban districts of Ashby Woulds and Coalville. [82] Ibstock parish council and many residents lobbied to join North West Leicestershire District, on the grounds that Ibstock's affinities and social ties were with Coalville, rather than Hinckley.[83] The Commission agreed to the request, and Ibstock became part of North West Leicestershire District in 1974.[84] For the purpose of district council elections, Ibstock comprised two wards in 2019, and elected two of the 38 district councillors.

The council's priority in the 1990s and early 2000s was the regeneration of Coalville,[85] the largest settlement and the designated 'principal town' in North West Leicestershire District, which had been badly affected by the closure of the Leicestershire coalfield. New housing and industrial development was concentrated along the Leicester to Burton-upon-Trent railway line, which passed through Bagworth, Hugglescote and Coalville,[86] although Leicestershire County Council decided in 2009 not to reopen this line to passengers.[87] Ibstock was designated a 'local service centre', where permitted development would be largely residential.[88] The addition of significant houses with few new jobs resulted in Ibstock becoming a dormitory settlement, although the village has in some respects been able to adapt, due to increasing employment at the brickworks, levels of car ownership, a bus service and because this repeated an older pattern of work, when the collieries stood on the fringes of the parish.

80 Above, Ibstock Parish, settlement.

81 ROLLR, DE 1524/129, pp. 705, 918; DE 3640/167, pp. 363, 375; W.W. Baum, *The Water Supplies of Leicestershire* (Leicester, 1949), 44–5.

82 *Local Government Boundary Commission for England, Report 1* (Parl. Papers 1972–3 [Cmnd 5148], xv), p. 465.

83 *Coventry Evening Telegraph*, 8 June 1972.

84 *Local Government Boundary Commission*, pp. 354, 466.

85 NWL DC, 'Adopted Written Statement, 2011–31', 12, 24.

86 North West Leicestershire Local Plan, 1991–2006, 15–16.

87 *Leic. Mercury*, 9 Sept. 2009.

88 North West Leicestershire District Council, 'Adopted Written Statement, 2011–31', 24.

GLOSSARY

THE FOLLOWING TECHNICAL TERMS MAY require explanation. Fuller information on local history topics is available in D. Hey, *The Oxford Companion to Local and Family History* (1996), or online at the VCH website (http://www.victoriacountyhistory.ac.uk). The most convenient glossary of architectural terms is Pevsner's Architectural Glossary (2010), also available in digital editions.

Advowson: the right to nominate a candidate to the bishop for appointment as rector or vicar of a church. This right was a form of property which was often attached to a manor, but could be bought and sold.

Attainder: an order made by a judge or Act of Parliament by which the real and personal estate of a convicted individual was forfeited and could not be inherited.

Bordar: a smallholder.

Brief: An appeal issued under the royal seal seeking donations for a deserving cause, addressed to the ministers and churchwardens of parishes, which had to be read out from the pulpit and a collection taken. The money and (from 1706) the document endorsed with the amount collected had to be given to a travelling collector.

Canon: one of a body of clergy (the chapter) who, with the dean at their head, form the governing body of a cathedral.

Cartulary: a register of the grants of property made to a landed estate, often that of a monastery.

Carucate: a unit of taxation and originally the amount of land that a team of eight oxen could plough in a year. The acreage varied from place to place, but was often about 120 acres.

Cess-pit: historically, a dung-heap under a privy (q.v.), where liquid drained through to the soil, and solid matter remained, which was emptied and taken away at regular intervals for use as manure. A modern cess-pit is a sealed underground tank that collects waste water and sewage in houses that are not connected to sewers. The unprocessed contents have to be emptied regularly and taken away.

Chancellor: an official who acted as the secretary to the governing body (chapter) of a cathedral.

Chantry: masses celebrated for the souls of the founder and anyone nominated by the founder, or for the souls of members of a guild (q.v.) or fraternity.

Cistercians: a monastic order, founded at Cîteaux in 1098 and distinguished by their white habit, which originally sought remote sites and gifts of uncultivated land, which were farmed by lay brothers.

Collation (by the Pope): the bestowal of a benefice or other preferment upon a clergyman.

Commons: areas of land governed by agreements made at the manorial court, giving specified rights (e.g. of grazing a certain number of animals, or collecting furze) to certain people (e.g. the occupiers of ancient cottages).

Conventicle: a meeting of religious Dissenters.

Copyhold: form of land tenure granted in a manor court, so called because the tenant received a 'copy' of the grant as noted in the court records.

Dame school: a school for young children held in a domestic house, which taught very basic reading skills.

Demesne: in the Middle Ages, land farmed directly by a lord of the manor, rather than granted to tenants. Although usually leased out from the later Middle Ages, demesne lands often remained distinct from the rest of a parish's land.

Dissenter: a person who dissented from the religious beliefs of the Anglican Church.

Enclosure: the process whereby open fields (q.v.) were divided into closes and redistributed among the various tenants and landholders. From the 18th century, enclosure was usually by an Act of Parliament obtained by the dominant landowners; earlier, more commonly done by private agreement, or by a powerful lord acting on his own initiative.

Fealty: an oath of allegiance to the king or to a lord.

Feoffees: trustees appointed to manage land or other assets for the benefit of others.

Frankpledge: a system of mutual responsibility for the maintenance of law and order. Every householder was part of a group of ten or twelve people responsible for the behaviour of the other members of the group, and for bringing members to the manor court to face charges.

Furlong: a block of strips in the open fields (q.v.).

Glebe: land belonging to the church to support a priest.

Grange: a monastic farming complex, usually on land which was remote from the monastery.

Guild: a religious organisation offering mutual charitable support to its members, who might all have a common occupation. In some small towns the guild might administer the affairs of the town.

Hearth tax: tax levied twice a year between 1662 and 1688, assessed on the number of hearths or fireplaces in a house.

Homage: formal and public acknowledgement of allegiance to the king or to a lord.

Husbandman: a farmer who often held his land by copyhold or leasehold tenure; the amount of land, between 6 a. and 100 a., was more than that held by a labourer or cottager, but less than that held by a yeoman.

Igneous: a type of hard rock produced by volcanic action.

Iron Age: a period of English history from 800 BC–42 AD, divided into early Iron Age (800–100 BC) and late Iron Age (100 BC–42 AD).

Knight's fee: a holding of land sufficient to maintain a knight, or enabling the landholder to perform knight service, that is, 40 days each year, equipped with horse and armour. In the 13th century, the amount of land was often valued at £40 yearly. As estates were divided up, smaller estates could be held as fractions of a knight's fee.

Ley: individual arable strips in the open fields (q.v.) which have been converted to grass for one or more seasons.

Manor: a piece of landed property with tenants regulated by a private (manor) court. Originally held by feudal tenure, manors descended through a succession of heirs, but could also be given away or sold.

Mark: a monetary unit used in accounting, equal to two-thirds of a pound.

Mercer: a shopkeeper who sold fabrics, and often other imported goods.

Messuage: a house with its surrounding land and outbuildings.

Moiety: a half (e.g. of a manor (q.v.) that has been split between two people).

Open (common) fields: communal agrarian organization under which an individual's farmland was held in strips scattered amongst two or more large fields, intermingled with the strips of other tenants. Management of the fields, and usually common meadows and pasture, was regulated through the manor court or other communal assembly.

Pail-closet: a type of toilet which had become common in many places by the 1870s. The waste matter was collected in a pail, usually deodorised with ash, and the pails were collected nightly by night-soil men. Some had an absorbent lining to collect the liquid. The pail-closet had the advantage of not contaminating the earth or ground water.

Pinder: a manorial officer in charge of the pound, where stray animals were kept.

Prebendary: a clergymen who received the income from an estate (known as a prebend) given to a collegiate church or cathedral to support its clergy.

Presbyterian: the Presbyterian Church rejected government by bishops and was governed by a body of ministers and lay people who were equal in rank.

Privy: a building, or room on the edge of a large building, containing a fixed wooden seat over a cess-pit (q.v.) and used as a toilet; the seat could contain several holes for more than one person to use simultaneously. A single privy might be shared by several families. Sometimes two or more separate privies drained to a common cess-pit.

Rectory: (1) a church living served by a rector, who generally received the church's whole income; (2) the church's property or endowment, comprising tithes, offerings and usually some land or glebe.

Roman: a period of English history from 42–410 AD, divided into early Roman (42–250 AD) and late Roman (250–410 AD).

Soke: in Domesday Book a soke was a dependent free territory covering several settlements where the land was held by free peasants.

Sokeman: a type of free peasant.

Stint: the number of animals a tenant was allowed to graze on common pastures, as agreed and enforced through the manor court.

Suit of court: a tenant's obligation to attend the lord's manor court.

Terrier: register of the lands belonging to a landowner, originally including a list of tenants, their holdings, and the rents paid, later consisting of a description of the acreage and boundaries of the property.

Tithe: a tax of one-tenth of the produce of the land, which originally went to the church. It could be divided into great tithes (corn and hay), which went to the rector, and small tithes (livestock, wool and other crops), which supported a vicar.

Turnpike: a road administered by a trust, which covered the cost of maintenance by charging tolls.

Vestry: (1) room in a church where clerical vestments are stored; (2) assembly of leading parishioners and ratepayers, responsible for poor relief and other secular matters as well as church affairs.

Virgate: a standard holding of arable land in the Middle Ages, of quarter of a carucate (q.v.), generally 15–40 a. depending on the quality of the land. A virgate usually generated surplus crops for sale at market; those with fractions of a virgate probably needed to work part-time for better-off neighbours. Also called a yardland.

Vitrified: converted by heat into a smooth glass-like substance or surface.

Warping: setting up the warp (lengthwise) thread on looms.

Yardland: see virgate.

Yeoman: from the 16th century, a term used for larger and more prosperous farmers, superior to a husbandman, sometimes owning freehold land, many of them socially aspirational.

NOTES ON SOURCES

Sources Used

THIS HISTORY OF IBSTOCK HAS been written using a wide range of primary source material, both printed and manuscript. This list includes the main sources used, but is best used in conjunction with the footnotes and the List of Abbreviations.

The National Archives, the Record Office for Leicestershire, Leicester and Rutland and the other repositories mentioned here have online catalogues and research guides, although the online catalogues do not include all their holdings.

Manuscript sources

The National Archives (TNA) at Kew holds the records of national government from the late 12th century onwards, with some earlier material. Calendars (brief abstracts) of some of the administrative records of government in the Middle Ages and early modern period have been published, and have also been used in this history.

The main classes of manuscript documents used in this history are:

BT 31 Board of Trade, files of dissolved companies.
C 2, C 3, C 6, C 8 Court of Chancery pleadings, Elizabeth I to 1714.
C 66 Patent Rolls.
C 101 Chancery Masters' account books.
C 142 Inquisitions Post Mortem, Henry VII to Charles I.
CHAR 2 Commissioners for inquiry into charities.
E 179 Exchequer taxation records, 1190–1690.
E 326 Ancient deeds.
ED 2 Elementary Education, parish files, 1872–1904.
ED 21 Public Elementary School, files, 1857–1946.
ED 49 Elementary education endowment files.
ED 70 Board of Education, practical instruction centres.
ED 103 Privy Council on Education, building grants, 1833–81.
ED 109 Board of Education, HM Inspectorate reports on secondary schools.
ED 161 Department of Education and Science, elementary and primary schools.
HO 1 Home Office, Denization and naturalisation papers and correspondence.
HO 107 Home Office, Census Enumerators' Returns, 1841, 1851.
HO 129 Home Office, Ecclesiastical Census, 1851.

IR 18 Tithe Files, 1836–70.
IR 23 Land Tax Redemption Office, quotas and assessments.
IR 24 Land Tax Redemption Office, registers of redemptions.
IR 58 Board of Inland Revenue, Valuation Office field books.
IR 130 Board of Inland Revenue, Valuation Office record sheet plans.
MAF 32 National Farm Survey Farm Records, 1941–43.
MAF 68 Agricultural Returns, 1866–1988.
MH 12/6566–6568 Correspondence of Poor Law Commissioners, Market Bosworth Union, 1833–53.
MT 6 Ministry of Transport, railway divisions, correspondence and papers.
PROB 11 Prerogative Court of Canterbury probate records.
RG 9–14 Registrar General, Census Enumerators' Returns, 1861–1911.
SC 6 Special collections, ministers' and receivers' accounts.
SC 11 Special collections, rentals and surveys.

Lambeth Palace Library in Lambeth and the **Church of England Records Centre** in South Bermondsey hold central records of the Church of England, including records of the Incorporated Church Building Society (ICBS), records relating to National (Church of England) schools (NS), the benefice (CC/OF/NB) and St Denys's churchyard (CC/OF/CB and ECC).

Record Office for Leicestershire, Leicester and Rutland (ROLLR) in Wigston, Leicestershire holds records of county administration, records of the diocese of Leicester (from 1926), some earlier archidiaconal records, and numerous parish, school and private records. The principal classes of documents used in this history are:

1D 41 Leicester Archdeaconry records.
1D 43/29 Whitwick colliery deeds.
3D 42/42/310 Sale catalogue.
5D 33 Farnham bequest.
9D 45/3–5 Deeds.
39'29/342 Deeds.
44'28/516 Bond.
109'30/94–5; PP 454 Estate Plans.
CC 4/16 Leicestershire County Council Education Committee minutes, 1909–66.
DE 40/26 Rental.
DE 40/17/4 Sale details Ibstock colliery and land, 1846.
DE 41/1 Coal and minerals.
DE 365 Paget estate records.
DE 380/1–24 Turnpike plans, Hinckley to Melbourne Common.
DE 380/45 Plan of Hugglescote, Bardon and Bagworth.
DE 390 Ibstock parish records.
DE 464/2 Tithe book.
DE 490 Snibston colliery records.
DE 630; DE 2480 School plans.
DE 1032/27; DE 4674/202; DE 4674/675 Sales particulars Grange and Park farms.

DE 1177/30–44 National Coal Board, Leicester District Miners' Welfare Committee, 1920–52.
DE 1524/129–130 Minutes, Coalville Urban District Council 1927–36.
DE 1536; DE 3541 Curzon estate papers.
DE 1717 Ibstock parish records.
DE 2072 Duties on Land Values records.
DE 3175 Market Bosworth Rural Sanitary Authority minutes, 1873–86.
DE 3627 Leicestershire County Council Education Department records, 1863–1989.
DE 3640/159–160 Market Bosworth Rural Sanitary Authority, minutes, 1886–97.
DE 3640/161–7 Market Bosworth Rural District Council, minutes, 1930–49.
DE 3640/170–73 Market Bosworth Rural District Council, composite minutes, 1930–49.
DE 3640/175–6 Market Bosworth Union, Guardians' minutes 1838–88.
DE 3806 Market Bosworth Rural District Council building plans.
DE 4094 Methodist records Ashby and Coalville circuits.
DE 4565 Ibstock parish records.
DE 4939 Ellistown colliery records.
DE 5174 Battram school records.
DE 8538/88 Market Bosworth Union, Guardians' minutes 1913–21.
DE 8666 Parliamentary enclosure award and map.
E/LB/155 School log books.
E/MB/B/155 Battram school managers' minute book.
EN/A/150 Hugglescote enclosure map.
G/9/8a/4 Market Bosworth Union, Guardians' minutes, 1922–30.
Ma 155/2 Plan of Ibstock, 1818.
N/B/150 Hugglescote Baptist church records.
N/B/155 Ibstock Baptist Church records.
N/M/9 Methodist records, Ashby-de-la-Zouch circuit.
N/M/73 Methodist records, Coalville circuit.
OS Ordnance Survey maps.
PR/I Leicester Archdeaconry, probate records, 1542–1812.
QS 44 Quarter Sessions Licences for Protestant Dissenters' meeting houses.
QS 62 Quarter Sessions Land Tax Assessments.
QS 73 Quarter Sessions Railways.
QS 95 Quarter Sessions Returns of Dissenters.
Ti/155 Tithe maps and apportionments.
Will and Inventory files, Leicester Archdeaconry, 1500–1603.
Will registers, Leicester Archdeaconry, 1515–33.
Will files, Leicester Archdeaconry, 1563–1858.

Lincolnshire Archives holds records relating to the Diocese of Lincoln, which included Ibstock until 1837. The most important classes used are:

COR B 5 Bishops' correspondence.
DIOC MGA 7 Mortgages of rectories under Gilbert's Act.
DIOC TER Glebe terriers.
DIOC PD, DIOC RES Presentations and resignations of incumbents.
MF visitation records of bishop Gibson (1718–21).

Northamptonshire Record Office holds faculties and visitation records relating to the parish church between 1837 and 1926, when Ibstock was within the Diocese of Peterborough:

ML 597, ML 601, ML 1116.
Boxes X920, X921, X923, X924, X926.

Staffordshire Record Office
D 641/1/2/262–3 Account.

St Denys Church, Ibstock
Parish magazines, 1886–2019.

St Denys School, Ibstock
School log books, 1890–1910, 1910–40.

Printed Sources

The most important printed sources, including calendars of major classes of records in The National Archives and parliamentary papers, are included in the List of Abbreviations. The Lincoln Record Society has published many original records of the ancient diocese of Lincoln which contain information about Ibstock. Transcripts of some other original documents have been published within the *Associated Architectural Societies, Reports and Papers* and within *Transactions of Leicestershire Archaeological and Historical Society.*

Good collections of Leicestershire trade directories and 20th-century telephone directories are held at ROLLR. National newspapers and local newspapers have also been used extensively in this research, both in digital form (through the British Newspaper Archive) and within the collections held at ROLLR.

Books and Articles

John Nichols' *History and Antiquities of the County of Leicester* remains an important secondary source for the history of the county. Transcriptions of the Garendon Abbey cartularies (in Latin) appear in volume III, part 2 (1804) and the Ibstock entry is in volume IV, part 2 (1811). The latter largely incorporates the earlier entry for Ibstock in *Description of Leicestershire* by William Burton (1622). Historian George Farnham published transcripts of many records relating to Ibstock in G.F. Farnham, *Medieval Village Notes* (Leicester, 1933), volume III.

The main sources used for architectural history are N. Pevsner (rev. E. Williamson), *The Buildings of England; Leicestershire and Rutland* (2nd edn, Harmondsworth, 1984), and the various listings of properties on the Heritage List for England.

ABBREVIATIONS

Ab. Placitor	*Placitorum in domo capitulari Westmonasteriensi asservatorum abbreviatio, temporibus regum Ric. I., Johann., Henr. III., Edw. I., Edw. II.* (Record Commission, 1811)
Accts	Accounts
Assoc. Archit. Soc. Rep. &Papers	*Associated Architectural Societies, Reports and Papers*
Book of Fees	*Liber Feodorum. The book of fees, commonly called Testa de Nevill* (1920)
Brit. Geol. Surv.	British Geological Survey
Burton, *Description*	W. Burton, *The Description of Leicestershire* (2nd edn, 1777)
Cal. Close	*Calendar of the Close Rolls*
Cal. Inq. p.m.	*Calendar of Inquisitions Post Mortem*
Cal. Papal Reg.	*Calendar of the Papal Registers*
Cal. Pat.	*Calendar of the Patent Rolls*
Cal. SP Dom.	*Calendar of State Papers, Domestic*
Calamy Revised ed. A.G. Matthews	A.G. Matthews (ed.), *Calamy Revised: being a Revision of Edmund Calamy's Account of the Ministers and Others Ejected and Silenced,* 1660–2 (Oxford, 1934)
Cawte, 'Report'	C.E. Cawte, 'Parish Warden's Report on Ibstock for 2000: Standing Archaeology'
CERC	Church of England Record Centre
CJ	*Journals of the House of Commons*

Colln	Collection
Complete Peerage	V. Gibbs, H.A. Doubleday and Lord Howard de Walden (eds.), *The Complete Peerage of England, Scotland, Ireland, Great Britain and the United Kingdom* (1910–38)
Dict.	*Dictionary*
Dioc.	Diocese
Dir.	*Directory*
Domesday	A. Williams and G.H. Martin (eds), *Domesday Book: A Complete Translation* (2002)
Eng. Hist. Review	*English Historical Review*
Eve.	*Evening*
Gaz.	*Gazetteer*
Hastings, I	*Report on the Manuscripts of the late Reginald Rawdon Hastings, Esq., of the Manor House, Ashby-de-la-Zouch* (Record Commission, 1928), vol. I
Indus. Hist. Soc.	Industrial History Society
L&P Henry VIII	*Letters and Papers of Henry VIII*
LJ	*Journals of the House of Lords*
Leic.	Leicester
Leic. Chron.	*Leicester Chronicle*
Leic. Jnl	*Leicester Journal*
Leics.	Leicestershire
Leics. CC	Leicestershire County Council
Leics. & Rutl. HER	Historic Environment Record for Leicestershire and Rutland
Libr.	Library

Lincs. Arch.	Lincolnshire Archives
Nat. Comm. Dir.	*National Commercial Directory*
NHLE	National Heritage List for England http://www.historicengland.org.uk/listing/the-list
Nichols, *History*	J. Nichols, *History and Antiquities of the County of Leicester* (1795–1815)
NWL	North West Leicestershire
NWL DC	North West Leicestershire District Council
ODNB	*Oxford Dictionary of National Biography*
OS	Ordnance Survey
Parl. Papers	Parliamentary Papers
Par. Mag.	*Parish Magazine*
Pevsner	N. Pevsner (rev. E. Williamson), *The Buildings of England; Leicestershire and Rutland* (2nd edn, Harmondsworth, 1984)
Poll Taxes 1377–81, (ed.) Fenwick	C.C. Fenwick (ed.), *Poll Taxes of 1377, 1379 and 1381*, pt 1 (British Academy Records of Social and Economic Hist. n.s. 27, 1998); pt 2 (n.s. 29, 2001)
Priv.	Private
RDC	Rural District Council
Rec. Soc.	Record Society
RO	Record Office
ROLLR	Record Office for Leicestershire, Leicester and Rutland
Rott. Lit. Claus	*Rotuli Literarum Clausarum* (Record Commission 1833–44)
Rpt	*Report*
Rutl.	Rutland

Tax. Eccl.	*Taxatio Ecclesiastica Anglie et Wallie ... circa AD 1291* (Record Commission, 1801)
TNA	The National Archives
Trans. LAHS	*Transactions of the Leicestershire Archaeological and Historical Society*
Univ.	University
Valor Eccl.	*Valor Ecclesiasticus, temp. Hen. VIII* (Record Commission, 1810–34)
VCH	*Victoria History of the Counties of England*
Walker Revised, ed. A.G. Matthews	A.G. Matthews (ed.), *Walker Revised: being a revision of John Walker's Sufferings of the Clergy During the Grand Rebellion*, 1642–60 (Oxford, 1948)
Youngs, *Admin. Units*	F.A. Youngs, *Guide to the Local Administrative Units of England* (1991)

INDEX

CPSIA information can be obtained
at www.ICGtesting.com
Printed in the USA
FSHW021503300121
78043FS

9 781912 702466